THE ADVENTURES OF A BLACK EDWARDIAN INTELLECTUAL

The Story of James Arthur Harley

PAMELA ROBERTS

Signal Books
Oxford

First published in 2022 by
Signal Books Limited
36 Minster Road
Oxford OX4 1LY
www.signalbooks.co.uk

A catalogue record for this book is available from the British Library
ISBN 978-1-8384630-6-9 Cloth
Cover Design: Tora Kelly
Typesetting: Tora Kelly
Cover Images: courtesy Pamela Roberts
Printed in India by Imprint Press

Contents

Foreword

Her Excellency Karen-Mae Hill
High Commissioner of Antigua & Barbuda to the United
Kingdom of Great Britain and Northern Ireland

The story of the life of James Arthur Harley is one that forces the reader to reflect on the complex issues of race, identity and class but not always in expected ways. Pamela Roberts has pieced together an intriguing narrative about an important and - before her work - hidden figure of black academia and politics at the turn of the twentieth century. His was an intriguing life which confronted prejudices across and within race and geography. The book is also a story of ambition that refuses to be shackled and of triumph over adversity.

The son of a white father of whom little is known and a seamstress mother of whom even less is known, Harley was born in Antigua in May 1873 and raised with an unquenchable desire to be more and see more than the limitations of his mixed-race heritage and Caribbean Island home could provide. He was of an era where the lighter hue of his skin afforded him certain enhanced privileges that those not of mixed race did not enjoy though he was still firmly placed in a lower class than those who were white.

Little is known of the role of Harley's father and mother in his life in Antigua. The figure of the strong, West Indian mother, however, is a well-known one. Mothers were often the main providers and would ensure that children made full use of education opportunities. Roberts herself notes in the book that 'it had been drilled into the young Harley, like many children, that education was the liberator that would set free the black population ... A good education was a passport to escape a life of servitude and menial jobs, a system that the white minority wanted to preserve and reinforce.'

The quality of the Antiguan education system in the time of Harley was evident as it gave him a sufficiently solid foundation to successfully navigate the academic requirements of first Howard University after leaving Antigua and then Yale, Harvard and Oxford Universities. His educational foundation from Antigua also seems to have been a rounded one as Harley's prowess as a musician and an orator served him well throughout his studies and career, earning him income at crucial times to make ends meet and top prizes in various competitions. Harley's impressive academic credentials included qualifications in the classics, law, Semitic languages, anthropology and theology from the best Universities in the US and UK - no trivial achievement for a man born and raised in Antigua and who received his formative education there.

The factors which consistently challenged Harley's academic and professional progress were his race, modest finances, prejudicial perceptions about his character based on his West Indian origins and resentment from those around him who despised his strong sense of self and purpose. These prejudices were shared by his white educators and contemporaries in the United States and later in the United Kingdom but also by the black elites of the US with whom he interacted. Harley was seen by them all as 'profoundly West Indian' and invariably described as quick tempered, arrogant and possessing the self-importance of the black Englishman. Attempts to assert himself or even to defend himself against perceived injustices were characterized as Caribbean or West Indian.

I found myself drawn to this story as an Antiguan by birth who like Harley studied at Oxford University as a Rhodes Scholar over 100 years after him and found the need to navigate the nuances of an institution steeped in tradition at times difficult. I was intrigued to read more about Alain LeRoy Locke, a contemporary and friend of Harley, and the first African American Rhodes Scholar at Oxford. Roberts provides some powerful comparative insights into these two lives thrown together by a shared racial identity and profound intellect. The pernicious and divisive nature of prejudice is highlighted by their shared experience. On the one hand, both men were of superior intellect to many around them but struggled to identify with other people of colour including people of colour of high intellect. On the other hand, Harley and Locke accepted no racial or social limitations to their ambitions and refused to see themselves or the extent of their abilities as inferior to that of their white counterparts. They were the 'New Negro' demonstrating in their numerous and impressive scholastic achievements that anthropological teachings prevalent at the time that the black race was intellectually inferior were false.

Uncovering stories like those of Harley and Locke are important to fill deliberate gaps in the black narrative. These gaps fail to recognize and honour the breadth and depth of black scholastic achievement not as anomalies to some black reality of servitude and underachievement but very much commonplace in the black world. The Caribbean, for example, is proud of its four Nobel Laureates - Sir Arthur Lewis in Economic Science and Sir VS Naipaul, Saint-John Perse and Derek Walcott in literature and of its many scholars who continue to thrive in an environment of opportunity. One of the most effective ways to confront prejudice and tear down barriers to advancement is with information that shines a light on the false foundations of those prejudices. Interestingly, both Locke and Harley were contemporaries of the prolific black composer and conductor Samuel Coleridge-Taylor whose musical genius is undisputed and today is enjoying a renaissance.

The story of Locke and Harley also highlights another layer of the issue of prejudice. Roberts points out in the book how some Black Americans held the perception that some West Indian blacks felt themselves to be superior to black Americans because of their 'Englishness'. To quote Roberts, 'Throughout the Caribbean, the colonial education system instilled an English sense of superiority, and a person's social class was also an intrinsic aspect of the black West Indian make-up and identity rather than colour consciousness alone.' Harley would be seen as not just West Indian but a mulatto West Indian adding yet another layer to the divisive perceptions. Harley often found himself fighting against white supremacy but also prejudice against him by a black American elite. That American black elite separated itself not just from the likes of Harley but from lower class blacks seeking to associate as closely to white as possible. Roberts describes in the book how the 'black elite saw themselves as separate from the run of the mill black person in Washington and frequently complained about the lack of manners and morals among the city's African Americans'.

It is Harley's marriage to Josephine Lawson which demonstrated one of the challenges he was unable to surmount with his characteristic zeal. Josephine was from an elite, educated black American class who maintained a steadfast devotion to Harley from the time they met when she was 17 and he was 29. Yet Harley failed to recognize or provide for her need for mental stimulation as a highly educated black woman exposed to the finer delights of good books, robust conversation and classical music.

Perhaps Harley was unable to focus on the needs of his young wife beyond the basic requirements of food and shelter as he would have wished given his daily struggles to secure a permanent position befitting his immense abilities. Perhaps Harley showed scant regard for the needs of his wife who for the years of their extended courtship wrote many letters which would have revealed important insights into her intellect and desires. Perhaps Josephine, removed from her family and country, lacked the stamina that was so second nature to Harley to endure the initial years of hardship. Whatever those reasons Josephine, having left the US to unite with Harley in England, was unable to sustain the marriage and eventually returned to her life in the US.

Josephine's story also reveals one further critical point. It showed how black elitism in the US at that time included elements of women empowerment, opening opportunities for education and careers for women of colour. She was, however, still among a small number of educated black women but a trailblazer in this regard.

Harley was later to enter local politics and was elected to Leicestershire Country Council as a Labour councillor. He enjoyed wide popularity as a politician demonstrating that ability he had as a priest to appeal to his audience even as a foreigner of a different race. This was a man who accepted no limitations on his life and fearlessly presented himself always as a man entitled to all that his abilities and his intellect suited.

The book does not tell us if Harley ever saw his mother or Josephine again. Indeed, very little seems to be known of how he weighted the impact of these factors on the various phases of his life. Pamela Roberts is to be commended for bringing this story to life. In so doing, she has unearthed a little-known piece of Antiguan history and brought to the world a powerful story of how James Arthur Harley navigated the 'complexities of racism, politics and survival' with tenacity and intellect.

Acknowledgements

James Arthur Stanley Harley's story was brought to life by many people. I am deeply indebted to them for their time, patience, ability to share in my enthusiasm and passion for this book. They opened their hearts, homes and archives and provided moral support, practical guidance and encouragement to enable me to tell Harley's enthralling story.

Thanks to Antonio Joseph, Antigua and Barbuda High Commission, and Michael and Margaret Wortley. Dr Ralph Norman, Canterbury Christ Church University, Canterbury, read the early incarnations of the manuscript. His excitement about Harley's story and encouragement that I had what could be considered a book was invaluable.

In Antigua my gratitude goes to: Ms Joseph, archivist, National Archives; Dr Reg Murray, Betty Hope Project, for showing me around the renovation project and explaining its history; the staff at the Pineapple Hotel, especially the waitresses, for being so welcoming, providing oral histories and Caribbean sat-nav guidance in searching for various locations on the island.

In Washington DC: Jo Ellen, Moorland-Springarn archivist, Howard University; Mrs Ali, Ben's Chilli Bowl Restaurant, for being so welcoming and reliving the restaurant's history. Mr Carlson graciously opened the door to his home, the former Frelinghuysen University. He furnished tea, knowledge, a historical overview of the area and allowed me to take photographs of his house. Tim Driscoll, Harvard University Archives. Thanks to David Winfield, Virginia Commonwealth University for his generosity in sharing his research about Locke and Kallen. And to Makiel Talley for hours spent on the phone, online, and in discussions and speculations. Thank you for the added layers and information you brought to Harley's story.

In England: Fawn Williams, Canterbury Cathedral Archives; Susan Killoran, archivist, Manchester Harris College, Oxford, provided information and greatly appreciated photographs and details about his fellow students; Simon Bailey, Keeper of the Archives, Bodleian Library; Jeremy Coote, Curator, Pitt Rivers Museum; Christopher Morton, Curator of Photographs and Manuscripts, Pitt Rivers Museum; the archivists at the British Library and the National Archives, Kew, for sourcing census documents and making suggestions for other sources to try; the archivists at Leicestershire Records Office sourcing the Shepshed Council minutes and newspaper cuttings.

Rev Richard Braddy, St Mary the Virgin Church, Chislet, spent a day as a tour guide. Thanks also to Rev Flewker, St Leonard's Church, Deal, and Freda Herbert, Reynolds Farm Guest House, Marshside. Thank you for going above and beyond to extend a welcoming hand and make me feel like part of your family. I am grateful to Sue and Allen Buckham and Margaret Willis, Deal Local History Group, for tea and cake in the Red Admiral pub while furnishing information about smugglers, St Leonard's Church and coffins transported along 'coffin way'.

Thank you to Professor Pippa Catterall, Professor of History and Policy, Westminster University, for reading the manuscript providing guidance, support, critical feedback and encouragement. I shall forever be grateful for the generosity of your time, grace, spirit and passion in enabling me to tell Harley's story.

Many thanks to the friends and family repeatedly asking, 'are you still writing about the black priest?', especially Canon Richards with his intermittent phone calls and sole question: where's my book? To Sybelle Prince, who would enquire, 'where have you returned from and where are you going to next?' Retelling her the stories became the catalyst for my blog and podcast. *Following in the Footsteps of James Arthur Harley* documents my research trips and the many incidents encountered in writing this book. They all kept me accountable and provided renewed passion and determination.

Of course, thanks to my beloved mother, who has been my fellow traveller, researcher and the source of motivation when I felt like I was wading through treacle; I am grateful for her unquestioning and unwavering support, and for the memories, we have made in undertaking this amazing journey.

Finally, thank you to James Ferguson and the team at Signal Books for bringing Harley's story to the world.

Preface

Discovering Harley

My 'discovery' of James Arthur Stanley Harley, a name completely unknown to me at the time, came about quite by accident. It began, strangely, in New Zealand when I was on holiday, visiting a Māori heritage and culture centre in Rotorua. During a tour of the centre, I mentioned to the guide a project that I had founded and developed - *Black Oxford: Untold Stories* - a project celebrating black scholars at the University of Oxford from the beginning of the twentieth century to the present day. She looked at me nonplussed, and I assumed she had not understood what I had said. At the end of the tour, the guide asked me to follow her to the gift shop, to encourage me to buy, I suspected, some obligatory tourist knick-knack. Instead, she led me to the shop's book section, took a book from a shelf and handed it to me, proudly announcing, 'this is Makereti, the first Māori woman to attend Oxford University.'

Reading the book, I learned that Makereti (1873-1930), also known as Maggie Papakura, was a true pioneer. Born to a Māori mother and British father, she worked from an early age in New Zealand's tourism industry as a guide, keen to explain all aspects of Māori culture to visitors. She led the Royal party of the Duke and Duchess of Cornwall and York around the famous Whakarewarewa geyser valley in 1901. Ten years later, she brought a troupe of performers and a reconstructed Māori village to the 1911 Festival of Empire at London's Crystal Palace. In 1927 she became a member of the Society of Oxford Home Students (which later evolved into St Anne's College), a body that enabled women to study while living in private homes. Makereti studied anthropology. She first lived in Oddington,

Makereti Papakura, the first Māori woman to study at the University of Oxford. (University of Oxford)

a village about ten miles outside Oxford, with her second husband Richard Staples-Browne, and then in Summertown, Oxford. She suffered from ill-health and lack of money and died with her thesis unfinished. Makereti donated her extensive collection of Māori artefacts to the University of Oxford's Pitt Rivers Museum, where several items are on display.

I contacted Jeremy Coote, Curator of the Museum, to view the collection. While I was at the Pitt Rivers, Jeremy introduced me to Christopher Morton, Curator of Manuscripts and Photographs. Christopher handed me a sepia photograph. The image portrayed four people, two white men, one white woman and a black man in Edwardian dress. Pointing to the black man, Christopher asked, 'Do you know anything about him?' 'No,' I replied. 'He's James Arthur Harley. All we know is that he came from Antigua and was the first black student to take the Diploma of Anthropology at Pitt Rivers Museum in 1909.' I took a copy of the photograph and 'filed' it. (Filed is a euphemism for being slung in a corner of my office on top of an ever-growing pile of papers.) In collating information for my first book, *Black Oxford: The Untold Stories of Oxford University's Black Scholars*, I reacquainted myself with the sepia image. I had much information about the lives and careers of other black men and women who had studied at Oxford but knew nothing about the man in the photograph.

In trying to find out about Harley, my starting point was that he came from Antigua. A letter quickly made its way to the High Commissioner for Antigua and Barbuda in London. The letter I received back contained six bullet points. Working my way through all of them, I reached the final point. It stated that Harley was a curate and lived in Shepshed, Leicestershire. I thought there must be a local history group in Shepshed that could know of Harley. A series of phone calls led to a series of dead ends. Months passed. Then I received a call informing me about a local historian who might have some information about Harley. Unfortunately, he was now very aged and no longer lucid. Another few months passed, by which time I had more or less forgotten about Harley, and I was busy researching others among Oxford's black scholars. A cold Monday morning brought yet another phone call. The caller inquired, 'Am I speaking to Ms Roberts?' He then asked, 'You want to know about Old Harley, do you?' My first thought was that this was the local historian I had been told about. He repeated the question and I asked whether he meant James Arthur Harley. 'Yes,' he replied. Still unconvinced, I continued, 'the black man who attended the University of Oxford?' Again, the caller affirmed yes. He then proceeded to tell me that he had 'a few bits and pieces' that might be of interest to me, and would I like to see them? My enthusiastic 'yes' resulted in an invitation to visit the next day.

Michael and Margaret Wortley, a retired couple in their seventies, welcomed me into their home, and strangely I felt that I had known them for years as we chatted easily like long lost friends - maybe because of our shared interest in Harley. Michael explained that his father had been handed a battered old suitcase after Harley's death in 1943. Michael and his sister had then cleared out their father's flat upon his death. His sister wanted to throw away the suitcase, but Michael, a historian, insisted on keeping it. He had already brought the suitcase downstairs from the loft - its usual resting place - into the dining room in readiness for my visit.

From the first sight of the sepia photograph in Oxford through the ensuing quest for elusive information, the opening of this suitcase felt like a turning point in what would become my search for Harley. I could barely manage to express my amazement when we saw that it was stuffed full of documents. Michael pulled dusty sheets of paper from the suitcase like a magician extracting a stream of coloured flags from his sleeve. Each time he handed me a piece of paper, he quizzically asked, 'Is this of any interest to you?' I could not digest and process the material quickly enough because I was astounded by what I was viewing and uncertain as to what it all meant. I was looking at a case containing what were effectively the elements of a life: letters, sermons, speeches, newspaper clippings, qualifications, all sorts of documents. I was handling history as I scanned each new item, and a flood of questions invaded my mind: who was James Arthur Harley, and what was his story? What secrets did the battered suitcase contain? How and why did Michael's father end up with the case?

*

Researching Harley's life since that fortuitous moment has been an extraordinary, ever-expanding process. The closer I looked, the more I unearthed, and sometimes the sheer volume of evidence I stumbled upon was almost overwhelming. But I found significance in the experiences and expressions of his life and wanted his memory to be recorded and persist and not to remain in relative obscurity.

Life got in the way at the beginning of 2014, and I had an emergency gall bladder operation. I combined a period of recuperation with my first research trip to Wookey Hole Caves, Somerset. I had gathered that Harley had excavated Palaeolithic flint scrapers at the site known as Hyaena Den Caves in 1909 as part of his Oxford Diploma of Anthropology. My curiosity in the place was again stimulated and I decided then that I would like to write James Arthur Stanley Harley's biography.

I soon realized that studying Harley's life was important both from a biographical point of view and as a broader exercise in documenting aspects of social, cultural, and intellectual change between the nineteenth and twentieth centuries through the perspective of an individual's story. And his story appealed to me because a determined, progressive and independent spirit filled the pages of his letters, articles and newspaper columns, and his voice, changing over time, spoke clearly through his writings.

At the beginning of 2015, I received the K. Blundell Award from the Society of Authors to undertake further research in England and Antigua. I did not know I would embark on a two-and-a-half-year journey of discovery, following in Harley's footsteps to absorb first-hand and archive material from the places he lived, studied and worked. I visited Antigua and its sister island Barbuda. I had hoped the Antiguan National Archives would provide details about Harley's family and his early life. Sadly, most documents, including parish records, are not digitized. I had the names of Harley's parents but no date or place of birth; and without this information I could not access any records. In addition, varying dates made cross-checking information problematic, and I had to rely to some extent on oral history. The joyful prospect of locating key facts or even some fascinating titbit had been effectively removed, making it a long, laborious and frustrating process.

Antigua had additionally experienced a misfortune that created a further setback in my attempt to access Harley's educational records. The Mico school he attended had subsequently burnt down - all its records lost in the fire. I visited All Saints, Betty's Hope Plantation, All Saints Church, the capital St John's, Potters Village and much more of the island. In Barbuda, the tiny sister island famed for its pink sand, the crushed pink conch shells, I visited Codrington House, Government House and several wells, watering holes and other sites where enslaved people would reputedly fetch water but also plot and plan their escape or death.

Later, as I learned more about Harley. I went to New York City, where I visited the General Theological Seminary and marvelled at its grandeur, experiencing a sense of *déjà vu* in the seminary's red-brick Gothic resemblance to Oxford's Keble College. In Washington DC, I immersed myself into the atmosphere and history of U Street and the landmark Ben's Chili Bowl, venue of a visit by Barak Obama shortly before his inauguration in 2009. I revelled in its history retold by its sprightly eighty-two-year-old owner Mrs Ali and in taking photographs outside with the historic True Reformer Building in the background. I marvelled at the gold signage still standing at the LeDroit Park neighbourhood entrance. British passport and my magistrate's identity card in hand, I summoned up the courage to 'gate-crash' the private residence of Mr and Mrs Carlson, owners of 2011 Vermont Avenue, once home of Frelinghuysen University. Mr Carlson was gracious with his time and in retelling the house's history.

In England, my travels took me to the windswept, flat land of Marshside in Kent, visiting the various places where Harley later lived, from the little Mill Cottage to the school in Chitty Lane. My research trips also encompassed the Kentish village of Reculver, St Leonard's Church in Deal, St Botolph's Church in Shepshed, Jesus and Manchester Colleges in Oxford, King's College University of London, and Canterbury Cathedral. I read through minute book after minute book of the Shepshed Urban District Council committee meetings and trawled through volumes of *Freeman's Shepshed Almanac* at the Leicestershire Records Office.

I was met with the challenges of incomplete, non-existent or destroyed records leading to dead-ends and forcing me at first to speculate and then to piece together information from other sources. Sometimes there was an abundance of documentation - copious exchanges of correspondence, records held in university archives, articles in a local newspaper. But at other times there were sudden and frustrating gaps and silences.

Documenting the life of Harley became an exercise in detailing the changing conventions of the late nineteenth- and early twentieth-century society. His early life reflected the economic changes resulting from the downward spiral of the once profitable sugar industry in the Caribbean and the resulting impetus for the first wave of Caribbean migration to America. The central part of his life revolves around his educational trials and tribulations as he asserts himself as a 'New Negro' (in the phrase of his friend and contemporary Alain LeRoy Locke) and navigates the complexities of racism, politics and survival. This revealed to me the significance of Washington's black elite history and brought into focus the key players who operated within the upper echelons of black society against the harsh realities of Jim Crow. Harley's later life in England, with his involvement in Church and local politics, was evidence of social changes paralleled in the transformation of American society through the progressive era of the early twentieth century.

Harley's seventy years were some of the most turbulently transitional times in history, and he was shaped by these profound changes. Yet he was also a product of his early years and Caribbean culture. His education revealed an extraordinary intelligence but did not remove a common touch. He could shake hands with the working man and speak elegantly about life's mysteries in the church pulpit to white congregations in small working-class towns and villages with perfect confidence and ease. He was profoundly West Indian, his quick temper (or sheer frustration) a feature of his character. He was sometimes an embarrassment, sometimes deeply passionate and inspirational, occasionally profound, at times egocentric and pompous. I believe that what follows will reveal that Harley was a deeply flawed character, but a man whose energy, drive and sense of justice won him many admirers, most tellingly among the poor communities in which he worked.

The African American and West Indian communities of Antigua-Barbuda, the United States and Britain have progressed significantly since Harley's time at the beginning of the twentieth century. His life thus provides context and meaning to a process of transformation that has continued to this day.

What started as an off-chance remark in a conversation in New Zealand would become an addictive compelling journey not only in search of Harley but also as a sort of self-discovery. I found many parallels between his story and the story of my parents. As a child with parents from the Windrush generation, I knew the difficulties they encountered daily as new arrivals from British Guiana in 1961: the overt racism of the demeaning housing colour bar ('No Blacks, No Irish, No dogs'); being qualified but barred from employment opportunities and taking a lesser job to survive and raise a family; and the impossible quest to be treated with equity, to compete on a level playing field.

Harley's determination and passion became my driving force, my motivation to enable me to realize what is possible and achievable despite seemingly insurmountable odds. My own determination to source new information and to identify people involved with my subject led me to trace and track down Makiel Talley, great grandniece of Josephine Lawson - Harley's wife - in Atlanta, Georgia. Makiel regaled me with oral histories that had been passed down through her family about Josephine. We had numerous discussions over the phone and via emails hypothesizing, speculating and questioning Josephine's and Harley's motivations and their relationship. Our conversations continue today over details of Makiel's current extended family and we remain good friends. I developed a profound respect and admiration for Harley and his wife Josephine, and their achievements.

I have done my best to present his story in an objective and accurate way and to avoid hagiography. Norah Lofts encapsulated my sentiments perfectly when she wrote:

> And so out of the bits and pieces I could gather, out of my own imagining and speculation, I built up a story... After all, how much near, even with much-documenting evidence, can we come to an understanding any one of the myriad deceased who has gone to their graves, carrying their secrets, of motive and essence and personality, into the silence with them?
> *The Brittle Glass*, 1942

1. Antigua

'Antigua is a small place. Antigua is a very small place. In Antigua, not only is the event turned into the every day, but the everyday is turned into an event.'

Jamaica Kincaid

The sight of the Statue of Liberty represented the start of James Arthur Stanley Harley's new life. He disembarked the ship that had brought him to New York City and entered the immigration facility at Ellis Island joining the confusion of passengers, porters and pickpockets. Gathering his senses and luggage, he made his way to the Great Hall for inspection. There he was processed with all the other hope seekers, successfully answering a series of questions and passing the requisite medical examination. Eventually he left the Great Hall and made his way to a series of stairs split into three sections. Two sections led to the new land of opportunities: the exits for New Jersey or New York. The third section, which no immigrant wanted to go to, led to disappointment and detainment for further tests and examinations.

New York assaulted Harley's senses on his first day. The buzz of the trolley cars with overhead electrical wires running along their rails. The sight of large black boxes on wheels pulled by horses - the Hansom Cabs. The city's aroma mingled with the smell of food from the street vendors hawking their wares with encouraging calls to buy. Buildings seemed to erupt out of the ground and touch the sky. New sights and sounds were far removed from the familiar soundscape of his island home. Harley would no longer hear the rustle of palm tree leaves, interrupted by whistling frogs, or witness the openness and colour palate of the lush green vegetation or hear the tall tawny stems of the sugar cane rustled by the trade winds blowing across the Caribbean island of his birth: Antigua.

James Arthur Stanley Harley was born on 15 May 1873 in the British colony of Antigua.[1] Named after the Church of Nuestra Señora de la Antigua in Seville, Spain, the island was 'discovered' by Christopher Columbus in 1493 on his second journey to the Americas. An island with an area of 108 square miles,[2] it was initially inhabited by the Siboney, also known as the stone people, who originated from Meso-Indian communities in South America and whose settlement dated back to about 2400 BC. Antigua was colonized by the English in 1632, and its plantations, established from the 1670s, were initially worked by white indentured labourers who produced cotton, tobacco and indigo. The island's climate, fertile soil, several accessible harbours and reliable trade winds meant that its potential for sugar cultivation was soon recognized by planters. Soon slavery was the mechanism that drove the profitable sugar industry, which relied on the enslavement and brutalization of Africans transported in large numbers across the Atlantic from the 1670s.

On the outskirts of All Saints village in the centre of the island was the site of one of the most productive sugar plantations, owned and operated by the English planter Christopher Codrington. Like many white settlers, Codrington came to Antigua, in his case from Gloucestershire, in the hope of making a fortune. Codrington's original 1,689-acre sugar estate, Betty's Hope, was named after his daughter, Elizabeth, and used the pioneering technology provided by its two- imposing brick-built windmills, which stood proudly together - a dominant landmark in the island's topography - to carry out more large-

---

1   Harley's personal archive.
2   ab.gov.ag

Betty's Hope Plantation, Antigua, 1823 by William Clark.
(British Library/Wikimedia Commons)

scale cultivation, extraction and manufacture of sugar than any other estate. Codrington and his family stamped their authority on the industry with hundreds of enslaved people and one hundred and fifty sugar mills throughout Antigua.[3] In its heyday in 1760, Antigua's sugar production made it the fourth largest in the West Indies despite the island's size.

This was an island where the plantocracy - and its colonial government - cultivated a system categorizing and keeping the races in their place, a system adopted determining a person's worth and status as defined by white supremacist ideology. Antiguans' ethnic make-up consisted of British estate owners and colonial government officials at the top of the hierarchical structure. Next came the mixed-race coloureds or mulattos, the derogatory term used to describe those of mixed African and

---

3   Susan Lowes, "'They Couldn't Mash Ants": the Decline of the White and Non-White Elites in Antigua 1834-1900", in *Small Islands, Large Questions: Society, Culture and Resistance in the Post-Emancipation Caribbean*, ed. Karen Fog-Olwig, London: Frank Cass, 1995, pp. 31-52.

white heritage. Located firmly at the bottom of the hierarchical scale were most of Antigua's population, Africans: Yoruba and Igbo from Nigeria and Akans from Ghana. To institutionalize separation and inequality between the races, ensuring that the white man retained his privileged position on an island where the black population outnumbered whites by nearly two to one, degrees of skin colour were used as a divisive tool of status. The lighter the complexion of the individual, the more acceptable to white society.

Not all blacks and coloureds were subservient on the island of Antigua. There existed a freed coloured population. These people were either born free, had purchased their freedom, or had subsequently been granted their release from their enslavers and could take advantage of the opportunities created after Emancipation (the freeing of enslaved people) in 1834.[4] By 1805, there were 1,300 free coloureds in Antigua.[5] The free coloured community also comprised a multi-layered society that included an upper class. They were the fortunate ones whose coloured fathers had been sent aboard for education or had set up businesses or those with the perceived good fortune of a white father.

4   Susan Lowes, 'The Peculiar Class: The Formation, Collapse and Reformation of the Middle Class in Antigua, West Indies, 1834-1930'. New York: Columbia University PhD. Thesis, 1994.
5   Ibid.

2. Son of the Soil

'The Black skin is not a badge of shame, but rather a glorious symbol of national greatness.'

Marcus Mosiah Garvey

Henry James Harley,[6] James' father, was a white man. But was he a father in the real sense of the meaning? Did Henry James play a part in Harley's life? Did he nurture, care for and look after his son, or was he just a white man who had made pregnant the woman who bore Harley? Harley's official documentation states his father's occupation as a landlord.[7] No further or specific information is provided to substantiate this claim. There is no name of the land or sugar estate property his father administered. There are two assumptions about Harley's father's occupation: he was a landlord, maybe an absentee landlord, or an overseer for a planter.

Harley's mother, Josephine Eleanor Lake, was a seamstress.[8] This was a respectable, skilled occupation, a step up from taking in washing to provide a living for her family. Her surname, Lake, originated from Anguilla,[9] an eel-shaped island smaller than Antigua, and the name can be traced back to Captain Jacob Lake, an Englishman born in 1605 who emigrated to Nevis in 1628. His son, John Lake, was one of the first settlers to arrive in Anguilla in 1650.

---

6   Harley's ordination papers, Harley's personal archive.
7   Ibid.
8   Greenleaf financial aid application Harvard University Archives call number UAIII 15.88.10 1890-1968, Box 2070.
9   The limitations of the material from Harley's personal archive about his parents, other than their names - no date of birth for either parent - means that it was extremely difficult to trace them through parish records. My conclusion is that Harley's mother's family at some point left Anguilla to travel the short distance and settle in Antigua.

Harley's parentage slotted him into the category of mulatto - a term that originated in the sixteenth century, a Spanish derivation from mule, an animal of mixed parentage, and one used to refer to the offspring of black African and white parents. As a mulatto, Harley embodied what was widely viewed as the social threat of race-mixing, where white blood, supposedly representing civilization, was thwarted by the inclination towards savagery, a consequence of black blood.[10]

A younger brother to his sister, Alice Maude, Harley was baptized in July 1873 at All Saints Church. He grew up in All Saints village, known initially as Hymens Village. It was one of the many villages or towns, including Liberta, Freetown and New Field, established to commemorate the abolition of slavery. All Saints was created around 1839 with a church at the crossroads, the most central location in the village. The crossroads pointed in four different directions, with three of the island's six parishes branching off from there: St John to the south-west, St Peter to the north and St Paul in the south-east. The village grew up from people who lived on plantations such as Burkes, Sanderson and Osborne, and then settled in All Saints. Like the other houses in the village, Harley's was built from cane trash with mud or cow dung using a daub technique applied by hand. The daub plaster gave the huts strength and resistance to the elements.

Harley's childhood growing up in a small rural village was typical of a Caribbean upbringing. This would have involved being fussed over and spoilt by his older sister and the women in the village, especially those who were unable to have children.[11] But the days of play did not last long in

---

10   Audrey Elisa Kerr, *The Paper Bag Principle: Class, Colourism, and Rumour and the Case of Washington D.C.*, Knoxville TN: University of Tennessee Press, 2006. p. 9.

11   Bridget Brereton, *Social Life in the Caribbean 1838-1938*, London: Heineman, 1985, p. 39.

Market place, St John's, 1902. (Library of Congress, Washington DC)

the Caribbean; as early as five years old, a child had chores to carry out, anything from fetching water, sweeping the yard and looking after chickens or goats.[12] A family's daily diet consisted of the fruit and produce from the land: chicken, fish, yams, sweet potatoes, eddoes, breadfruit, plantains, mangoes and pineapples. The smell of Antigua's traditional dish, fungee and chop up, permeated the kitchen on Sundays. Fungee consisted of yellow cornmeal grain mixed with milk into a smooth paste, formed into a ball, wrapped like a parcel in a banana leaf and boiled. Chop up was dried salted codfish, boiled, shredded to skilfully remove its fine bones, fried with onions and peppers, and served on the unwrapped banana leaf as a plate with the fungee.

Religion, faith and different forms of cultural practice were essential aspects of life for many Antiguans.[13] Blacks recognized and acknowledged that their Emancipation was made possible by the significant role missionaries and ministers had played.

---

12   Ibid, p. 39.
13   Brereton, p.48

Support for the Church remained strong after Emancipation, with ministers and preachers held in high regard.[14] Antigua witnessed the establishment of various religions, the two most significant being the Moravians and the Methodists.

Established in the early fifteenth century by the Czech Jan Hus, the Moravian Church was founded in reaction to the Roman Catholic Church's teachings. The Moravians arrived in the 1700s to convert and educate the enslaved people. They began work in the Spring Gardens and St John's area of the island and erected a stone chapel in 1773. By 1818, the Church had 12,000 followers. The Methodist Church came to Antigua because of Francis Gilbert, the disgraced grandson of Nathaniel Gilbert, an early settler. The Gilberts were reputed to be descended from the great English navigator, explorer, colonist and privateer, Sir Humphrey Gilbert, and his half-brother Sir Walter Raleigh.[15] Francis disgraced himself in Antigua through 'loose living' and a fraud. Left out of his father's will, he fled to England to avoid his creditors. Gilbert's acquaintance with the Wesleys, John and his brother Charles, converted him to the faith. Such was Francis' conversion that he wrote to his older brother, also Nathaniel, a lawyer, slaver and Speaker of the House of Representatives in Antigua, about the religion and sent him material by John Wesley. Nathaniel sailed to England to hear Wesley preach from *An Earnest Appeal to Men of Reason and Religion*. He returned to Antigua in 1759 and started preaching in front of the steps of his great plantation house to his enslaved people and those from neighbouring estates. To devote more time and energy to his preaching, Nathaniel gave up his position as Speaker.

Nathaniel's evangelizing increased the number of people

---

14   Ibid, p. 48.
15   John C. Neal, "The Methodist Episcopal Church and Early Wesleyan Mission in the Caribbean", *Methodist History*, 50:1, October 2011.

converting to the religion and attending meetings. The congregation began to outgrow private homes and the dirt grounds of the estates where he preached. In 1783, the first chapel on St Mary's Street, St John's, was constructed.

The Church of England and the Anglican religion arrived with the English settlers during the seventeenth century.[16] The clergy came as chaplains to governors, tutors to the families of wealthy planters or merchants and rectors of parishes.[17] The Anglican Church became the institution of most upper and middle-class people. Harley worshipped at the church of respectability: All Saints Church,[18] where the congregation was predominately 'Baccra',[19] an Antiguan term for white people. At the front of the church were the designated pews for the significant white families. If no family members attended, no one else was allowed to sit in the empty seats.

Presbyterians, Baptists, Catholics and Lutherans were the other religious groups present. For those who believed in mystical and spiritual wonders, there was the Obeah, a man or woman with powers to conjure up spirits and evil shadows to harm people. A visit to the Obeah man was carried out in secret, as inconspicuousness was a requirement. Such was Obeah's influence and the belief that it could exert a malign influence on people that the practice was made illegal after Emancipation.

In 1887, aged fourteen, Harley committed to strengthening his relationship with God. Charles James Branch,[20] the Barbadian, Codrington College-educated (a college established in 1875

---

16   World Council of Church - Church in the Province of the West Indies https://www.oikoumene.org/en/member-churches/moravian-church-eastern-west-indies-province

17   Ibid.

18   Candidate for Deacon's Order application, Harley's personal archive.

19   Antiguan oral history.

20   Thompson Cooper FSA, *Men of the Time: A Dictionary of Contemporaries*, London: George Routledge and Sons, 1884.

with a bequest from the slave owner Christopher Codrington III) Coadjutor Bishop of Antigua, undertook Harley's rites of passage - his confirmation ritual.[21] Harley's vocation as a young boy was to become a priest in the Protestant Episcopal Church (the American branch of the Church of England).[22]

It had been drilled into the young Harley, like many children, that education was the liberator that would set free the black population; it was the instrument to enable them to compete on a playing field that would soon start to become level, especially after the broken promises of Emancipation. For many, the purpose of an education was 'to get on and get out'. A good education was a passport to escape a life of servitude and menial jobs, a system that the white minority wanted to preserve and reinforce.

Before Emancipation, mass education was largely provided by Sunday schools, which multiplied in number in the 1800s.[23] By 1823, the Moravians had established Sunday schools at all their stations and on nineteen estates.[24] Spring Gardens was the largest, created in 1810 and teaching 640 students. The Methodists established sixty-one schools between 1812 and 1831.

The era of Emancipation slowly introduced a process to develop a formal education system. The British government made grants available to the various church mission societies to provide primary schooling for all. The formalization of teaching was not received as a positive step by everybody and was interpreted by the white plantocracy and some middle-class coloureds as a destructive force. Education, they suspected, would give the black population ideas above their enforced and entrenched station in life. Aspirations to develop a career in

---

21   Ibid, Harley's personal archive.
22   Candidate for Deacon's order application, Harley's personal archive.
23   Lowes, p. 111.
24   Ibid.

medicine, law or the ministry would not be encouraged. In 1836, Henry Loving, an Antiguan coloured man, the first to be appointed chief of police, a newspaper editor, and ironically a campaigner for civil rights, through his paper wrote:

> The only universal complaint, or rational cause of alarm, is the withdrawal of the younger persons from any proportion of Plantation labour, or trivial occupation, for the purpose of education, or being placed out to learn different trades of Mechanics or Artisans, and the general impression is, that the System of Education has been overdone and that the rising generation will grow up without the ability or inclination to engage, at any future period, in the different branches of Field Labour, or Cultivation of the Soil.[25]

Thirty-seven years before Harley's birth, Loving's view was still a notion that was applied to the impecunious black masses, and even after his birth and during his schooling, these views were still current and pertinent in Antigua and the Caribbean. William Russell, a Guyanese planter and politician, reinforced the point when he told the Guyana Legislature in 1876: 'We do not want a population of simple penmen. What we require is knowledge of the shovel and the hoe'. When he heard about a newly qualified black lawyer, the same man is said to have muttered, 'another good shovel man spoiled...'[26] A retired Trinidad Inspector of Schools remarked in 1898: 'How often have sugar planters and others said to me, What do you want to educate little niggers for? Put hoes in their hands and send them into the cane pieces.'[27]

Parents understood the benefits of education, but many

---

25   Ibid, p. 110.
26   Brereton, p. 42.
27   Ibid.

could not afford the fee of less than a penny or the potential wage loss.[28] Students paid for the privilege of being taught to read or write. The additional learning would occur before the start of the school day; otherwise schooling consisted of Bible education.

Harley was aged three when the 1876 Education Act required parents to ensure their children attended school.[29] A system of government control was also implemented for regulation and to set standards. The standards ensured schools met specific criteria to receive their government grant.[30] Like the curriculum, though, education for the masses was still limited. Its main aim was to promote Christian values and morality, best served by instruction in Bible study and the teaching of scripture. The Bible was the most common textbook and often the only one. Donors congratulated themselves on the noble cause of converting heathens in far-flung regions of the British Empire.[31] Samuel Smith, a black Antiguan born in 1877, reported the cynical use the British made of the Bible at the Methodist school he attended in Freeman's village. Rendered in the patois of the time, he said:

> They gave us the bible and hymn book and told us we must be obedient to our masses (masters), for Christ was obedient to death. I think that there was hardly one Englishman in this land that was not telling neg (sic) people good was heaven and what we must do to get there.[32]

The grammar school was only for Antigua's legitimate children.

---

28 Lowes, p. 111.
29 Ibid, p. 111.
30 Ibid, p. 111.
31 Howard A Fergus, *A History of Education in the British Leeward Island 1838-1945*. Kingston: University of the West Indies Press, 2003, p. 24.
32 Ibid, p. 24.

The Bishop of Antigua implemented the rule in 1834. Despite protests, the rule was not overturned until a century later, in 1934.[33] But Harley had a father. He could have gone to the grammar school with all the well-bred plantocrats' children. But from the age of five, the All Saints primary school was his playground.[34] School for most working-class children took place in a large room in a small, dilapidated building crowded with other children, who were seated on wooden benches with a minimum of books, slates and copy books. Chalk, talk and rote learning were the order of the day.[35] Teachers were strict, switch in hand, any misbehaving met with a quick flick of the wrist - the switch alighting on the skin and setting it on fire with stinging pain.

Harley remained at All Saints primary school until the age of fifteen.[36] He then left to study as a teacher at the Mico school, considered the best on the island. In 1898, the *Antigua Times* referred to the school that had educated 'the majority of the middle-class people in the city'.

Sir Samuel Mico, an English trader, died in 1666, leaving his wealth to his wife, Lady Jane Mico, and his nephew, Samuel; they established the Lady Mico Charity. The charity funded 300 elementary schools in the British colonies of the West Indies. The London-based Lady Mico Charity had embarked on a teacher training project in the West Indies.[37] Initially encountering resistance from the Anglicans, who felt that all education should be under their control, the Mico trustees persisted with their programme. By 1840, over 196 Mico schools had been established in the region, including

---

33 Lowes, p. 11
34 List of schools attended, Harley's personal archive.
35 Fergus, p. 20.
36 List of schools attended, Harley's personal archive.
37 Lowes, p. 115.

the non-denominational Mico Training School.[38] In 1841, the Mico Charity founded a permanent centre and a practice school at Buxton Grove,[39] a small village located about five miles from St John's. The Mico Normal School provided a two-year course and certification for high school graduates preparing to become teachers. It was non-denominational but profoundly religious - emphasizing morality and a disciplined character.[40] General knowledge of scripture was among the entrance requirements. The applicant's parson had to vouch for their moral character and recommend them as a person of deportment for the teaching profession.[41]

Harley studied a full curriculum of subjects at the Mico school. Mr Buckley, Harley's tutor, marked his progress in 1891 as satisfactory. His concluding remarks rated his conduct at 80% and diligence at 92%.[42] Harley finished his studies at the Mico school in 1892 and proceeded to the Teachers' Training College at Spring Gardens.[43]

In 1894, Harley reached two milestones; he turned twenty-one, and completed the Government Certificate and so became a teacher in elementary schools. But the oversupply of teachers, pay not equating with experience, and lack of teaching opportunities in Antigua all became the catalyst for Harley to embark on a journey of 251 miles to Puerto Rico to seek new opportunities.

Puerto Rico was a staunchly Roman Catholic territory, and Catholicism had been the only religion permitted since the beginning of Spain's colonial rule in 1493. In 1869, however,

---

38   Ibid, p. 115.
39   Ibid, p 115.
40   Fergus, *op. cit.*
41   Ibid.
42   Mico certificate, Antigua, Harley's personal archive.
43   Ibid.

Harley's half year examination results from the Mico School,
Antigua 1891. (Private collection)

religious freedom was granted in Puerto Rico,[44] and the first Protestant church was established in 1873, when Bishop William Walrond Jackson, Lord Bishop of Antigua, provided for the creation of the Holy Trinity Anglican Church in Ponce.[45] He was the first Anglican Bishop to visit the neighbouring island of Vieques (attached to Puerto Rico) on 24 February 1885,[46] where he was received and attended throughout his stay by Joseph Nathaniel Bean.[47] A native of Bermuda, Bean, a British government employee in Jost Van Dyke, the smallest island of the British Virgin Islands, had become aware of a colony of Bermudians who had sought work in the burgeoning sugar industry in Vieques without any spiritual counsel. Bean arrived in Vieques in November 1880 with his wife, Lucinda.

Harley and Bean's paths would cross, and Bean would play a pivotal role in his life and destiny. Bean, a layman, read prayers and conducted Sunday school services. Wishing to be licensed as a catechist, he travelled to America after the death of his wife to undertake training for the priesthood in Raleigh, North Carolina. He returned to Vieques and was ordained on 25 February 1893 at the parish church of St John. Rev Bean was instituted Rector of All Saints Episcopal Church, Puerto Rico, and inducted at a public service on 22 February 1894. Adjacent to All Saints Church stood the Vieques School, where Harley had secured a teaching position. Rev Bean provided a role model for the young Harley as a black man who travelled to America to receive his clerical training, and who returned to administer to his fellow countrymen. Bean proved instrumental in crystallizing Harley's decision to study in America.

---

44 Charles L. Colmore, *Historical Magazine of the Protestant Episcopal Church*, vol. 11, no. 4 (December 1942), pp. 398-406.
45 From the journal of The Bishop of Antigua papers.
46 Ibid, p. 4.
47 Ibid, p. 12.

At the end of the centurry, the political climate in both Puerto Rico and Antigua started to change. On 25 July 1898, US troops invaded Puerto Rico at the start of the Spanish-American War. Harley returned to Antigua. Like many islands throughout the Caribbean, Antigua had begun to suffer a change in fortunes and prosperity. For centuries the sugar industry had afforded its white planters wealth, status and identity. From the 1840s, the industry started to decline. Now a real crisis was looming.

Many factors contributed to the Caribbean's economic woes. The Sugar Duties Act of 1846 gradually removed the differential tariff protection that had protected the market for sugar coming into Britain from its colonies.[48] A riot in March 1858 led to five days of fighting when Thomas Barnard, a Barbudan, and Henry Jarvis, an Antiguan, both stevedores, argued in a rum shop about Bernard receiving preference over Jarvis from shipmasters entering St John's harbour and gaining more jobs for his men. The riot may have started as a drunken argument, but it was an explosive reaction by people to the discontent bubbling away as the economic downturn took hold of their ability to get work, feed their families and survive. The year 1862 saw the worst drought in fifty years, drastically reducing production.[49] European sugar beet began to compete in the British marketplace when imports began in the 1860s and rapidly increased. West Indian production declined steadily after 1862.[50] The future was grim, with no immediate signs of improvement. In 1862, 12,920 tons of sugar was produced; in 1863, 10,124 tons; in 1864, 2,613 tons; in 1865, 7,906 tons. Prices were at an all-time low, and

---

48 Lowes, p. 2.
49 Ibid, p. 32.
50 Ibid, p. 3.

the combination created a severe crisis.[51] Estates were sold off, and planters headed home to England. By the 1890s, Antigua had become an island where absentees were the largest owners.[52]

Antigua's economic crises of the 1890s provided no opportunities for Harley to participate fully in the dawning of the new era Emancipation had promised. Improvements in social and political conditions had not materialized and would not be realized for the black population. Harley's lighter skin may have gained him certain privileges, but these were limited. Lighter-skinned blacks could aspire to little better than clerkships. Any real prospects of advancement lay outside of the island, especially when pursuing a professional career as a minister. Harley had become a headmaster at the Mico Normal School, training pupil teachers for government examinations. He saved and amassed the requisite funds to leave the island. His goal of being a minister lay in the land of opportunities - America. He was equipped with references from Rev Bean of Puerto Rico for the General Theological Seminary in New York.

A man short in stature, five feet six inches, his round-edged glasses framing his face, but with lofty dreams and ideas, the twenty-five-year-old Harley departed Antigua's shores for the United States in 1898 to start on his journey to achieve his vocation.

---

51 Ibid, p. 3.
52 Ibid, p. 4.

3. A West Indian in New York

'Success is to be measured not so by the position that one has reached in life as by the obstacles which he has overcome while trying to succeed.'

Booker T. Washington.

Harley's eyes were soon opened to America's direct, overt, endemic and entrenched racism. He had arrived on the cusp of the twentieth century, an era steeped in horrific racial prejudice. In 1896, the historic Plessy v. Ferguson case had implemented the overt racial separatist laws in the South – the doctrine of 'separate but equal', or Jim Crow laws. He had arrived in an America that still held ingrained beliefs that black people were intellectually inferior and could not function efficiently without the plantation's rigorous and disciplined work. Black men were often portrayed as savages, uncontrollable without the slave master's whip, sexualized, predatory beings lusting after the revered white woman. Whites used lynching and the ever-present threat of violence to effectively keep blacks in place and to intimidate any white people who sympathized with them.

Caribbean immigrants generally settled in already existing or evolving African American communities.[53] Many were well educated. Winston James notes that 'of those who arrived, quite a few were skilled craftsmen, teachers, preachers, lawyers, and doctors.' Hubert H. Harrison observed: 'It was taken for granted that every West Indian immigrant was a paragon of intelligence and a man of breeding.' Once in New York, however, most immigrants took menial jobs.[54] For men, this

---

53 Irma Watkins-Owens, *Blood Relations: Caribbean Immigrants and the Harlem Community*, Bloomington IN: Indiana University Press. 1996, p. 5.

54 David Reimers, *Other Immigrants: the Global Origins of the American People*, New York City: New York University Press, 2005; Winston James, *Holding Aloft the Banner of Ethiopia: Caribbean Radicalism in Early Twentieth Century America*, London: Verso, 1998.

meant working as a labourer, porter or an elevator operator.[55] A railroad porter job was considered middle-class in the black community, as was a job at the post office.

Having coloured skin in America did not automatically classify Harley as black. White America only saw one label - Negro - while black communities in the North used more subtle differences and categories. To black America, he was a black man, not a Negro. A black man would hold his head up, look a white man in the eye and converse with him. He would not be reduced to the head lowering appeasement of a man known as a Negro, subjected to being belittled, dehumanized and emasculated in 1900s America. Harley had no intention of lowering his head to anyone. As a West Indian in New York, it became apparent that he would have to navigate the both the simple racism of white America and the complex racism of black America. But Harley's colonial upbringing equipped him with self-confidence bordering on arrogance.

It was thought by some African Americans that West Indian blacks thought themselves superior to them.[56] This was a belief predicated on the notion of Englishness. Throughout the Caribbean, the colonial education system instilled an English sense of superiority, and a person's social class was also an intrinsic aspect of the black West Indian make-up and identity rather than colour consciousness alone. The black West Indian became the black Englishman abroad, a caricature of an Englishman filled with self-importance, arrogance and aloofness. Not only was Harley a West Indian: he was a mulatto West Indian.

---

55 Ibid.
56 Harold T. Lewis, *Yet With a Steady Beat: the African American Struggle for Recognition in the Episcopal Church*, Valley Forge PA: Trinity Press International, 1996.

Ambition, education, and pride, according to the poet and playwright, Lennox Raphael, are three words dear to the West Indian heart, and since he is hung up on these three words, he sometimes accuses Afro-Americans as having no ambition, wishing no education and possessing no pride.[57]

Such attitudes created tension between Caribbean and American blacks. Black West Indians were incredibly insulted by the demeaning colour bar enforced on American blacks and which they seemed to accept. The Guyanese writer Eric Walrond wrote:

On coming to the United States, the West Indian often finds himself out of patience with attitudes he meets there respecting the position of white and Negros. He is bewildered ... at being shoved down certain blocks and alleys 'among his own people.' He is angry and amazed at the futility of seeking certain types of employment for which he may be specially adapted. And about the cruellest injury that could be inflicted upon him is to ask him to submit to the notion that because he is black, it is useless for him to aspire to be more than a tap drummer at Smalls, a red cap at Pennsylvania station or a clerk in a Bowling Green Post Office.[58]

Clarence Coleridge, one of two Caribbean Bishops in the American Episcopal Church, shared the following:

I was trained, and in most West Indian families, I know it was the same to be upwardly mobile. One knew one could make it. One perhaps knew one had to go abroad

---

57 Eric Walrond, *Winds Can Wake up the Dead: an Eric Walrond Reader*, Detroit MI: Wayne State University Press, 1998, p. 14.
58 Ibid, p. 14.

to get, as they said, your papers - higher education, but one had the confidence that one could succeed. And I suppose that this is responsible for the sense of arrogance which many West Indians are accused of. You already knew you could make it.[59]

*

Harley had travelled to America to pursue his vocation, to become a minister in the Protestant Episcopal Church. Established after the American Revolution, the Episcopal Church has its roots in the Anglican Church and was formed when most of America's Anglican clergy refused to swear allegiance to the British monarch as was required.[60]

The first black priest of the Protestant Episcopal Church and founder of the first black Episcopal church in America was Absalom Jones. Born into slavery in Delaware, Jones taught himself to read using the New Testament. Sold to a shopkeeper in Philadelphia aged sixteen, Jones attended a black night school operated by Quakers. Following the purchase of his freedom in 1784, Jones served as a lay minister for the black membership at St George's Methodist Episcopal Church. The active evangelism of Jones and his friend, Richard Allen, increased black membership at St George's, and in 1794 Jones and Allen established the African Episcopal Church of St Thomas in Philadelphia with local Quakers and Episcopalians' assistance. Shortly afterwards, he applied to join the Protestant Episcopal Church and was accepted into the Diocese of Pennsylvania. Jones became a Deacon the following year but was not ordained a priest until 1804. He founded a day school (blacks were then excluded

---

59   Lewis, *Yet with a Steady Beat.*
60   The Anglican Communion, Episcopal Church Archives (www.
     episcopalchurch.org, accessed 17 February 2016.

from attending public school), the Female Benevolent Society and an African Friendly Society. Jones died in 1818.

The reality of Harley's goal - training at the General Theological Seminary - the oldest seminary of the Episcopal Church and a leading centre for theological education in the Anglican Communion - was near. In the decades following the Civil War, scores of West Indians came to the United States at American Bishops' invitation to study for the priesthood. They were ordained to serve black parishes both in the North and South. The American Church establishment perceived West Indian blacks as superior in education, intellect and refinement when compared to prospective minister candidates in their dioceses, especially in the South.[61]

Harley arrived at the General Theological Seminary with recommendations from the Rev Bean of Puerto Rico for Dean Hoffman.[62] The New York Chelsea landowner, Clement Moore Clarke, best known as the author of the poem 'The Night Before Christmas', had donated the Chelsea Square block for the location of the Seminary.[63] Established by a General Convention on 27 May 1817, the red brick building occupies 440 West 21st Street, a quiet street in the otherwise busy Chelsea area of New York.

Rev Eugene Augustus Hoffman, Doctor of Divinity (Oxon), Doctor of Civil Law and Doctor of Laws, presided over the General Theological Seminary as its dean. The eldest son of Samuel Verplanck Hoffman and Glorvina Russell Storm Hoffman, he received degrees from Rutgers College, Harvard, Oxford, Sewanee: the University of the South, Trinity University, Toronto, and University of King's College, Windsor, Nova

---

61   Lewis, *op. cit.*
62   Greenleaf Financial Aid Application, 1903-1904 Harvard University Archives call no: UA 15.98.10 1890-1968, Box no. 2070 Folder title: Harley, James Arthur - 1906.
63   General Theological Seminary information leaflet.

The General Theological Seminary of the Episcopal Church, New York.
(Wikimedia Commons)

Scotia. He graduated from the General Theological Seminary in 1851 and became its dean twenty-seven years later.[64] He was known as the wealthiest clergyman in the world because of his extensive property holdings.

Dean Hoffman implemented the Seminary's grand design. His attendance at Oxford influenced the choice of neo-Gothic buildings facing onto a central quadrangle. The Seminary's heart, the 161-foot tower of the Chapel of the Good Shepherd, was inspired by Magdalen College's fifteenth-century Tower in Oxford. Dean Hoffman introduced many of the distinctive marks of student life and community and collegiate customs: commencement ceremonies in 1880 and 1881, student academic gowns for class and chapel in 1880, and in 1892 the Oxford cap.

---

64 GTS Catalog 1892-1893 p. 39.

But Harley's excitement and anticipation at starting religious instruction for Holy Orders in the Episcopal Church were short-lived. To his surprise, he was firmly directed to King Hall in Washington DC. He was unfamiliar with American life, its locations and states, and despite his objections, he had no choice but to follow this order.[65] The newly arrived young West Indian had protested he was in the right place, but turned away from the General Theological Seminary, Harley was never acquainted with its dormitories, halls or chapel.

Because of the limitations of Harley's archive and with no further information available from the Seminary it is difficult to ascertain whether Harley actually met Dean Hoffman and why he was turned away. The reasoning behind for Harley's rejection could not be based purely on his colour; the Seminary had previously educated black clergymen.

Despite his objections, Harley travelled to Washington DC. He discovered that King Hall was a theology school preparing black students for Holy Orders at Howard University. Harley now found himself in an American state where he had not planned to live and at a college which he had not planned to attend.

---

65 Matthews Scholarship application Harvard University Archives 1903 call no: UA 15.98.10 1890-1968, Box no. 2070 Folder title: Harley, James Arthur 1906.

4. The Washington 400

'I've never seen such a collection of Black, brown, tan, beige, yellow colour-struck bourgeois, blue-vein, prim, high-minded, unfeeling go their own way intellectually, hopelessly, ineffectual quiet and clean Negros in my life as I have seen moving in confused circles in and around Washington D.C., all on U Street alone.'[66]

Despite his unpromising arrival, Harley was to remain in Washington DC; the state capital, the seat of democracy, a city where slavery 'officially' ended in 1862, and home to the largest percentage of African Americans of any city in the country. Harley enrolled, but not for the clergy course. Instead, he registered for the preparatory certificate at Howard University in 1899.[67]

The Historically Black College or University (HBCU) dubbed 'Negro Oxford' sat on a hilltop in north-west Washington, two miles from the US Capitol. It was founded in 1866, its initial and humble beginning as a teachers' training school. The founding concept for the university began in meetings between members of the First Congregational Society of Washington, as an institute for African American clergymen, although the aim was soon broadened to encompass medicine and the liberal arts.

The university acquired its name from Oliver Otis Howard, a white Civil War general. Born in 1830 and educated at West Point Miltary Academy, Howard commanded thirty-six battles during the Civil War, starting with Bull Run in 1861. He lost his left arm in 1862 in the battle of Fair Oaks.[68] General Howard became a

---

66   Kerr, *op. cit.*
67   Harley archive.
68   Paul K. Williams, *Greater U Street (Images of America)*, Mount Pleasant SC: Arcadia Publishing 2002.

General Oliver Otis Howard, Commissioner of the Freedmen's Bureau.
(Wikimedia Commons)

commissioner of the Freedmen's Bureau, a government agency established by Congress in March 1865 to help the transition from slavery to freedom in the South.[69] Howard University was designated as a university in 1867 by charter in Congress and approved by President Andrew Johnson; early financial support came from the Freedmen's Bureau. Howard University made significant strides in its progressive development by establishing medical training and making history in 1869 by creating the first black law school in the country. General Howard served as the university's first president from 1869 to 1874.

The university campus was a hive of activity close to U Street. Formerly agricultural land and orchards, the cleaned and open land served as a settlement for Camp Cambell during the Civil War. After the war, thousands of soldiers, freedmen and whites, flooded into the district.[70] Imposed segregation elsewhere in the city made the U Street Corridor, which ran from 14th Street to 4th Street,[71] the focal point for Washington's black culture and commerce. Standing at 1200 U Street was the True Reformer Building, built by the United Order of True Reformers, a Richmond, Virginia-based Benevolent Society that offered insurance and banking services to African Americans. Twenty-eight-year-old John A. Lankford, alleged to be the first black architect in Washington, designed the building. Upon its completion in 1902, the headline in the white-owned *Washington Post* read: 'Erected by Negros; White race Had No Hand in Any Part of work'.[72] The True Reformers was a building of prominence and elegance, and a fitting space to entertain and host black elite dances, socials and society events.

---

69   The Episcopal Church Archives www.episcopalarchives.org/discover/african-american-episcopal-collections, accessed 17 February 2016.
70   Williams, p. 9.
71   John DeFerrari, *Historic Restaurants of Washington D.C.*, Mount Pleasant SC: Arcadia Publishing, 2013, p. 102
72   Williams, p. 28.

The black community frequented restaurants, diners and cafés in the neighbourhood. The Delmo-Koonce Café, on the ground floor of the Odd Fellows Hall, was popular, while Gray and Costley offered its black clientele dining rooms upstairs and cigars and liquor purchased on the ground floor.[73] Gaskins & Gaines' Academy Restaurant was part of the local, black-centred economy, and further uptown was the black-owned saloon Moore and Prioleau's Sparta Buffet, famous for its cocktails.

*

While at Howard, news reached Harley about the closing of the Mico school. The school had played a role in providing him with the academic and social skills that were the foundation of his early life. The depression of the 1890s in Antigua had affected the Mico Charity, and in 1898, after several years of financial struggle, it had to put its property up for sale. In a three-page letter to the Editor of *The Antigua Standard* he voiced his disgust at the closing of the Mico. His message was also a call to arms to his fellow Antiguans to motivate and develop themselves, to follow in his footsteps and those of other Antiguans.

The letter was difficult to transcribe, and some words are missing because of its degenerated state.

Dear Sir,

Please permit me to address a few words to my countrymen through the medium of your columns.

Brave young men of Antigua, I cannot reconcile myself to the closing of the Mico. Are you? The Mico! Most potent, albeit unobtrusive, in the intellectual development of Antigua's sons! True, there is the Grammar school, but to this, while the few are not the

---

73   DeFerrari, p. 102.

many so far? Bright lads of the village, hopelessly you sit 'amid the encircling gloom'. But what would you do if a gift presented itself into the darkness? Would you remain seated in your dull, despairing chair if the shadows of night were to be chased away by the smiling rosy-cheeked morn? I know not. Therefore this letter is written to light the cheerless subject to point a path out of the difficulty.

Let us survey the Giants in the way. In the first place, do we not well know Wrangler took his theological course at the famous New York General Theological Seminary? Have we forgotten that Trinity College, New York State, conferred D. Dow, the late Archdeacon Clarke when he wrote De Apostolical Succession? Is it not well-known that our own intrepid Dr Wykham received fully ninety per cent of his medical within these walls of Howard University? Above all, did not that incomparable mathematical and all-rounded scholar Rev. R. John E. M.A. B.C.L. leave West Indies shores to study medicine in New York?

There is a prejudice against our American education, or rather, there WAS. (…)

We find the total of the reports about the Great Land of Opportunities constitutes the triple-faced giant of lynching, race prejudice, and menial work.

Difficult the lynching to take, greet the name of race prejudice with silent disdain. And so for menial work, dare you, craven-hearted, forget what is at stake. Nay, as if door be low, just stoop to conquer. Or should the door be very low? Why crawl to conquer? But be a conqueror bold.

Our next step reveals a mountain with its top touching the sky across our road – Expenses! Young men, find your way here and register. Let it be granted that to you it proves steep, unusually; others have climbed; why cannot your mother's son distinguish himself? To him with the grit to do that, the rest is easy; all is clear. It is not more difficult than was learning your alphabet. Attempt something, go to Lincoln, Shaw, Come to Howard. Here are Law, Dental, Medical and Theological departments. Choose. Expenses are not high. Do not win the fees. Earn them here. That is more modern, cannier, more ideal. Can you print? Do you know photography and music (I get three shillings per hour to teach vocal music)? A Student's Aid Association helps new men to find employment to defray expenses.

Whatever your hand, find, make do, do it with all your might.

Besides – oh, you no longer need expense? Do not see the mountain?

That mountain was a mirage. But some irascible forgery will raise still one more objection regarding a 'field' [profession]. My fellow-Antiguans despising American Institutions, dreading lynching, blaming prejudice, fearing to soil your ten dainty West Indian fingers, waiting for your expenses to be mailed from heaven, uncertain about finding a 'field' after graduating? Have you ensconced so long? And there I ask whether you will continue to sit bemoaning your melancholy fate any longer?

Harley's character and determination, driven by ambition, anger and a strong sense of purpose is evident in his letter to his fellow Antiguans. He is prepared to undertake whatever is meted out to him to achieve his goal.

*

Harley received his certificate from the Howard Preparatory Department in 1900.[74] He found employment at the United States Postage Stamp Agency to support himself as a student and to secure income for his room, board and living expenses.[75] He also worked as a lay preacher, a Sunday school teacher and choirmaster at St Luke's Church.[76] The church, situated at 1514 15th Street, was the city's first independent black Episcopal congregation and one of the most influential churches among Washington's black elite. The Episcopal Church was the denomination that included more aristocrats of colour than any other and was considered a high-status church by whites. The ranks of those attending black Episcopal churches constituted a 'privileged' group and included a disproportionately large number of the most respected 'old families', professionals and others whose education and affluence often set them apart from other blacks.[77] St Luke's was no different, Sunday brought an array of the best dressed and polished men and women to take their place in pews alongside the white members of the congratulation.

The many local whites who attended St Luke's distinguished it from the other elite black churches. George Freeman Bragg Jr, a well-known black Episcopal clergyman, admitted that the church contained 'a small contingent of dandiacal coloured people', who used the church 'to get as far as possible from the ordinary Negro'.[78]

St Luke's may have employed a colour bar door policy, its solid beige door keeping Washington's harsh winters at bay but

---

74 The Directory of Graduates, Howard University, 1870-1963.
75 Ibid, 1903-1904.
76 Ibid.
77 Willard B Gatewood, *Aristocrats of Colour: The Black Elite 1880-1920*, Fayetteville AR: University of Arkansas Press, 2000, p. 285.
78 George F. Bragg Jr in *New York Age*, 13 June 1907.

also used to check the parishioners' shades of pigmentation. A God-worshipping person who was darker than the church door was politely but firmly told by the minister or a congregation member that this was not the church for them. The sedate, sombre services at St Luke's and Episcopal churches demonstrated severity and good manners, behaviours to illustrate to whites that they were different from the black masses and could be accepted; there would be no emotional outbursts or exaggerated whooping, wailing and fainting spells.

The imposing stone structure of the church, with a large stained-glass window behind the chancel, was established in 1875 by Rev Dr Alexander Crummell, the son of an ex-slave. Crummell travelled to England to raise money for his church and lectured on anti-slavery. He is recognized as the first officially recorded black student to study and graduate from the University of Cambridge in 1853. An alumnus of Queens' College, his three-year tuition fee and expenses were supported by British evangelicals. After graduating, Dr Crummell spent a period teaching in Liberia before returning to America to develop St. Luke's. After his resignation, Dr Owen Meredith Waller, born in 1868 in Eastville, Virginia, succeeded Crummell. Waller was a student at the St Mary's Home for Little Colored Boys in Baltimore.[79] He was then accepted by the Society of St John the Evangelist, based in Marston Street, East Oxford, England, also known as the Cowley Fathers. The Society was founded by Richard Meux Benson in 1866 as the first Anglican male monastic order since the Reformation. Waller received an Associate of Arts (A.A) from the University of Oxford in 1887, a certificate awarded to young men who had passed the Senior Local Examination.[80] Waller returned to America and entered the General Theological Seminary in 1892 by competitive

---

79 *Afro American*, 1 August 1936.
80 University of Oxford, Bodleian Library.

scholarship.[81] Ordained in 1893 by Bishop Potter,[82] Waller held a brief tenure at St Thomas from 1896 to 1905 followed by a fruitful period of service at St Luke's from 1896 to 1905.[83] Rev Waller later became a founding member of the National Association for the Advancement of Colored People (NAACP), founded on 12 February 1909 in New York City.

At St Luke's Harley was introduced to a young woman, Josephine Maritcha Lawson; she would become his wife. Like many of St Luke's congregation, the Lawsons were not typical of the average black Americans who occupied Washington's tenement buildings and alleys, or the construct of the usual narrative and imagery associated with African Americans at the beginning of the twentieth century. They were associated with Washington's black elite - a concentration of 'old families' bound together by background, good breeding, occupation, respectability and colour, making them an exclusive group known as the 'black 400'. Washington's black elite numbered fewer than a hundred families out of a black population of 75,000 in 1900.[84] Even so, the city was still referred to as the centre of 'negro blueblood and aristocrats'.[85]

Through their efforts and endeavours, the black 400 were families who had utilized the negativity of segregation as the principal driving force for building and establishing successful black-owned businesses. Banks, insurance companies, newspapers and social and entertainment venues provided a service for the community and made them wealthy. They owned homes in the fashionable areas of the city, furnished

---

81 *The Colored American*, 20 June 1903.
82 The Reverend Owen Meredith Waller Fifth Rector (1893-1896). African Episcopal Church of St Thomas: aecst.org.
83 St Thomas Church, Washington DC, (https://stthomasdc.org, accessed 20 February 2016).
84 Gatewood, p. 38.
85 Ibid.

with antiques, cushions and drapes that demonstrated not only their style and taste but projected their wealth and status to the other families within the 400. The educated, sophisticated and refined black elite existed in an insular goldfish bowl: removed spatially, economically and socially from the black masses who occupied the crowded dwellings in places such as Hog Alley, Coon's Alley, Goat Alley and Tin Can Alley, and this enabled them to avoid the daily humiliating experiences of Jim Crow.

An 'old' family name synonymous with the Washington black elite, which oozed prestige, was Cook. Association with the Cook family carried considerable cachet and influence. The patriarch, John Francis Cook, was a freeman who founded the 15th Street Presbyterian Church in 1841. A white acquaintance described Cook in 1849 as 'a gentleman in all his departments, whose complexion placed him about halfway between pure Anglo-Saxon and the doomed race.'[86] His two sons, George Francis Cook and John Francis Cook, were both graduates of Oberlin College, Ohio, which played a pivotal role in educating many members of the Washington black elite. Founded in 1833 by a Presbyterian minister and missionary, Oberlin was a leader in the education of African Americans with a reputation as a centre for abolitionist activities. Oberlin's founding trustees agreed that 'the education of people of colour is a matter of great interest and should be encouraged & sustained in the institution.' Carter G. Woodson, the scholar of Afro-American history, observed: 'Oberlin College did so much for the education of the Negroes before the Civil War. As a result, it was often spoken of as an institution for the people of color.'[87]

---

86   Carter G. Woodson, *The Mis-Education of the Negro*, Washington DC: Associated Publishers, 1933, p. 26.
87   Woodson, p. 26.

The young John Cook was referred to as a 'leader of the aristocracy among the darkies',[88] who looked down on poor blacks, particularly the Virginia contrabands (escaped enslaved people from the South) flooding into Washington. Cook and his friends thought such people unfit for decent coloured society. A black critic described George Cook and his coterie of aristocratic friends in Washington as 'constituting something of a mutual aid society which manifested no concerns for ordinary blacks and was solely concerned with promoting the welfare of their social group.'

Several families among the '400' were accepted by Washington's white society, and exceptions were made for what white society defined as "refined and genteel Negroes".[89] The Syphaxs, Wormleys, Shades, Francises, Grays and Bruces fitted comfortably into this prescribed mould. The Shades, Francises, Grays and Wormleys began as restaurateurs and caterers. Joseph Wormley founded Wormley House, the first African American hotel, in 1871, located near the White House. It represented a pinnacle of black achievement for its time. The five-storey structure had offices, an acclaimed dining room on the first floor, which served European-style dishes, and parlours and apartments on the upper floors. It could accommodate a hundred and fifty guests, primarily the capital's wealthy white political leaders, but the black community also used the hotel, which had the newest facilities such as elevators, telephones and electric bells. The basement had a bar that was widely known for its excellent wines and a first-class barbershop.[90]

Blanche Kelso Bruce became Washington's first black Senator. An ex-slave born to a white father - his master - and a black mother, Bruce's fortune was that his father took an

---

88 Gatewood, *op. cit.*
89 Ibid.
90 John M. Ingram and Lynne B. Feldman, *African Americans Business Leaders: A Biographical Dictionary*, Westport CT: Greenwood Press, 1994, p. 710.

Senator Blanche Kelso Bruce. (Library of Congress, Washington DC)

interest in him and his education; he shared lessons with the master's legitimate son. Bruce attended Oberlin College for a short period and went on to work as a steamboat porter on the Mississippi before becoming a wealthy landowner in the Mississippi Delta during Reconstruction. A rising star in the Republican Party, Bruce quickly progressed from his election as sheriff in Bolivar County and took other county positions, including tax collector and supervisor of education; he was elected to the US Senate in 1874. William Syphax, meanwhile, became chief messenger at the Interior Department and the first head of the city's black school system.[91]

As a group, the Washington black elite socialized almost exclusively among themselves,[92] setting up their clubs, societies, organizations and churches, where their 'good breeding', culture and sophistication could be displayed for both black and whites to witness. The black elite saw themselves as separate from the run of the mill black person in Washington and frequently complained about the lack of manners and morals among the city's African Americans.[93] 'They would never be anything - except nothing - of the flimsiest and poorest, weakest and meanest quality at that,' noted Bruce Grit, a syndicated columnist from New York. Bruce Grit was the pen name of John Edward Bruce, an African American journalist, historian and civil rights activist. He held the Washington black elite up to ridicule for their shallowness and meaningless sense of distinction.[94]

---

91   Tucker Carlson, 'Washington's Lost Black Aristocracy', City Journal, New York, Autumn, 1996.
92   Jacqueline M. Moore, *Leading the Race: The Transformation of the Black Elite in the Nation's Capital*, Charlottesville VA: University of Virginia Press, 1999, p. 11.
93   Wendell E. Pritchett, *Robert Clifton Weaver and the American City: the Life and Times of an Urban Reformer*, Chicago IL: Chicago University Press, 2008, p. 12.
94   Moore, p. 9.

5. The Interlopers

'Mrs. Lawson may be regarded as one thoroughly alive to the needs of the race. She is full of holy race pride, and is ever ready to lend a helping hand to any effort that has in view the elevation of the Afro-American and the betterment of the condition of mankind. To say that she is liberal, wise, kind, prudent and just is to tell only a part of her good traits.'

L.A, Scruggs, *Women of Distinction*, 1892

Harley's future in-laws, the Lawsons, existed on the periphery of the Washington black elite through their association with the Cook family and members of the other families that made up the exclusive enclave. 'If one was educated and exhibited "true gentility" but lacked a distinguished family heritage, admittance to the upper tens was highly likely.'[95] The Lawsons were undoubtedly members of the upper class, but were not - and would never be considered to be - members of the Washington black elite. William Calvin Chase, for instance, a free-born, educated and socially prominent native of Washington, the editor and publisher of the *Washington Bee*, and related through his mother, Lucinda Seaton, to 'one of the best and purest families in the Commonwealth of Virginia', was never in the top stratum of Washington's black society but on the rung below it.[96]

The Lawsons were both interlopers from neighbouring Maryland and Virginia; not from an 'old' Washington family. The old citizens and their descendants drew a sharp line of

---

95   Ibid, p. 9.
96   Gatewood, p. 57.

distinction between themselves and those from the outside who also 'possessed culture and affluence, but who lacked the longevity of residences in the district that bestowed considerable status'.[97] The Lawsons were not in industry or commerce, and were intellectually elite individuals, but they remained '*people*, but not our kind of people.' Old citizens exercised caution when considering new entrances into their social circle. They not only investigated a newcomer regarding their character, background, education and respectability, but also required a proper introduction, meaning that someone had to vouch for them to verify that he or she would not be unfit or uncordial.[98]

The Lawsons resided within the enclave of the black elite at 2011 Vermont Avenue in the historic LeDroit Park, a neighbourhood of Washington lying south-east of Howard University. The district was founded in 1873 by Amzi Barber, a former teacher and Principal of the Normal and Preparatory Department at Howard University. Barber purchased forty acres of land from Howard University and hired architect James H. McGill to develop a new sub-division. McGill designed sixty-four houses in the neighbourhood; no two houses were alike. Developed and marketed as a romantic district, it was exclusively for whites only. The development had black wrought-iron gates with the inscription LeDroit Park in large gold letters at the entrance of 14th Street. The tree-lined streets, landscaping and flower beds aimed to attract the 'right' city professionals, not extending to or including the black professionals who were flowing into the city to take up professional and teaching positions at Howard University. The neighbourhood was gated and guarded to ensure LeDroit kept 'undesirables' out and provided safety and security.

---

97   Ibid, p. 57.
98   Ibid, p. 46.

By then, Washington's black elite had existed for decades, and the new generation of blacks was no longer willing or forced to capitulate. They saw themselves as part of the brand-new elite and refused to accept gates and fences to segregate them. Numerous protests, notably by the students at Howard University, led to the fences being torn down in 1888 and the resulting racial integration of the neighbourhood. Octavius Augustus Williams, a barber, was the first black to move into the LeDroit Park neighbourhood in 1893. The Lawsons' home on Vermont Avenue was a sizeable three-storey row house with a series of open-planned rooms with polished wood floors, and six fireplaces.[99]

Jesse Lawson, Harley's future father-in-law, was a small, dark-skinned man with a receding hairline, and a purposeful expression. His ancestry was traced back to his great-grandmother, Sara Price, an enslaved woman who bought her freedom in 1834 when she 'signed' her manumission papers with her thumbprint. Mr Lawson, born in 1856, was from a family that had lived in the enslaved state of Maryland. His parents, Jesse Lawson and Charlotte Price, migrated to Washington to take advantage of the better education and employment opportunities the state offered. Jesse obtained his BA degree from Howard University, graduating *cum laude* in 1881, and then from the Law Faculty in 1884, the same year he married his wife, Rosetta Evelyn Coakley.

Jesse Lawson had steady employment as a legal examiner at the Bureau of Pensions in Washington, a tenure that would last forty-four years. His political affiliation lay with the Republican Party and he was a socially active campaigner for improvement to the working and living conditions of African Americans. He became a sociology lecturer in 1890 at the Lyceum of the

---

99   Makiel Talley oral history.

Second Baptist Church and held the dual roles of legislative and financial director for the National Afro-American Council (AAC). The Council was established in 1898 by Thomas Fortune and Bishop Alexander Walters of the African Methodist Episcopal Zion Church and was a forerunner to the National Association for the Advancement of Colored People (NAACP).

The Afro-American Council was a pioneering organization of its time; it welcomed women as equal members, being one of the first black organizations to do so. The AAC made great strides to establish itself as a body with real influence by meeting regularly with President William McKinley each year between 1898 and 1901.[100] Lawson was directly involved in 1889 with the historic election of the first black man in Virginia to represent Congress: John Mercer Langston, Dean of Howard University Law School. Langston had run for Congress in Virginia but seemed to lose the vote; contesting the result, Lawson successfully made representation to the Virginia electoral committee to recognize his election and seat him in Congress.

Lawson held a two-year editorship of *The Colored American* newspaper from 1895-1897. The newspaper, like Lawson, was staunchly Republican and promoted itself as a national newspaper, carrying stories about the achievements of African Americans across the country and articles on politics, education and military affairs. Lawson used the paper as his personal vehicle to promote his meetings and report on the progress of the Afro-American Council. The paper's society feature, 'City paragraph', highlighted events in Washington. To ensure its continued existence, the paper had to make concessions. It relied on subscriptions and, more importantly, much-needed income from advertisers; skin lightening creams and hair straightening kits were promoted on its pages.

---

100 Cyrus Field Adams, *The National Afro-American Council, Organized 1898, A History*, Washington DC, 1902.

Margaret Dischman, a midwife,[101] gave birth to Rosetta Evelyn Coakley, Josephine's mother, on 1 January 1856 in the state of Virginia, in the county located at the gateway to the Northern Neck, between the Potomac and Rappahannock rivers and named after the British King George I. Rosetta Coakley was a small woman, five foot four inches, with a pleasant, homely face, a button nose, long black hair (which looked of mixed - but Indian, not white like Harley's - heritage) that cascaded down to her shoulders. Rosetta attended M Street School, Washington's first school for black children and one of the first in the United States. Known initially as the Preparatory High School for Negro Youth, it was founded in 1870, after schooling was made accessible to black children.

In the early part of the nineteenth century freed blacks who wanted their children educated created private schools.[102] In 1807, one year after the first public school opened for whites, three former enslaved men - George Bell, Moses Liverpool and Nicholas Franklin - organized Washington's first school for black students.[103] George Bell was a carpenter while Franklin and Liverpool were caulkers at the Washington Navy Yard. None of these men was literate. George Bell's wife, a market woman, had purchased his freedom through her dedicated efforts of saving from the income she made by selling produce. The Bell School, the name given to the institution to acknowledge Bell's efforts, leadership and determination in developing educational opportunities for black children, was located at 3rd and D Street in south-east Washington. The school was a modest, one-storey wooden building.

---

101 Taylor archives.
102 Kenneth Mitchell, 'The Story of Dunbar High School: How Students from the First Public High School for Black Students Influenced America', Washington DC: Georgetown University thesis, 2012, pp. 6-11.
103 Ibid.

The opening of the Bell School was momentous, with many whites viewing the practice of educating blacks with disdain. The black community had risen from a history that had denied education to them, and the prospect of being taught amidst open hostility carried risks. Caution was paramount. An agreement was made with the authorities to enable the school to remain open despite threats to shut it down from white dissenters. Yet those students who were still enslaved were not permitted to write, nor was any teacher allowed to write anything down for them. The school also had to convince white critics that it was only providing basic education and not operating as a centre for abolition. The school's first instructor, Mr Lowe, a white man, supported the students by paying for their tuition.

The establishment of public schools for black children finally came about after Congress passed the District of Columbia Compensated Emancipation Act on 21 May 1862, freeing enslaved people in Washington.[104] George Francis Cook and William Syphax had the vision for a Preparatory High School, Cook stating that 'the purpose of the high school was to economize teaching by concentrating under one teacher, several small classes of the same grade of attainment, and to present to the pupils of the school's incentives to aim higher in education.'[105]

The M Street School was later renamed Dunbar High School after the poet Paul Laurence Dunbar,[106] and had a reputation as the best black high school in the country with the ability and reputation to attract the best teachers. The rollcall of its first teachers reads like a black Debrett's of historical achievement: Richard Greener, the first black graduate of Harvard University; Carter Goodwin. Woodson, the historian

104 Ibid, pp. 6-11.
105 Ibid, pp. 6-11.
106 Ibid, pp. 6-11.

M Street High School (Colored), Washington, D. C.

M Street School, Washington DC, early 1910s. (Creative Commons)

and founder of Negro History Week, now celebrated in America in February and the UK in October as Black History Month; and Anna Julia Cooper, the first black woman to graduate from the Sorbonne in Paris. The calibre and wealth of knowledge the school attracted were primarily due to the prevalent racism; most colleges did not hire black professors.

Emma J. Hutchins, a white woman from New Hampshire, had an interest in the education of the black population. She became M Street's first principal and teacher. The school enrolled forty-five students in its first year; four took classes on the high school level, and the other forty-one students took classes to prepare for high school.

Rosetta was one of the first four students in the high school class. Classes took place in the basement of 15th Street Presbyterian Church, in a room equipped with fifty seats. Rosetta's course of study included arithmetic, algebra, geometry, trigonometry, astronomy, English grammar, composition, literature and elocution; there were also lessons in United States English and general history. The school's first class was expected to graduate in 1875, but demand for teachers was increasing and Rosetta and her classmates joined the teaching faculty of the school before they had completed the prescribed course.[107] Rosetta then worked as a high school teacher before attending and graduating with a diploma from the Chautauqua Literary and Scientific Circle in 1884. In the same year, aged twenty-eight, Rosetta married Jesse Lawson.

The Lawsons had four children: Wilfred, Edward, James and Josephine. Josephine Maritcha Lawson, born on 3 November 1885, may have been named after two women her parents admired - Josephine Bruce, the wife of Washington's first black Senator, Blanche Kelso Bruce, and Maritcha, after Maritcha Redmond Lyons. Josephine Bruce, nee Beal Wilson, was a striking, light-skinned, wealthy woman[108] with a distinguished elite Philadelphia pedigree. Her father, an esteemed dentist, published a controversial and anonymous book aimed at educated whites and upper-class blacks in Philadelphia, *Sketches of the Higher Classes of Colored Society of Philadelphia*, in 1841, the same year Blanche Bruce, Josephine's husband, was born. A graduate of Cleveland High School, a teacher and accomplished linguist, Josephine enjoyed literature and classical music. She spent four months in Europe on her honeymoon visiting Paris, London, Vienna and Berlin. Her wardrobe attire came from Saks, the luxury department store on Fifth Avenue in New York. Upon their return from Europe, the couple were celebrated in black and white society alike, entertaining at their residences, Hillside Cottage, and a brownstone on M Street. The *Baltimore America* newspaper maintained that 'her attractive personal traits were sufficient to preclude any embarrassment', and another commentator noted 'a quiet dignity that besets the perfect lady' and 'more education than most of the women who

---

107 Mitchell, pp. 6-11.
108 Gatewood, p. 4.

intend to snub her'. But no matter how fair her complexion, she was still classified as a Negro.

Active in the promotion of women rights, Josephine Bruce was a member of the Colored Women's League of Washington DC and became the first vice-president of the National Association of Colored Women and Dean of Women at the Tuskegee Institute. The Lawsons' naming of their daughter after Josephine Bruce may have been in tribute to her class, status, education and personal achievement as a black woman.

Josephine's usual second name was Maritcha.[109] Maritcha Redmond Lyons was a free black woman born on 23 May 1848 in Lower Manhattan. Her parents owned a seaman's outfitters store and also ran a boarding house for black sailors. The house doubled as a stop on the Underground Railroad, the network of clandestine routes and safe houses used by escaping slaves from the South. It is estimated that her parents helped to liberate 1,000 people.

In July 1863, poor whites in New York, upset at being drafted to fight in the Civil War, turned against blacks in the city. The Draft Riots destroyed the family's business, and Maritcha's home was ransacked and firebombed; she and her family had to flee. Eventually they settled in Providence, Rhode Island, making their decision on the basis that the town's schools had good reputations. Maritcha and her parents had to fight the school district for her right to attend the previously all-white high school. She made history when at the age of sixteen she addressed the Rhode Island state legislature to be allowed to participate in the school of her choice. She was subsequently the first black to graduate from Providence High School. A gifted orator, Marichta's delivery style

---

109 Taylor archive.

had a unique quality: her voice was audible through a large hall, at a time when young ladies were taught to speak softly, and she spoke at numerous events in a long career of supporting education.[110]

Rosetta Lawson's cousin had attended providence High School after Maritcha Redmond Lyons. It is believed Josephine's second name is given in recognition of Maritcha's achievements.

A shy young girl, Josephine Lawson's round face and delicate features combined with her mother's light skin colour and her father's dark skin made her complexion a beautiful mocha chocolate brown colour with 'good hair'. This was a term adopted and used in the black community to signify hair that was not kinky, curly or perceived as ugly; it was soft, silky, smooth, straight, long and easy to manage.

The Lawsons' children's upbringing was in complete contrast to that of Harley as a small child in the rural Antiguan village of All Saints. They grew up in a busy metropolis as members of Washington's upper class, closeted from the harsh realities of Jim Crow. Their social activities included the theatre, attending lectures, poetry readings, lawn parties in Lincoln Park and musical programmes. Josephine was like a canary in a gilded cage, and the mirror did not reflect the suffering of the majority black population. Her parents ensured that she partook in events and activities that indicated that she was a member of the elite: a social diary of pink tea parties (parties for light-skinned blacks[111]) and soirees with genteel friends. The Lawsons escaped Washington's sweltering heat by decamping to Asbury Park, a coastal resort town in New Jersey favoured by some of the elite. Josephine and her brothers could run and skip along the promenades, enjoy fun and games on the beach, indulge in long cold drinks and ice-

---

110 Jessie Carney Smith, *Notable Black Women: Book II*, Detroit MI: Gale, 1996, p. 417.
111 Kerr, p. 37.

creams. Rosetta noted of summer in Asbury Park: 'much of the time is whiled away in some of the numerous pavilions dotted along the coast, watching the restless ocean and drinking in the cool, health-giving breezes constantly wafted landward from the sea.'[112]

Josephine benefitted from her parents' educational achievements. Her life with her brothers centred around their political energy in a household filled with books, committee papers, agendas, speeches and religious and political leaders. Conversations and debates permeated the hall, lounge and dining room as Rosetta and Jesse entertained and hosted meetings for the various societies and committees they were both involved in organizing or assisting. Their meetings regularly featured in the notices of the *Evening Star*, or the 'City paragraph' column of *The Colored American*.

> Mr John W. Thompson, a prominent lawyer of Rochester, New York, and a treasurer of the National Afro-American Council, was in the city Tuesday, the guest of Editor T. Thomas Fortune. He met the general finance committee of the Council Tuesday evening at the residence of Prof. Jesse Lawson.[113]

When Harley met Josephine, she was a shy seventeen-year-old girl, open and trusting with romantic ideals, and a student at the M Street School, the school her mother attended. Harley was a twenty-nine-year-old student at Howard University. The nascent courtship took place at church socials, perhaps under the watchful eye of her parents and elder brothers. As choirmaster at the principal church for the black elite, Harley had some cachet, but realistically he was twelve years her senior and a financially challenged West Indian mulatto student.

---

112 Ibid.
113 *The Colored American*, 18 April 1900.

The Lawsons were members of the Bethel Literary Historical Society, an African American society that consisted mainly of members of Washington's black elite and its upper classes. The organization believed that association with literature was one way of asserting a positive, learned identity far removed from the intellectual poverty associated with slavery. It would thus expose participants to useful knowledge through which black Americans would enlighten themselves, thus becoming better prepared for the demands of citizenship and the particular challenges of the twentieth century.[114] Jesse Lawson regularly attended the society's meetings, usually held on a Tuesday evening at eight o'clock at the Metropolitan African Methodist Episcopal Church, 1518 M Street. This was no ordinary church. Built under the leadership of Daniel Payne in 1886, it functioned as a 'cathedral' for black America.[115] National and international presentations were as varied and lofty as the invited guest speakers who delivered them. The topics ranged from 'Heroes of the Anti-Slavery Struggles' by Mary Ann Shadd Cary, 'Reconstruction' by Pinckney Benton Stewart Pinchback, former Governor of Louisiana, "A Glimpse of Europe' by Mary Church Terrell, 'The Emancipated Races of Latin America' by Congressman John Mercer Langston and 'The Commercial Importance of the High Seas' by Jesse Lawson.

A trailblazer of her time, Mrs Lawson was the first woman to serve as a clerk and assistant to Colored Schools' Superintendent George Francis Cook, one of the original visionaries for the M Street High School. She was active in the promotion of women's issues, while her friends and colleagues including Belle

---

114 Elizabeth McHenry, *Forgotten Readers: Recovering the Lost History of African American Literary Societies*, Durham NC: Duke University Press, 2002.
115 Lewis C. Sheafe, *Apostle to Black America*, Hagerstown MD: Review and Herald Publishing, 2010.

Cox Francis, Anna Evans Murray and Mary Church Terrell were engaged in similar charitable works and activities. Anna Evans Murray, a graduate of Oberlin in 1876, was a staunch advocate of nursery schools, kindergarten education and teacher training.[116]

The Grande Dame of Washington black society, Mary Church Terrell, was the daughter of one of the first black millionaires, Robert R. Crunch of Memphis. A graduate of Oberlin College and a linguist with a command of four languages, Terrell taught Latin at M Street School, where she met her husband, Harvard graduate Robert Terrell. Terrell's father, Harrison Terrell, served as a nurse companion to General Ulysses S. Grant, worked for the banker George Washington Riggs and served in the Department of the Interior for twenty years. Robert became Principal of M Street School, received his Law degree from Howard University[117] and after a series of appointments became the first black judge in the capital. The lynching of her good friend Thomas Moss ignited Mary's activism. A white mob killed him because his business was, in their eyes, too successful. A staunch anti-lynching campaigner, she also campaigned when segregation started to creep into Oberlin College and for universal suffrage. Into her eighties, she worked tirelessly on the desegregation of Washington diners which became the catalyst for the modern-day Civil Rights Movement.

The lives of the Lawson, Terrell, Evans and Francis families differed vastly from those of the black women and poor whites whose daily routine consisted of house cleaning for the rich and, in some instances, the families that made up the Washington elite. In their own circles, Mrs Lawson and her many cohorts were celebrated for the good works they did to elevate and advance the poorer classes. Outside these social

---

116 Smith, p. 493.
117 Moore, p. 11.

Mary Elizabeth Church Terrell. (Wikimedia Commons)

circles, however, they were widely despised, scorned for their snobbery and because they were seen to align themselves with the racially oppressive system that kept the majority of blacks subjugated. Their work and efforts, often viewed with suspicion and interpreted as 'doing good', were thought to be motivated by appeasing their own consciences, aiding their progression up the ladder of social mobility, and advancing their personal and political ambitions.

No matter how superior this elite may have felt as educated, sophisticated or light-skinned blacks who moved effortlessly from soiree to soiree, the Jim Crow culture and the violence of white supremacy threatened all - the masses, the upper classes and the elite.

*

Harley decided to stay in Washington after graduating from Howard University Preparatory Department and enrolled for the University's Law degree. Howard University's School of Law was created to provide legal education for those traditionally excluded from the profession, especially African Americans. The objective was to produce superior professionals capable of achieving positions of leadership in law, business, government, education and public service. The early Law School did not have traditional classrooms; students met at night in the homes and offices of faculty members, all of whom were part-time. Initially, two years were required for the Bachelor of Law (LL.B.) degree. The new three-year programme began in 1900, the year of Harley's matriculation.

In 1900, Rosetta Lawson as Chairwoman of the Women's Temperance Movement travelled to Scotland to deliver a series of lectures in Edinburgh, visiting London and Paris on her return journey. Her visit was reported in *The Colored American* newspaper: 'Mrs Jesse Lawson Hearty Reception at

Edinburgh – Scotland Ability and Character Not Colour the Measure of Mankind. An Ideal Representative of Afro-America - Speaks Eloquently on Temperance at a Leading Presbyterian Church'.[118]

In Harley's second year of Law School, the dramatic event of 6 September 1901 changed America's political landscape when two bullets rang out from the gun of Leon Czolgosz, a Polish immigrant anarchist from Detroit, and lodged in the chest of William McKinley as he was attending the Pan-American Exhibition in Buffalo, New York. The assassination of President McKinley saw Vice-President Theodore Roosevelt sworn in as his successor. The Lawsons were Republicans, and like most of the Washington black elite had some loyalty and expectations of Roosevelt delivering on what was aptly and dismissively called 'the race problem'. Initially, Roosevelt did, speaking out about lynching. He also made a momentous and historical gesture by inviting Booker T. Washington, his adviser on race, the founder of the Tuskegee Institute and considered one of the leading voices on race issues, for tea at the White House. Their meeting overran, and Washington stayed at the request of the President and had dinner, becoming the first black man to dine with a President.

The event caused outrage, especially in the Southern states, and was met with a mixed reaction in the North. The philosophy of Booker T. Washington centred around the black race empowering itself through the acquisition of skilled and manual craft trades; Washington's ideology did not extend to or comprehend blacks developing professional careers in the field of arts, literature and sciences. Some saw him as acquiescent, promulgating a cause that would elevate the black race proportionally, so as not to challenge white supremacy.

---

118 'In the land of Bobby Burns', *The Colored American*, 11 August 1900.

Law graduates from Howard University, c 1910.
(Library of Congress, Washington DC)

Harley achieved his degree from the School of Law in May 1902[119] and won a gold medal for his debating skills.[120] He then set his sights on reaching his second academic goal - Harvard - but a tempting offer was laid across his path. Dr Algernon Sidney Crapsey of Rochester, New York, Rector of St Andrew's Episcopal Church, offered to purchase a scholarship for him at Columbia University.[121]

A member of one of the city's most prominent families, Dr Crapsey was a man late to education, ridiculed because of his poor background and status[122] when he attended St Stephen's

---

119 The Directory of Graduates, Howard University, 1870-1963. Harvard University Archives.
120 Harvard Scholarship application 1903-1904, Harvard University Archives call no: UA 15.98.10 1890-1968, Box no. 2070 Folder title: Harley, James Arthur - 1906.
121 Ibid.
122 Emma Pollock, *Algernon Crapsey, Rochester's Heretic*, University of Rochester, 2013 p. 7.

College, Annandale. His reception and time at the General Theological Seminary School were more positive.[123] Harley may have met Rev Crapsey when he spoke at the Metropolitan African Methodist Episcopal Church in 1901, delivering a constitutional defence of the black race and presenting the doctrine that 'in the Kingdom of God, there is neither white nor Black, bond nor free, but all are one in Christ Jesus'. For preaching that doctrine, he was mildly admonished by those in high authority within the Church. He was told, in effect, to mind his own business, and leave matters to those men who knew better.[124]

Harley's early educational efforts probably resonated with Rev Crapsey and his own experience and determination to attend the General Theological Seminary. Harley may have interpreted his gesture as vindication of his belief in his commitment to enter the ministry. Nonetheless, Harley rejected Crapsey's generous offer. Instead, he wrote to a Mr Cobb, Bursar of Harvard University, and was informed that he would need at least $400 (some $40,000 in today's value) in hand to be able to study at the college.[125] Harley made a late application to secure a Matthews Scholarship to attend Harvard. Founded by Nathan Matthews of Boston in 1870, the Matthews Scholarship made provision for an income of $300 for needy and deserving students who intended to study for the ministry of the Protestant Episcopal Church. He failed to secure the scholarship. Harley now started the arduous process of investigating other American colleges and he decided to try for Yale.[126] He spent the summer of 1902 studying for the Yale subject-based entrance examination and teaching music to support himself.[127]

---

123 Ibid, p. 7.
124 Proceeding of the Sociology Conference, University of Michigan, 1903, p. 229.
125 Harvard 1903-1904, Harvard University Archives.
126 Ibid.
127 Ibid

6. Second Best

'Optics is an example of the different ways a human is able to see things in the world. The same goes for the color of a person's skin and even though optics present that there are differences in color, these do not state that they should necessarily be treated as different.'

Edward Bouchet

Yale is the archetype of an elite private college in New Haven, Connecticut. It was founded in 1701 as the Collegiate School at Saybrook before being renamed Yale College in 1718, after a former official of the British East India Company, Elihu Yale, in recognition of his gifts to the college. His offerings consisted of books and several bales made up of various cloths - calico, muslin, black and white silk crepe and poplin. These were all sold and raised the sum of £525 for the school. The black crepe was kept and used to make robes for tutors.

A teaching institution for ministers from Connecticut, the college provided instruction in theology and sacred languages, later incorporating humanities and sciences into its curriculum. As the third oldest educational institution in the country, Yale's philosophy and approach were similar to Harvard's. Officially, 'membership was open to all students, and the selection was by personal accomplishment rather than social origin.' Still, to Harley, Yale was just a temporary stop-gap - second best, until he could make it to Harvard's historic seat of learning.

The first black student to enter Yale was Edward Bouchet; documented and celebrated by the university, he had a hall named after him and his portrait hangs in the transept of Sterling Memorial Library. Edward Bouchet attended the Hopkins

Yale University, c 1910 (Chaplain's Office, Yale University)

Grammar School, a private preparatory school for young men to enter the classical and scientific departments at Yale College. Graduating first in his class, he entered Yale in 1870, becoming the first black to graduate there in 1874; he ranked sixth in a class of 124. He then completed his dissertation in 1876 on the new subject of geometrical optics, again making history as the first black person with a Ph.D. from an American university, and sixth American of any race to achieve a Ph.D. in physics. (While this book was being written, another name came to light that has questioned Bouchet's prestigious title of the 'first'. Richard Henry Green, born in New Haven on 14 November 1833,[128] is thought to be the first black to graduate

---

128 Rick Stattler, an archivist at Swann Auction Galleries, New York City, stumbled across this information by accident while researching the Green family papers.

from an Academic Department of Yale in 1857. While at Yale, Green was a member of Brothers in Unity, a literary society, and the Sigma Delta fraternity. He attended medical school at Dartmouth and served as an assistant surgeon in the US Navy, earning his degree in 1864.)

Harley entered Yale College in September 1902 on scholarship by subject examination, passed in Latin, Greek, English and Ancient History. He was a member of the Class of 1906,[129] and the only West Indian student in the university that year.[130] It is interesting to note that Mary Goodman, a laundress of modest means who died in 1872, saved tirelessly and left her life savings of approximately $4,000 to the Yale Divinity School to fund scholarships for black students.[131]

New Haven experienced a wave of migration from the South, like many cities in the North, beginning in the 1870s. This was prompted by the depression of 1873, which saw cotton prices slump, the rise of the Ku Klux Klan and the end of Reconstruction. Between the 1880s and 1890s, Italians were the most significant immigrant population to arrive in New Haven. By the turn of the century, jobs traditionally undertaken by African Americans were being taken by European immigrants, as white employers often preferred to hire whites rather than integrate their workforce. Poorly paid and labour-intensive jobs as janitors and messengers, or drilling and digging inside tunnels, tending coke ovens or carrying heavy loads were often all that was left.[132]

Harley initially lodged at 386 Berkeley Hall,[133] the residence halls at the northern terminus of Old Brick Row, and then took

---

129 Yale Alumni Yearbook, Class of 1906, Harley's personal archive
130 *The Sun*, New York, May 1902.
131 'An Ethnic History of New Haven: Pre-1638 to 2000 and Beyond', New Haven CT: The Ethnic Heritage Center, n.d., p. 12.
132 Ibid, p. 12.
133 Yale alumni records.

lodgings at 75 Edgewood Avenue.[134] He later lived in a poor area of New Haven, at the home of Mrs Eliza Simmonds, at 39 Sperry Street,[135] located off Whalley Avenue in the Dixwell neighbourhood.

Harley satisfactorily completed his freshman year, except for a deficiency of one hour in French.[136] He achieved a standing of 250th out of 400 students. He then suddenly declared that he would be leaving Yale, writing to inform the Board that the reason for his withdrawal was his 'oratorical ambitions' and that he wished to be near the Emerson School of Oratory, Boston, Massachusetts.[137] He declined a lucrative offer to teach music at the Tuskegee Institute, Alabama, for $75 a month and an accompanying house. Harley also rejected the request of many friends to practise law in Washington.[138] His aim was Harvard.

To pursue an education at Harvard required an extensive outlay. The tuition fee alone was $150 - $90 paid at the beginning of the academic year and the second instalment of $60 upon the first term bill. The Bursar had previously informed Harley he would need $400 to attend the college.[139] The $400 was itemized as a $200 bond and security for the payment of dues, which had to be filed with the Bursar.[140] The bond had to be signed by two bondsmen, of whom one had to be a citizen of the United States, or the employee of a surety company duly qualified to do business in Massachusetts. The other two options were a $200 deposit in US bonds or a $50 security deposit and payment in full of sums that became liable

---

134 Ibid.
135 Ibid
136 Ibid.
137 Matthews Scholarship application, 1903-1904 Harvard University Archives.
138 Harvard Scholarship Application 1903-1904, Harvard University Archives.
139 Bursar to Harley, Harvard University Archives.
140 Bursar to Harley, Harvard University Archives.

to the university. The other expenses estimated for an academic year were rent and care of a furnished room ($40 to $150), board for thirty-eight weeks ($133 to $266), fuel and lighting ($11 to $25) and textbooks ($25 to $35).

Harley had been in higher education for several years, and his savings were exhausted.[141] His work as a lay preacher and teaching music would not generate the funds required to attend Harvard. He made two applications to Harvard on 25 April 1903. The first was to the Committee on Admission from other Colleges and the second another request for a Matthews Scholarship. In his application for the Matthews Scholarship, Harley explained:

> I was all alone in America, struggling to go through college. Without a scholarship,I could not continue in college. I had twenty dollars acquired from teaching music during the present school year, and my rent was fifty dollars. I had given up many tempting offers to continue my studies and that my heart is set on Harvard.[142]

The scholarship application form asked, 'If the applicant fails to get a scholarship, does he wish to be regarded as an applicant for Price Greenleaf Aid?' Harley wrote 'yes' for another scholarship, 'NO' for aid, capitalizing and emboldening the word to stress that he did not consider himself a charity case in need of 'aid'. A scholarship was different; it was what scholars should expect to receive if they were capable students of high rank who could not meet the expenses of the college fees.

Harley received a letter from Byron Satterlee Hurlbut, the Dean of Harvard, telling him what he already knew. He had no

---

141 Greenleaf Financial Aid Application 1903-04, Harvard University Archives.
142 Harley to Dean Hurlbut, 21 May 1903, Harvard University Archives.

proper security for the payment of his deposit, and he would be deprived of the privileges of the university unless he provided adequate security. Harley now sought the assistance of Henry Yates Satterlee, the Bishop of Washington, John Patterson Green, his former boss at the US Postage Stamp Agency, and James Bundy, secretary and treasurer of Howard University, to write to the secretary of Harvard University, J.G. Hart, and to vouch for him and provide testimonials for his Harvard scholarship application.

Satterlee was an alumnus of Columbia University and the General Theological Seminary, President of the Board of Trustees at King Hall, and was consecrated the first Episcopal Bishop of the newly-created Diocese of Washington in 1896.[143] As a student at the GTS, Satterlee worked periodically at the Church of the Messiah on the Lower East Side of New York. He was deeply committed to working with poor and black people, seeking to advance the status of African Americans but, according to some, tinkering only at the margins and not going as far as to integrate the parishes of the capital.[144] Green was appointed to a high-ranking position in the Post Office Department in 1897. A postage stamp agent, he was responsible for inspecting and ensuring that stamps matched the contract between the government and the Bureau of Printing and Engraving concerning paper, colour, perforations and adhesive. The 1899 Official Register lists Green as the head of the Postage Stamp Agency, earning an annual salary of $2,500, with a chief clerk, six clerks and three labourers working for him. Bundy, an alumnus of Oberlin College, was also one of the candidates along with Jesse Lawson, Josephine's father, to be recommended by Booker T. Washington in 1901

143 Frederick Quinn, *A House of Prayer for All People: A History of Washington National Cathedral*, New York: Morehouse Publishing, 2014, p. 6.
144 Ibid.

for consideration for the appointment to the position of Civil Magistrate in the District of Columbia.

The men provided the following references.

My dear Mr Hart, (sic)

In answer to your letter, regarding Mr J.H. Harley (sic), I would say that I believe he made a good record for himself in his studies in the Law Department of Howard University, in this City. It is one year since he left the University here; and last year, I think he was at Yale University. I believe him to be sober moral: but our experience with him was that he was a quick-tempered man, and hard to get along with.

Faithfully yours,

Henry Satterlee

Dear Sir,

I am in receipt of your letter dated the 25th relating to Mr James Arthur Harley. Permit to say, I am well acquainted with Mr Harley, and that he is a fit subject for help and encouragement: - he is earnest, industrious, honest, and capable: By all measure, aid him.

Respectfully,

John P. Green.[145]

To whom it may concern.

This is to certify that the bearer, J. Arthur Harley, Esq, now a student at Yale University, New Haven, Conn, completed the regular three-years' course in law at the Howard University Law School in the city. I am pleased to state that in point of scholarship, Mr

---

145 Green to Hart, 4 June 1903, Harvard University Archives.

Harley ranked easily among the foremost students of our school. It is but simple justice to him to say that during his stay with us, he showed himself to be a young man of high character, splendid decorum, and exalted purpose. Along these lines, his example was a variable inspiration to his fellow students.

The following averages attained by him in the respective studies of the course clearly indicate the thoroughness and efficiency of his work. Domestic relations 89, Torts 93, Commercial Paper 83, Crimes 93, Contracts 62 (Passed) Personal property 82, Pleading and Practice 92, Constitutional Law 49 (Passed) Commericial Law 87, Real Estate 92, Corporations 96, Administrators and Executors 91, International Law 83, Evidence 76, Equity Jurisdiction 82, Criminal Procedure 80.

This standing, coupled with uniformly excellent conduct, constitutes the basis for the high regard and esteem in which he was ever held by both Faculty and fellow students. It is with a deep sense of pride that I heartily commend this young man to the most favourable consideration of all those who are ever seeking to assist the worthy.

Very truly yours
James F. Bundy.

*

The summer of 1903 brought good news; Josephine graduated from the M Street School, her graduation ceremony reported in *The Colored American* newspaper.[146] Josephine then matriculated at Oberlin College to read for a BA degree. She was based in Ohio while Harley was in Connecticut, separated by 518 miles

---

146 *The Colored American*, 20 June 1903.

and a nine-and-a-half-hour journey. They continued to write to each other.

Harley was not successful in acquiring the Matthews Scholarship. His academic dreams were now slipping through his fingers. At thirty, he was already older than his fellow sophomore students; this, he feared, could be his final chance of reaching Harvard. There would be no chance of him acquiring the tuition fee or deposit for the start of the academic year. And so Harley utilized what was available to him: his skills of preaching and persuasion. He negotiated with the Bursar to defer his payment and was clearly convincing. He achieved his goal, matriculating at Harvard in September 1903 as a sophomore in the class of 1906. He finally became a Crimson Man.

7. A Crimson Man

'Tis once in life our dreams come true,
The myths of long ago,
Quite real though fairy-like their view,
They surge with ebb and flow;
Thus thou, O haunt of childhood dreams,
More beauteous and fair
Than Nature's landscape and her streams,
Historic Harvard Square.
Harvard Alumnus Edward Smyth Jones, 1910[147]

A Harvard man is the very epitome of a college man - cultured, educated, respected, with sound moral fibre and values. But a Harvard man was certainly not perceived to be a black man when the oldest institution of higher education in America, established in 1636 and named after its first benefactor, John Harvard of Charlestown, opened its hallowed doors. The doors remained firmly shut to black students for its first 214 years of existence. An attempt to address Harvard's discriminatory admission practice took place in 1850 with the admittance of three black students, Daniel Lang Jr., Isaac Humphrey Snowden and Martin Robison Delany, to its Medical School.

The criteria for admittance to the medical school were three years' training with a regular physician, evidence of good moral character and a college degree or a demonstration of knowledge of Latin, mathematics and basic science, deemed satisfactory by the medical faculty. Yet, qualified though the three were, entrenched racism was not to be easily dissolved. The medical

147 Werner Sollors, Caldwell Titcomb and Thomas Underwood, *Blacks at Harvard: A Documentary History of African American Experience at Harvard and Radcliffe*, New York: New York University Press, 1993.

school administration faced immense pressure from white students after the admittance of the three black students. Their objections were that the presence of blacks would cheapen the Harvard medical degree; that the quality of education would suffer; and that 'the presence of an inferior race was socially offensive'.[148]

Stressing their unhappiness at the medical school's decision, a number of students organized, signed and presented a petition. The petition read:

Petition
To the Medical Faculty of Harvard University,
Gentlemen,
The undersigned members of the medical class would respectfully submit to the Medical Faculty their desire to be informed whether coloured persons are to be admitted as students at another course of lectures. This request is offered not with the view of influencing any action of the faculty, but simply that the undersigned may have the opportunity to make such arrangements for the future as all be most agreeable to their feelings in the event of Negroes being allowed again to become members of the school.[149]

The Dean, Oliver Wendell Holmes, explained the medical students' action: 'The intermixing of the white and black races in their lectures rooms is distasteful to a large portion of the class and injurious to the interest of the school.'[150]

The medical faculty called a meeting, bowing to pressure from the students, where it passed a resolution - despite strong objections - that as the three students were already in possession

---

148 Ibid, p. 26.
149 Countway Library, Dean's File, Harvard Medical Archives.
150 Sollors et al, p. 29.

of their tickets of admission to the various courses, they were entitled to complete the semester. But after a few weeks, the three black students had reached the point where they decided to withdraw.

Fifteen years later, the medical school reversed its policy, admitting Edwin Clarence Joseph Turpin Howard. In the same year, 1865, Harvard admitted its first black student to the College - Richard Greener. Greener, in a speech at the Harvard Club, said, 'There is but one test for all. Ability, character, and merit - these are the sole passport to her favour.'[151] Greener obtained his degree in 1870, having won the Bowdon prize for elocution and for his English essay, which criticized the system of land tenure in Ireland entitled 'The best way of Crushing the Agitator is to give him Grievance'. He became a philosophy professor, law school dean and foreign diplomat, serving as a consul in India and commercial agent in East Siberia. His services were recognized by the Chinese government when he received the Order of the Double Dragon for aiding victims of the Shanxi famine.[152]

Fifty years after Harvard accepted its first black medical students and thirty-eight years after the first black student entered the College, Harley made the 135-mile journey from Connecticut to Massachusetts. Massachusetts had been the first state to abolish slavery in 1783 and as a result it attracted the largest concentration of freed blacks in the country.[153] In 1830, the black community made up 1,900 residents, 3 per cent of Boston's population,[154] and 1900 there were 11,500 blacks in the city.

---

151 Ibid, p. xx.
152 Ibid, p. 40.
153 Robert Hall, 'Boston's African American Heritage', ASA Footnotes, Northeastern University, 2008.
154 Ibid.

Harvard Yard, 1906. (Library of Congress, Washington DC)

Unlike Howard University, situated in the bustling metropolis of Washington DC, Harvard was located twelve miles from downtown Boston, the small, peaceful town of Cambridge on the banks of the Charles River. Harvard Yard, twenty-five acres of parkland, made up the focus and central hub of the university campus. The Yard contained red-brick accommodation halls, faculty and classroom buildings and libraries.

Harvard's walls, built with the mortar of prestige and elitism, could not and did not protect black students from the rampant racism of Jim Crow America. Regardless of their allegedly privileged position, challenges and barriers were faced both inside and outside the campus. William Edward Burghardt Du Bois (W.E. Du Bois), an undergraduate at Harvard in 1886 to 1890, recalled:

Sometimes the shadow of insult fell: being mistaken constantly for a servant, being turned away from local barbershops on account of colour, knowing better than to even ask the white families who rented lodgings to white students whether they would be willing to rent the same lodgings to Blacks, suffering exclusions from various extra curriculum activities because of race.[155]

155 Ibid.

Herbert W. Nickens remembered:

> Being black exacerbated the already difficult freshman adjustment in addition to raising questions all its own. We not only had to live with strangers but white strangers whose attitudes towards us were rarely indifferent to our colour. We often bear the burden of being cultural and anthropological curiosities: inspired, sometimes devalued, frequently overvalued, but never regarded in the absence of the Black factor. We found ourselves spread-eagle between Black and white.

Harley finally entered Harvard in the autumn of 1903, to work for a degree in Semitic Languages, the study of the ancient histories and cultures of Israelites, Ammonites, Moabites, Edomites, Phoenicians, Arameans, Akkadians, Babylonians, Arabs. But he did so with a considerable disadvantage - the issue of his fees still hung over his head.

Renowned for its academic excellence, Harvard's extra-curricular and social activities were just as relevant, if not more important than its academic teaching. Harvard's social clubs were where long-term friendships were forged, networks and associations developed. Harvard had a number of noted elite clubs from the Porcellian, founded in 1791, to The Signet Society, established in 1870, and its famous theatrical company - The Hasty Pudding Club - produced musical revues where actors dressed in drag to play female roles. All these clubs had one factor in common: they were elitist and exclusive, although not advertised or promoted as such. It was an unwritten rule that was not questioned. The members of these clubs resided in the 'Gold Coast', the name given to the elusive halls of residence situated on Massachusetts Avenue and Mount Auburn Street, between Dunster and Bow Streets, along with Holyoke, Linden and Plympton Streets. They had facilities

JAMES ARTHUR HARLEY
Home address, Antigua, British

Harley's yearbook photograph, Harvard University 1903. (Private collection)

such as steam heat, electricity, private bathrooms and elevators.[156] Claverly Hall set the standard for accommodation. The largest hall had fifty suites with prices ranging from $250 to $500 per year, offering its residents such amenities as electric bells, speaking tubes, a swimming pool, and squash courts. Other dormitories offered valet and maid service, round-the-clock doormen and elevator operators.[157] *The Cambridge Chronicle* noted that 'a student seeking rooms for $50 per year, would have to travel at least a mile from the Yard if accommodations in the college could not be found.'

Harley's accommodation stood in stark contrast to the luxury of the Gold Coast, in lodgings away from the university. He lived at 57 Museum Street. The poorer students and Harley had to contend with the Harvard Union, a club established and open to all Harvard students, and Phillips Brooks House, opened on 23 January 1900, in memory of Rev Phillips Brooks, a Harvard graduate and preacher at Trinity Church. Philips Brooks House enabled students to engage in charity work in the community. Harley was also a member of the St Paul's Society, a fellowship organization.

---

156 Charles M. Sullivan, *Harvard Square History and Development*, Cambridge
    Historical Commission (www.cambridgema.gov/historic) accessed 25 March 2016.
157 Ibid.

Harley, like many other black students, had to work to support himself. William Monroe Trotter, Harvard alumnus (1896), supplemented his income by selling desks door to door in the neighbouring towns. He said, 'I am more among the labouring people than the better class. No house is too small for me to call.' To earn income for his room and board, Harley juggled three jobs at Memorial Hall, St John's Mission and St Augustine's Church, in between his studies. He worked for eight hours at Memorial Hall,[158] the centre of university life. Memorial Hall consisted of three buildings, its high chamber dedicated to the fallen men of Harvard in the Civil War. The Sanders Theatre, inspired by Christopher Wren's Sheldonian Theatre in Oxford, was used for student registrations, graduations, significant performances and the official ceremony of commencement, and the refectory provided the university's dining facilities.

St John the Evangelist Mission Church[159] was situated on Bowdoin Street, which ran from the top of Beacon Street down Beacon Hill to Cambridge Street, where the black population was concentrated. The area was referred to as Beacon Hill, while its white residents gave it the derogatory name of 'Nigger Hill'. The church was built in 1831 for the Bowdoin Street Congregational Society, and led by Rev Dr Lyman Beecher, the father of Harriet Beecher Stowe, the celebrated author of *Uncle Tom's Cabin* (1852). The mission brought Harley into contact with the poor, destitute and dispossessed.

Harley worked five hours a week as a lay preacher and Sunday school teacher at St Augustine's,[160] a storefront church in the West End area of the city. It had outgrown the living room

---

158 Greenleaf financial aid application, 1 January 1904, Harvard University Archives.

159 Ibid.

160 Harley to Dean Hurlbut, 20 January 1904 - Harvard University Archives call no: UA 15.98.10 1890-1968, Box no. 2070 Folder title: Harley, James Arthur - 1906.

of one of its parishioners, Sarah Jackson, at 17 Westminster Street in the South End in 1899.[161] The Rev Charles Neal Field was the priest in charge, a man described as firm but fair. Harley from his pulpit on a Sunday saw and shared the pain, frustration and sense of injustice of his congregation. Many parishioners were West Indians from his island[162] who had also made the arduous journey in search of a better life in America. He watched grown men, like himself, relegated to menial positions as porters, janitors, messengers, boot blackers, waiters and busboys. In all, 73 per cent of 4,510 black males worked in poorly paid occupations,[163] while employment at the docks, shoe, confectionery and textile industries remained the preserve of the white European communities in the city. The women, some of whom were skilled seamstresses, like his mother, took the only employment opportunities open to them in the domestic service industry - as maids, cleaners and housekeepers. Ironically, West Indian women became sought-after commodities as their heritage enabled their middle- and upper-class employers to boast who had the maid from the most 'exotic' island. St Augustine also served as a centre to teach young men marketable skills.

Harley's residential address and series of jobs did not result in him harbouring any notion of inferiority or jealousy. His roommate, Jacob Loewenberg, a Russian Jewish immigrant, noted: 'Harley was British to the core, an insufferable snob and quite neurotic'. He treated his peers with an air of formality. Loewenberg, who would become a professor of philosophy, attributed Harley's attitude to his non-American origin.[164]

---

161 The Church of St Augustine and St Martin: http://www. saintaugustinesaintmartin.org
162 David Wallen to E. Hart, 30 July 1904 - Harvard University Archives.
163 Hall, 'Boston's African American Heritage'.
164 Jacob Loewenberg, *Thrice-born: Selected Memories of an Immigrant*, New York: Hobbes, Dorman and Company, 1968, pp. 40-41.

January 1904 brought Harley no respite from his financial difficulties. He wrote to the Dean to inform him he had received $100, which went towards his rent and books.[165] He still required additional funds if he was to study and compete on an equal level with the other students. His work suffered because of the amount of work he had to undertake to make ends meet.[166]

Harley now had to concede on his principles and made a retrospective application to the Price Greenleaf Aid, dated 1 January 1904 (the application should have been submitted in May 1903), for the sum of $150 for the academic year 1903-1904. Harley provided three names as referees: Jeremiah Eames Rankin, President of Howard University from 1889-1903, was a white minister of Washington DC's First Congregational Church and an abolitionist; Charles Cook was Professor of English Language and History at Howard University; and F.W. Fairchild was Dean of Howard University.

> Dear Sir,
> Mr J. Arthur [sic] possesses beyond question high education and good relationship. His ideals and purposes are lofty. As a writer and speaker, he bade fair while here to excel. I warmly commend him and endorse his application for aid as given to a needy student, while at Howard University he supported himself in part at least by services as minister at St. Luke's Church.
> I am
> With thanks
> Charles Le Cook
> Prof of Eng. Lang and History at Howard University

---

165 Greenleaf.
166 Ibid.

Mr A. J. Harley. [sic] is a member of the Law Department of Howard University, but he also resides with some of the classes in the College Department and so in some senses, under my care in the past year. I take pleasure in commending his honesty and character.
F.W. Fairchild
Dean of College.

Harley's application also required a physician's testimony to certify his physical and mental health. Mr Bailey, at 47 Brattle Street, carried out the examination on 20 January 1904, and provided his statement to the committee.

I, M.H. Bailey, of the town of Cambridge county of Middlesex, and State of Mass, being a practising physician, and having carefully examined *J. Arthur Harley* hereby certify that to the best of my knowledge and belief he is physically and mentally sound, capable of hard study, and strong enough to lead a life of active usefulness.
Signature *M.H. Bailey*

Harley followed up his application with a personal letter to the Dean of Harvard to illustrate the importance of the application, his current situation, and how much the aid was needed and why his application was so late.

I can hope for nothing from the letter of the law which governs this case. But the spirit which gives the law interpretation will I trust extend my case its favour; since in these four months I have fought hardest of student-life's battles and won the two points of board and lodgings, and the third point tuition is one lying wholly within the clemency of your committee. I am simple handed in my struggles. I earnestly pray the

Committee to grant me the tuition for as I have no means of paying debts for years to come and summer work provides clothing.

Harley was also struggling with the course subjects and wanted to change from Semitic Language 2 to Semitic Language 16. Semitic Language 2 covered Hebrew for graduates, syntax, interpretation of parts of the Prophets and the Poetical Book and criticism of selected portion of the text, while Semitic Language 16 covered History of Hebrew Literature. Harley petitioned the board explaining,

In every seminary or college in the country where Hebrew is studied, three years are devolved to the subject. Here at Harvard we have to master the language in two years, a task by no means difficult for the majority of men who take the course, for they are generally graduates of Semantics, who came to Harvard having previously had three years in Hebrew, or they are Jews who have diligently addressed themselves to the mastery of their beloved language from their earliest boyhood. Those of us, however, who take Semitic 2 after the preliminary training of a simple year in Semitic 1 find it difficult to keep abreast of the lessons, and when it comes is the thoroughness expected of men who need for honours the task is simply Herculean; if not an impossible accomplishment. I begged to be allowed to change Semitic 2 for Semitic 16 on the list of subjects for final honours Semitic Languages and history.[167] During the past school year, I took six courses; I was working two hours daily and about five hours on Sundays, this was a curse, as it made it difficult to obtain high grades.[168]

167 Harley to Board, Harvard University Archives.
168 Matthews Scholarship application 1904-1905, Harvard University Archives.

Harley made a second application for a Matthews Scholarship for the academic year 1904-05 on 26 April 1904, supplying the names of David Wallace, assistant priest, St Augustine's Church, and Rev Field as his references.

Dear Mr Hart,

I have known Mr J. Arthur Harley for a year, the length of his residences in Boston since coming from Yale. He came highly recommended by the Reverend Mr Waller, Rector of St. Luke's Church, Washington D.C. and immediately found favour with the Reverend Field of St Augustine's Church, Boston and myself, the assistant at St. Augustine's.

He has been assisting at St. Augustine's and St Martin's as lay reader and Sunday School Superintendent and has performed his duties quite satisfactorily. There are a number of people in the congregation of these two churches who come from his West Indian home from whom I have heard nothing but good concerning Mr Harley.

I am anxious that men entering our ministry should be of the very best and would refrain from assisting Mr Harley in this way did I not think him entirely worthy. Had I money enough, I would assist him in his preparation and am very glad to think that these few words may help you to determine to award him a scholarship.

I do not at present see how Mr Harley can meet his expenses without it from you and sincerely hope that you will award him a scholarship
Yours truly,
David R.W. Wallace
Assistant priest in charge
St Augustine's Church
Boston.

Dear Sir,

J. A. Harley is an excellent young man and has been my Sunday Schools Superintendent for a year and acted as lay preacher in one of my missions. The poor fellow has been hard work to get along but has taken to his work meaningfully. I am sure that Mr Matthews would be very pleased if Mr Harley could have one of the scholarships.
Truly yours
C.N. Field

Harley was determined this time to secure the Matthews Scholarship; in a typically tactical move he tried to enlist the support of the founder's son, Albert. A note was made on his application file by the secretary indicating 'late applicant - was trying to secure *recommendations* of Mr Matthews'.

Harley's moral character also had to be assessed before the scholarship could be made. The following is an extract from a letter by Henry Satterlee, Bishop of Washington, to the Dean of Harvard with regard to his suitability:

Mr Harley was formally a student at King Hall, Washington. He is bright, intelligent, a good, industrious student - moral with an unblemished character. His fault was that he feels himself above his fellow students, was conceited and had the usual West Indian irritability of temper. But white students have similar faults. Harley may have outgrown and overcome his. I saw him four or five years ago, I commend him for the prize, so do this Board of King Hall.
Faithfully
Henry Satterlee[169]

---

169 Satterlee to Hart, Harvard University Archives, call no: UA 15.98.10 1890-1968, Box no. 2070 Folder title: Harley, James Arthur - 1906.

Harley possessed all these attributes - as a black man who was not afraid of telling white or black what he thought of them. His irritability, described as the usual West Indian temperament, could be interpreted as sheer frustration at injustice, an inability to do anything because of a lack of power, resources, status and the environment he had to navigate daily; the intermittent eruptions were a necessary release valve.

Harley was finally successful in obtaining the Matthews Scholarship for the academic year 1904-05.

The summer of 1904 saw the town of Cambridge buzzing with scholars and teachers from all parts of the globe who were attending Harvard's prestigious summer school,[170] which began on 5 July and closed on 12 August. Harley was at the summer school to study philosophy as an opportunity to take an extra course to make up his grades. His recently acquired philosophy knowledge immediately made him an attractive candidate for the Harvard Ethical Society, and he was elected a member of the executive committee of the society.

---

170 Summer school certificate, Harley's personal archive.

8. Alain LeRoy Locke: 'The New Negro'

'I am not a race problem. I am Alain LeRoy Locke, and if these people don't stop I'll tell them something that will make them.'

Alain LeRoy Locke, letter to his mother, 1907

In the autumn of 1904, a shy nineteen-year-old man from Philadelphia, Arthur Roy Locke, arrived at Harvard to study philosophy. Locke was a small-framed individual, only five feet three inches in height, a result of him contracting a severe bout of rheumatic fever in his early childhood which permanently damaged his heart. He entered Harvard with an impressive pedigree. The only son of Pliny Locke and Mary Hawkins Locke, he was born into a distinguished Philadelphia family, with interests in education and culture. His grandfather, Ishmael Locke, was a free African American and teacher. The Society of Friends (Quakers) had sponsored his time at Cambridge University, after which Ishmael spent four years in Liberia establishing schools. Returning to the United States, he became headmaster of a school in Providence, Rhode Island, and then principal of the Institute for Colored Youth in Philadelphia. Arthur's father, Pliny Ishmael Locke, graduated from the Institute in 1867, then taught mathematics there for two years before leaving to teach newly freed African Americans in North Carolina. Locke had been raised by his mother after the death of his father when he was six years old.

Locke's illness provided him with the opportunity to spend his time reading and learning to play the piano and violin. He adopted the French spelling of the name Alan, Alain, at the age of sixteen and added the Le to Roy.[171] He graduated from the Central High School in 1902 and proceeded to study at the Philadelphia School of Pedagogy, where he moved up to first in his class. The Philadelphia African American journalist William Carl Bolivar wrote in 1902 that

> It was a remarkable achievement for anyone; not to mention an African-American during this highly segregated era - while many white American scholars were seeking to prove the intellectual inferiority of African Americans to justify racial segregation, Locke became a symbol of achievement and a powerful argument for offering African Americans equal opportunity at white educational institutions.

Harley met Locke at the Ethical Society.[172] Locke wrote to his mother:

> There is a coloured West Indian by the name of Harley here, and of course he is different to the rest. He is a graduate of Howard, spent two years at Yale, is here for the year, and expects to go to England to study for the ministry, and incidentally to study at Oxford - the two schools are connected. He is a very nice fellow and has become very friendly. He criticizes the coloured fellows here, said that they were conscious of their inferiority and justly so, and the house in which they were huddled was a 'nigger-Hell', he knew because he had been there, that he had noticed that I had been criticized as he was, and would like to know me. Where I met him was at the Ethical Society - and I think he became so very pleasant

---

171 Rudolph Alexander Kofi Cain, *Alain LeRoy Locke: Race, Culture and the Education of African American Adults*, Leiden: Brill, 2004.

172 Alain LeRoy Locke to Mary Locke, 2 April 1905, ALP Box 49, folder 2.

as he was that I was 'in the ring' there - I don't think it is patronizing, however, for he is very prominent here, a good debater - and has a scholarship. He is very well thought of, of considerable ability, believes in social equality, is the typical West Indian with their fault of being conceited - But you know what I think of conceit - when a man has something to be conceited over - I call it self-respect.

Harley wrote, more succinctly: 'Locke and I became good friends communicating almost daily.'

The two men should have been distanced by the following factors: age, sexuality and countries of birth. Harley was twelve years older than Locke, a heterosexual and a West Indian; but they shared one bond, one commonality - their dislike of their fellow African American students. Harley and Locke had become 'very chummy' because they had a 'common enemy' in the other black students at Harvard.[173] Locke appreciated Harley, writing that he was 'different from the rest'.[174]

Both men shared a sense of entitlement and superiority. Locke employed a system of referring to black people as 'coons', 'the uneducated', 'the herd' and gentlemen and ladies.[175] Locke was a gentleman, had spent time carefully crafting an image of cultural sophistication and importance which he used as his calling card, and the thought of associating with what he called nigger behaviour was abhorrent. Too much association with his own kind could jeopardize his acceptance into white elite society.

---

173 David Weinfeld, 'What Difference Does Difference Make? Horace Kallen, Alain Locke, and the Development of Cultural Pluralism in America,' New York University, May 2014.

174 Alain Locke to Mary Locke, 2 April 1905.

175 Jeffery Stewart, *The New Negro: The Life of Alain Locke*, Oxford: Oxford University Press, 2017, p. 52.

Alain LeRoy Locke, 1918. (Harvard Magazine)

Locke had positively sought to ingratiate himself with predominately white students. He felt quite comfortable among more tolerant whites, especially educated and assimilated Jews.[176] Locke ascribed a different label and set of values to himself to illustrate to others at Harvard that his educational merits and family background indicated that he should not be perceived and treated as the other African American students. Locke's and Harley's arrogance and elitism meant that they saw themselves as among the intellectual elite at Harvard and chose their friends accordingly.[177] Locke had little time for the black student 'that carries prejudice along with him'. As he explained to his mother: 'You can't get along anywhere unless you prove by your actions that you are a gentleman. Those fellows up here eat, walk, sleep, and do everything else together - they are isolated as if they were quarantined, and they hate Harley of course.'[178]

Like Locke, Harley wanted to enjoy the status and introductions that associating with white students brought. But he was a contradiction, aware of his colour and its impact. When Harley and his roommate, Loewenberg, went to have lunch at Randall Hall and sat at a table, the two students already there got up and left abruptly. When Harley 'pointed to his wrist', Loewenberg asked, 'And what is the matter with your wrist?' Harley responded with sad amusement: 'what innocence, what incredible innocence!'[179] (The rubbing of the back of the hand by a black person signifies colour and discrimination.) Absurdly, Harley claimed to have a disregard for blacks at Harvard, but he 'seemed to associate exclusively with them'.[180] To Loewenberg, Harley displayed the same

---

176 Weinfeld, *op. cit.*
177 Alain Locke to Mary Locke, 28 November 1905, Box 50, folder 17.
178 Alain Locke to Mary Locke, 3 May 1906, Box 51, folder 36.
179 Loewenberg, pp. 40-41.
180 Ibid.

ghetto mentality as those Harvard students of African origin. Though 'A British subject' who 'enjoyed rights and liberties unheard of in Alabama or Mississippi', Harley had an 'almost pathological' preoccupation with his pigmentation.[181]

Locke made Harley his sole black friend at Harvard. He had witnessed traits in Harley that reminded him of his father, notably, his fiery temper.[182] In a country and at a time when the norm was for black men to bend their heads and accept their situation and circumstances, Harley shattered this norm; he made no apology for being an outspoken, sometimes abrasive, black polymath, challenging and provoking any white man.

In 1905, Harley was residing at 49 College House, 1172 Massachusetts Avenue, student lodgings in Harvard Square. His rent had increased to $75.[183] He was still a lay reader at St Augustine's Church. He wrote: 'My work during the past year has been of a far higher-grade owing to the lack of pressure which the scholarship offered, however, through a technicality I may not finish my work this year as I have striven to do.'[184] The anticipatory examinations, also known as advanced standing - the process which allowed students to anticipate required work and which counted towards their degree - could be completed within three to three and a half years. It could be utilized to make up outstanding shortfalls which Harley had in Algebra A and B and German. He was unaware of the process, stating, 'There was the real prospect of failing in college this fall.' Harley made another application on 31 May for a Matthews Scholarship for the academic year 1905-1906. On 23 June 1905, he wrote to the Committee on Admissions with regard for advanced standing. His spidery writing filled two pages,

---

181 Loewenberg, pp. 40-41.
182 Stewart, p. 68.
183 Matthews Scholarship. Harvard University.
184 Harvard University. Examinations, 1836-2009: an inventory, Harvard University Archives.

setting out in detail to Dean Hurlbut the work he had done in Solid Geometry (mathematics) during his year spent at Yale and Harvard's equivalent. Harley made the point that the work he offered was no less than similar work at Harvard.[185]

The committee did not accept Harley's impassioned plea and explanation regarding his work, and his petition was rejected. Harley's failed request may have been a casualty of Dean Hurlbut's improving instructon committee. The committee reported that most students did not devote enough time to their studies and called for reforms of the elective system. Various means were developed to both require and encourage students to strive for greater academic achievement. The Administrative Board began to place more students on academic probation.

A further letter dated 24 July reminded him that to complete the requirement for his degree he must pass with a C grade in a half course and remove his admission conditions in Algebra and Plain Geometry.

*

Harley and Josephine meanwhile maintained their long-distance relationship by corresponding from their respective colleges. But was Harley involved in a duplicitous game of love? Locke reported to his mother:

> Harley went to 'see white girlfriends out at Wellesley[186] (the women's college) - has white girl pupils and brings them to chapel' while his black Harvard peers 'nearly choke[d]', and Harley simply laughed 'his devilish West Indian laugh and sneers'.[187] Over the summer,

---

185 Harvard University. Examinations, 1836-2009: an inventory, Harvard University Archives.

186 Wellesley is a private woman college, founded in 1870 by Henry and Pauline Durant, who were passionate about the higher eduction of women.

187 Weinfeld, p. 109.

Harley had gotten himself into a sticky situation when he tutored 'one of his Jewish girls' in his room without a chaperone. Harvard dean Byron Satterlee Hurlbut got wind of the story, giving him yet another weapon against Harley.[188]

Harley's 'tutoring' resulted in him being excluded from his dormitory room at College House for violating the university rules.[189] Locke further confided:

Don't breathe a word of this to anyone, but Harley is engaged to a white woman at Wellesley and has taken us into his confidence. He is like all of the West Indians - they leave a trail of enemies everywhere. They are always doing exciting and preposterous things.[190]

Who was this white woman? Was the engagement real, or one of Harley's attempts to further alienate his fellow black cohorts at Harvard? Whatever the explanation Harley wrote to Josephine and sent her cuttings detailing his prize successes with the masthead from the *Harvard Crimson* as a header. The first cutting reported the winning of the Hill essay prizes. It reported on the students who received varying financial awards for the essay on the subject 'Why should a student chose Harvard University?' Harley received the second undergraduate and professional school prize of $50. The second headed 'Harvard Prizes Awarded' reported on the same Hill prizes. The final cutting, 'Coloured Student's success', reads:

Mr J. Arthur Harley, Harvard '06 has been elected as a member of the executive committee of the Harvard

---

188 Ibid, p. 147.
189 Dean Hurlbut to Harley, Harvard University Archives, call no: UA 15.98.10 1890-1968 Box 2070 Folder title: Harley, James Arthur - 1906.
190 Stewart, p. 58.

Ethical society, the object of which is 'to promote an earnest interest in problems of practical ethics towards the highest ideals in personal, political, and social life'. Mr Harley was awarded one of the four-second prizes of $25 each, offered by a graduate for the best essay on 'The Feasibility of Introducing the English College Hall System at Harvard'. He has also received this year a Matthews' scholarship of $300, which, possibly, but one other Harvard student beside himself has ever received. In the fall, Mr Harley leaves for Oxford university, England, where he will receive a scholarship of $300 a year for three years.[191] Mr Harley is to be congratulated upon his splendid scholarship which might be an answer to Prof. Bigelow's vaporings.[192]

The pasted articles on the *Harvard Crimson* headed paper gave the impression that the newspaper had published them, but the articles were in the *Boston Guardian*. The *Boston Guardian* was an African American newspaper, co-founded by William Monroe Trotter and George Forbes, both Harvard alumni, in 1901. The paper's motto was 'For every right, with all thy might'. The paper provided an alternative to the usual images portrayed in the mainstream media. There were no depictions of the black man as the obedient clown, smiling, happy, bringing joy to many as a 'good Negro' or the wholesome, buxom mammy cuddling a white child. These stereotypical and caricatural images portrayed the lives of many in subservient jobs, but the paper was different: it carried a regular 'Men of Honour' feature, political articles and reports on black life, movers and shakers, and the successes of black graduates. Except for its

---

191 The article reporting Harley's scholarship of $300 for three years to attend Oxford University is somewhat perplexing. I have been unable to find any record of any scholarship application to Oxford University.
192 *Boston Guardian*, 18 March 1905.

Harley's press cuttings from the *Boston Guardian*. (Private collection)

advertisements for Black No More skin lightening creams and products that claimed to straighten curly hair, the paper did not portray images that colluded in a negative discourse. It was also the first paper to openly criticize Booker T. Washington. W.E. Dubois wrote:

> *The Guardian* attracted wide attention among colored people; it circulated among them all over the country; it was quoted and discussed. I did not wholly agree with the *Guardian*, and indeed, only a few Negroes did, but nearly all read it and were influenced by it.

Harley's decision to paste these three small cuttings onto the *Harvard Crimson* headed paper was significant. His successes were not reported in the venerable pages of this highly regarded publication, named after the university's iconic colour. Staffed by white elite students, the *Crimson* did not deem a black student's success newsworthy. There was also a tone of posturing from Harley that said, 'Look how well I am doing.' Was he trying to impress Josephine through the reporting of the Matthews Scholarship and a scholarship to attend Oxford at $300 per year for three years?

It appears that Harley adopted some creative licence in reporting his scholarship to Oxford. His verbose claim may have been intended to illustrate to Josephine that he would be a man of some means when he arrived in Oxford. Moreover, this could be construed as sufficient reason for her to seriously contemplate marriage. Harley, it seems, was determined to impress Josephine, but was he trying to resuscitate a relationship, salvage one, or secure one that would be beneficial to him in the long term?

At the close of 1905 and the beginning of a new year, Josephine's parents, started to operate a school for Bible study in their home at 2011 Vermont Avenue in Washington.

This was the forerunner to what would later become the Frelinghuysen University (see Chapter 22). In contrast, the new year brought the same old problems for Harley. He wrote to the Administrative Board in February 1906 to ask for the work he had done for his degree to be accepted and to have an honourable mention. He states:

> I understood that my deficiency must be offset by good work in other branches; I pointed out that last year I made the second of scholarship man, and most of my work was Semitics and social philosophy. Beside my remaining two conditions in Mathematics, during the past half year I had attained grades A. B. and C. in Semitic work, and as a member of the Princeton and Yale second debating teams, I had put extra time on outside work which during the regular work in Semitics. I stated that should I not obtain final honours I shall at least have an honourable mention.[193]

The Administrative Board informed Harley that they could not give him any statement about his standing for his degree until they had acted upon the recommendation of the Committee on Admissions.

Harley had preached as a lay minister since his arrival in America. His noted skills in oratory carried passion and conviction. He thus seized the opportunity to enter the university's Boylston Prize for elocution. Two reason attracted Harley to enter: prestige and the cash prize. Established by Ward Nicholas Boylston in 1817 in recognition of his uncle Nicholas Boylston, who established the Boylston Professorship of Rhetoric and Oratory, the prize was open to seniors, juniors and sophomores in good standing and awarded for the ability

---

193 Harley to Administrative Board, 28 February 1906, Harvard University Archives.

to memorize a text selected from English, Greek or Latin literature. The presentation could not exceed five minutes; delivery, style and presentation were also critiqued.[194] Harley achieved the first prize with his presentation entitled 'The Roll Call on the Philippine Question' and received a $60 prize.[195]

Harley's run of good luck continued for a short while, the $60 award helping to relieve his continual financial difficulties. Furthermore, his petition to change from Semitic Languages 2 to 16 was approved by Professor David Lyons, and his marks were changed on his application for honours. Harley at first failed the examination for Honours in Semitic: Professor Lyons' diary entry states: 'Examination of J.A. Harley for honours in Semitic. Unsuccessful.' But five days later, Professor Lyons wrote to inform him that one of his essays received positive attention, that some slight changes in the composition would make it worthy of a place in a good magazine, and that these changes he could easily make. 'Hammurabi was a man of the first importance, and you have told his story in a very attractive way. I hope that some editor will think as well of your paper as I do.' Harley's archive does not contain the article or any evidence of its publication.

Harley once again petitioned the Board for honours and for his degree to be recognized as *cum laude*. He wrote to the Dean on 21 June 1906 to inform him that he had passed all the written examination for honours in Semitic Languages but owing to lack of time to prepare thoroughly for the detailed oral examination, his first attempt was unsuccessful.[196] He stated:

Seeing that I am making Theology my first, it was my wish to get credit for the special work I have done on

---

194 Harvard University corporate records, Harvard University Archives.
195 *The Cambridge Tribune*, 12 May 1906.
196 Harley to Dean Hurlbut, 21 June 1906, Harvard University Archives call number UAIII 15.88.10 1890-1968, Box 2070.

that subject here at Harvard. I beg to remind him, [the Dean] however, that I had the required 2/12/ honour grades in English Composition, and the three honour marks in Semitics to get an honourable mention in both these subjects, and therefore as you are aware of the rule that effect, I am entitled to a Cum Laude. I outlined the point 5. 11 of the pamphlets entitled Harvard College 1905-06. The rule read 'If he has attained Grades A or B in nine courses or their equivalent, or has received honourable mention twice, he is recommended for a degree cum laude.[197]

NO in large black letters dominated the letter Harley received from Dean Hurlbut. There was no room for misunderstanding or negotiation; the subject was firmly closed. Whether offence was taken at Harley for reiterating the rules to the Dean, or his request was rejected because of his constant demands since his arrival, or even there was a more covert reason for the dismissal of his request, it is impossible to know. Yet the haggling and negotiations over his marks in order for his degree to be recognized with honours or *cum laude* would soon pale into insignificance with what loomed on the horizon. The impending situation would seriously threaten his degree and was to trigger a series of letters that raised questions about his moral conduct, nature, fitness for the ministry and, ultimately, whether he was suitable to follow his ultimate vocation in the Church.

---

197 Ibid.

9. A Looming Crisis

'In times of crisis, people reach for meaning. Meaning is strength.'

Viktor E. Frankl

To the Harvard Faculty

I understand that Mr. J. Arthur Harley is a student in the academic department of Harvard University. He is in debted to me ten dollars for board while he was here in New Haven. [Yale]. I write to ask you to pledge me that this bill is paid before you grant him a degree. Please oblige me, if you wish to be advised further, I will be glad to advise you.
I am forever.
Eliza Simmonds.[198]

Harley was informed by the Board that a Mrs Simmonds had contacted them, on 19 June 1906 and his degree was in danger of being witheld if the bill was not settled. Mrs Simmonds wrote again on 21st June.

Dear Sir,

I have just received your communication. I also received one from Mr. Harley saying that you had written him about the bill. But he did not pay the bill. All that I ask of him is that he pays a just debit, and he ought to pay it not only because he owns it but also because I need my

---

198 Mrs Simmonds to Dean Hurlburt, 19 June 1906, Harvard University Archives call number UAIII 15.88.10 1890-1968, Box 2070.

money. I find that I have given him time enough within which to pay it. So, I again ask you to please see that he pays the bill before you dismiss him from the university. Obligingly yours,
Eliza Simmonds.[199]

The Dean had already received Mrs Simmonds' letter, hence the unambiguous NO in response to Harley's request for *cum laude* status. Harley then responded to Mrs Simmonds' and the Dean's letter of 21 June.

Dear Sir,

Your letter about Mrs Simmonds is hard and is ugly. I beg to say that my bill with Mrs Simmonds was contracted at Yale; it has nothing whatever to do with Harvard College. I am not evading payment of the bill in question; every time I pass through New Haven, I go quickly to the house of Mr Simmonds to tell his wife that I shall pay her as soon as possible. I have written to fix the debt of payment now that I know I shall not have an expensive college to face this fall. Harvard College rules do not undertake to say that no graduate shall own a bill anywhere. I have my hands full trying to pay a twenty-dollar fine for graduating in less than four Harvard years. So long as I pay all my debts contracted during my Harvard undergraduate days, as long as I do not refuse to pay either debt, as long as I show no intent to defraud man or woman, boy or girl, I fail to see what such a matter as presented me has to do with my seven-year 'toiled' for a degree in any way whatsoever.

---

199 Mrs Simmonds to Dean Hurlbut, 21 June 1906, Harvard University Archives call number UAIII 15.88.10 1890-1968, Box 2070.

James Arthur Harley.

On 23 June, the Administrative Board voted to strike Harley from the list of candidates for his degree.[200] The Board proposed, however, to recommend him for the degree if he discharged the debt to Mrs Simmonds. But worse, this latest incident gave Dean Hurlbut carte blanche to rigorously investigate Harley, his superior attitude, his association with white elites, the unthinkable fraternizing with white women in his room, and the whisper of an engagement to a white woman. The Dean now had enough ammunition to justify a letter-writing campaign to ascertain Harley's credibility not only as a Harvard man but a man of God. He wrote to Dean Wright at Yale:

Dear Dean Wright,

I am writing about a student, a J.A. Harley, and his time at Yale in the year 1902-03, I think. I wish you would write to me as fully as you can your opinion of the man. He has been a most perplexing case ever since he came to Cambridge. He was very indignant this year because I refused to recommend him for his degree. A poor woman in New Haven wrote protesting his receiving his degree because he had not paid her for the board. He maintains that since the bill was indebted at New Haven it had nothing to do with his degree at Harvard, but the Administrate Board had a very different opinion. He secured work when he first came here with Father Field, who has a mission for the Episcopal Church, worked to a considerable extent among the coloured people of Boston. His work there was not done satisfactorily. Altogether I

---

200 Harley's record, Harvard University Archives call number UAIII 15.88.10 1890-1968, Box 2070.

question the fitness of Harley for the ministry.
Sincerely yours
B.S. Hurlburt

A note was received back from the Bursar of Yale stating:

> He seemed to have good standing among the coloured
> people of New Haven and had the appearance of activity
> in religious work. No complaint was ever made to me
> that he did not pay his bills. All his college bills were
> paid before he left us.
> Yours sincerely
> Charles Masons
> Bursar[201]

Yet more concerning than whether Harley had paid his debt
or not, a number of questions were now being raised about
his moral conduct and general character. The Dean of Harvard
wrote to Father Field at St John's Mission House, where Harley
was a Sunday School Superintendent.

October 21st, 1906

Dear Sir.

I write to request your opinion of Mr. J.A. Harley;
he is at present registered in the Senior class. This
week Harley has been to see me in regard to financial
assistance. He told me he needed money to pay for
coal and his dues for the Phillips Brooks House, the
Union, and the Debating Club. He is the holder of
a Matthews Scholarship, which is assigned to him
because he is preparing himself for the ministry of the

---

201 Bursar of Yale to Dean Hurlbut, 19 August 1906, Harvard University
Archives call number UAIII 15.88.10 1890-1968, Box 2070.

Episcopal Church. From this scholarship, I have already authorized the advance of a sufficient sum to cover his tuition, more than this I cannot give him. Do you know of any work whereby he can earn money necessary for his support? I wish much that I could talk Harley's case over with you, for am I a good deal pleased with him and the advisability of giving him further help, for it seems to me that it is time for him to be at work to support himself. He is now over thirty years old. I have been told that instead of going to work at the end of the present year, he plans to go to Oxford for further study. I should like to know your opinion of the man.[202]

The Dean also solicited the opinion of the Cambridge Theological Seminary School's Dean Hodges.

October 29th, 1906

Dear Dean Hodges,

I would like to have a talk with you sometime about J.A. Harley. He has asked me for a larger assessment of preliminary help from his Matthews Scholarship than I can give him. I am allowed by the rules of the Corporation to have credited to him that amount necessary to pay the first instalment of tuition. He now needs further help to buy coal, and tells me that he should like to pay his dues to Brooks House, the Debating Union, etc. I wrote to Father Fields, for whom Harley worked last year. Harley expressed regret that I had done so and did not speak very pleasantly of the Church. I told him that I should write to Bishop Lawrence, but as Harley

---

202 Dean Hurlburt to Father Field, 21 October 1906, Harvard University Archives call number UAIII 15.88.10 1890-1968, Box 2070.

has been to see you (I draw this conclusion from Father Field's letters), I thought that I would write first of all to you. I question the advisability of giving him more help that I have. Father Field tells me that the work he did for him last year was done with 'constant grumbling' and that Harley speaks very bitterly of white people. I would like to know your opinion of the man.
Sincerely yours
B.S. Hurlburt[203]

A response arrived:

Dear Sir,

Your letter has been forwarded to me here, and I am sorry for the delay in the answers to your questions. The case of Mr J.A. Harley is difficult to understand. He is as you know coloured. He came to me asking for work among the coloured people, and I gave him Sunday school work and some lecturing for which I could not afford to pay him more than ten dollars a month with an occasional present. He did this work for about a year with continual grumblings. Before I went to Europe in July, he told me that he was going to Oxford in September and was giving up working for me. To my great surprise, Dean Hodges told me that he was at the Theological Seminary in Cambridge and asked me if I would like to engage him in coloured mission work. He is very able but bitter against white people; is dangerous among his own people. He takes it as a slight, if not helped. He complains about his grievances. He lectures and teaches elocution and has a good many points, but

---

203 Dean Hodges to Dean Hurlbut, 29 October 1906, Harvard University Archives call number UAIII 15.88.10 1890-1968, Box 2070.

his bitterness prevents his usefulness. I return to Boston at the end of next week. I shall be glad to answer any questions.

With Mrs Simmonds' debt still hanging over him and because of his failure to complete sufficient courses in his senior year, Harley's degree was not awarded. To resolve this situation, Dean Hurlbut wrote to Mrs Simmonds in February 1907 to ascertain whether the matter had been settled.[204] She responded the next day that Harley had written to her the previous June to inform her that he would settle the matter on or about 10 September. However, up to this time, he had failed to keep his promise, and she had not heard from him since.[205]

---

204 Dean Hurlburt to Mrs Simmonds, 6 February 1907, Harvard University Archives call number UAIII 15.88.10 1890-1968, Box 2070
205 Mrs Simmonds to Dean Hurlburt, 7 February 1907, Harvard University Archives call number UAIII 15.88.10 1890-1968, Box 2070.

10. Oxford Beckons

'The world surely has not another place like Oxford; it is a despair to see such a place and ever to leave it, for it would take a lifetime and more than one to comprehend and enjoy it satisfactorily.'

Nathaniel Hawthorne

Harley's dream of attending the General Theological Seminary of the Episcopal Church in New York had evaporated as a result of either an unintentional mistake or a predetermined order. Now his financial situation was dire; he depended mostly on the Matthews Scholarship administrated by the Dean, which gave the humiliating impression of a child awarded pocket money. His remuneration at the mission house and church appeared to be incommensurate with the time and effort he gave. His moral character and potential as a spiritual adviser were seriously compromised, and he was 'charged' with possessing what could be seen as the worst character trait of all: bitterness towards white people. Those four words could have devastating, -threatening consequences for him.

Harley existed in an America that did not value black life, especially that of a black man perceived as 'uppity'. An educated black man, who thought he knew better than the people he was working with, and who was not shy in coming forward to articulate his views and opinions, was a dangerous man. America was a country which in 1906 exhibited a black man in a cage in the monkey enclosure at Bronx Zoo for people to view. People flocked to see Ota Benga, the Congolese pygmy brought over by Samuel Philips Verner, an American anthropologist, and businessman from South Carolina. An estimated 40,000 people a day visited the zoo to marvel and gawp at the 'monkey man' - satisfied that the black man was still a subspecies, and their white superiority reinforced. Talk of animosity towards white people could result in Harley being dangled from the end of a noose.

Dean Hurlbut's series of letters to the ministries Harley had worked for and their reports back were largely unfavourable. The prospect of achieving admission into the General Theological Seminary School with so many questionable stains against his character, attitude and behaviour, would definitely eliminate him. The next best option was for him to remain in Massachusetts and attend the Cambridge-based Episcopal Theological School. Founded in 1867 by Boston businessmen, the school was the foundation and preparation for students taking Holy Orders and the Episcopal presence at Harvard. Harley enrolled as a student while completing his degree and the exact dates when he attended the seminary are not recorded.

*

12 March 1907 was a significant day for two reasons; Booker T. Washington delivered a speech at Harvard, introduced by Charles Elliot, the President of the University. Washington had agreed to meet with black students after his address to recruit entrants for his Tuskegee Institute. Secondly, Harley's young friend, Alain LeRoy Locke, received good news - he would be the first African American scholar to receive the prestigious Rhodes Scholarship at Oxford University. This scholarship was founded by Sir Cecil Rhodes (1853–1902), an alumnus of Oriel College, Oxford. A Bishop Stortford Grammar School boy, Rhodes earned his Master of Arts degree in 1881 after an extended period from 1873 when he was only intermittently in Oxford. He was not a model student, according to his tutor A.G. Butler: 'His career at Oxford was uneventful. He belonged to a set of men like himself,

'not caring for distinction in the schools [examinations] and not working for them, but of refined tastes, dining, and living for the most part together, and doubtless discussing passing events in life and politics with interest and ability.'[206] Rhodes interspersed his academic life with his business adventures. He amassed his fortune by obtaining a large interest in the newly-worked Kimberley diamond mines in southern Africa and amalgamated then into the De Beers Consolidated Mines, amassing a multi-million-pound fortune in gold and diamonds. An advocate of British imperialism in Africa, he dominated the country which took his name – Rhodesia.[207]

The Rhodes scholarships, administered by the Rhodes Trust, were a feature of Rhodes' sixth and final will, drawn up in 1899 at the age of forty-six. Rhodes' vision of world peace was expressed in financing Rhodes Scholars, a move to educate future leaders of the world by allowing them to study for three years at Oxford. Rhodes laid down the following criteria by which categories of Rhodes Scholar were to be selected: 30 per cent for literary and scholastic attainments; 20 per cent for a fondness for and success in manly outdoor sports such as cricket and the like; 30 per cent for qualities of truth, courage, devotion to duty, sympathy for and protection of the weak, kindliness, unselfishness and fellowship; and 20 per cent for exhibiting during their school days signs of moral force of character and instincts to lead and take an interest in their schoolmates.[208]

Rhodes chose to endow these postgraduate scholarships at Oxford because he believed 'its residential colleges provided an environment especially conducive to personal development.' His view was unashamedly elitist: 'Wherever you turn your eye

---

206 Sir Lewis Mitchell, *The Life of Rt. Honourable Cecil John Rhodes*, Ithaca NY: Cornell University Library, 1912.
207 Association of American Rhodes Scholars, *The American Oxonian.*
208 Rhodes Scholarship information, Rhodes House Trust, University of Oxford.

- except in science - an Oxford man is at the top of the tree.'

For the Rhodes Scholarship, Locke passed the qualifying examination in Latin, Greek and Mathematics, scoring the highest mark and beating seven white student candidates in the process. He was awarded the Scholarship before the committee discovered he was black, but after careful consideration, the committee decided to let the award stand. Locke would now be making applications to Oxford colleges. Harley sent him a letter of congratulations: 'I say I am glad, Old Boy, glad, glad, glad; glad without thinking of self, save to say I wish I were going to be near you [in Oxford] so that I might have the pleasure of your fellowship. Go & prosper Locke. You have acted the part of a man always.'[209]

Not everyone was so pleased with Locke's achievement. The New York *Evening Post* observed: 'A negro has won the Rhodes scholarship at Oxford University... Mr. Locke gives offense beyond that of the race. He announces: "I intend to devote myself to study while in England." To be a Negro beating white competitors is bad enough; but to advertise oneself, in addition, as mollycoddle, is to strain even the impossible beliefs of Oxford.'

Now Harley also made his plans for an Oxford education and applied to Manchester College. Manchester College was a Unitarian establishment. The Unitarian movement and its beliefs were far removed from the teachings of the Anglican Church, and Unitarians' rejection of credal forms, the Thirty-Nine Articles and the triune nature of God - all of which were central to orthodox Anglicanism - were paralleled by their practice which was based on the principle of social justice and the conviction that religion should make a difference to the local community. The religion provided individuals with the opportunity to accommodate a broad range of opinions and express any doubts.

---

209 Harley to Alain Locke, 12 March 1905, Moorland-Spingarn Research Center.

Harley had to apply to the Manchester College committee on admission, stating his line of study, and to present testimonials signed by at least two disinterested persons as to his character and attainment and his willingness to conform to the regulations of the college.[210] Locke and Horace Kallen were his two signatories. Kallen, a German-born Jew, met Locke in 1905 in a Greek philosophy class as a teaching assistant to George Santayana, the celebrated philosophy professor, when he was undertaking his Ph.D. He had studied philosophy at Harvard graduating in 1903, and the President of Princeton University, Woodrow Wilson, personally hired Kallen. His appointment made him the first Jewish scholar to teach at Princeton. Yet his tenure there was short-lived; after two years his contract was not renewed. Rev David Wallace also provided a testimonial for Harley:

> This is to certify that I personally know James Arthur Harley to be of an excellent moral character and splendid natural endowments such as to qualify him for becoming a student at your college. Furthermore, he is qualified by disposition and abilities to become a student for the ministry which I know he seeks of his voluntary choices.
>
> David R. Wallace
> Assistant Priest in charge
> St. Augustine.

Harley had also requested a testimonial from Bishop Satterlee, and he sent a letter from Professor Lyons. Lyons had stated that Harley's essay was of such high quality that it merited, with slight amendments, inclusion in a magazine.

---

210 Harris Manchester College Archives, University of Oxford.

Harley's vocation as a child, we have seen, was to become a minister in the Protestant Episcopal Church. What then precipitated his application to study at a Unitarian college? Was it an opportunity for Harley to explore his theological orthodoxy and broaden his knowledge of other religious concepts, or was there an underlying pragmatic reason? Did Harley harbour theological misgivings, or was Manchester College a useful stepping-stone in his long-term plans?

Now ensconced at the Theological School, Harley took advantage of one of the awards available there - the Pierre Jay Prize, given to students who produced the best essay. The Pierre Jay award was in recognition of Peter Augustus Jay, the son of John Jay, one of the founding fathers of America. Jay, a staunch supporter of social justice and equal rights, gave consistent support for African Americans to receive equal rights, manifested through his work as President of the New York Manumission Society. As a Federalist delegate, he argued that the right to the vote should be extended to free African Americans at the New York State Constitutional Convention in 1821.

The essay prize, to aid meritorious students, had to be on a subject related to the topic of 'The Motives for Foreign Missions' and it carried a reward of $100. With his mind now set on Manchester College, the award of the prize would provide for Harley's travel to Oxford. And so he entered for the prize, the topic of his essay 'Japanese Shintoism - What is It?' He was duly awarded the Pierre Jay Prize.

With the situation over Mrs Simmonds' debt apparently resolved, the Board at Harvard now recommended the awarding of his degree. Harley received his AB degree in 1907, the same year Josephine graduated from Oberlin College. She would henceforth be entering the profession of teaching, but on specific conditions. Denied access to white schools, elite blacks realized they would have to train members of their race to prepare them for the few colleges that would accept them. Josephine, like other members of the elite, had the responsibility of uplifting the race. In 1890, only thirty black women in the United States held Baccalaureate degrees as compared with 300 black men and 2,500 white women.[211] Seventeen years later, when Josephine graduated, a conservative estimate revealed only fifty black women acquiring a degree: Josephine was still a rarity.

Josephine secured a position at Cheyney State Normal School in Pennsylvania. The school had developed from the historical and groundbreaking Institute for Colored Youth, founded in 1837 and became the first establishment to provide higher education for African Americans. During the following year, Josephine taught in public schools in West Chester, followed by a year of substitute teaching in Washington DC.[212]

Locke also graduated in Philosophy in 1907, *magna cum laude*, and was elected to one of the oldest academic honour societies in the country - Phi Beta Kappa. Established in 1781, Phi Beta Kapp members are recognized for excellence in the liberal arts and sciences. Membership signifies that an undergraduate has demonstrated exceptional reach, originality and rigour in their course of study. Locke also won Harvard's most prestigious award, the Bowdoin Prize, for an essay, 'The Literary Heritage of Tennyson'. It carried with it a medal, the public presentation of a thesis and $250.

*

Harley had completed his academic quest - a Harvard degree. Why did he want to pursue an education in England, why was an elite education important to him, what was he trying to

---

211 Linda M. Perkins, 'The Role of Education in the Development of Black Feminist Thought, 1860-1929', *History of Education*, vol. 22, 1993.
212 Josephine Lawson Oberlin College record, Oberlin College Archives.

prove, or whom was he trying to impress? The constant quest for his educational goal had taken its toll on him and had been made at great financial cost. Harley would now travel to another foreign country, to further his experiences and knowledge. As a man in his mid-thirties, his motives regarding his age and prospects had already been questioned by the Dean of Harvard. Harley had navigated a political, social and cultural landscape that conspired to break and brutalize a black man who did not conform to prescribed norms. Like Sisyphus, he had managed to roll the stone to the top of the summit, for it now to roll back down, and to start all over again in England. On 25 September 1907, the thirty-four-year-old Harley left New York for England and set sail for the port of Liverpool[213] to begin his Oxford journey.

---

213 Harley to Locke, 11 September 1907, Moorland-Spingarn Research Center, Howard University.

11. Dreaming Spires

'Let us turn a deaf ear to criticism and slander and push forward to the goal.'

Alexander Walters

As Harley set out to commence his studies in Oxford, *The Antigua Standard* newspaper carried the following report of his achievements:

> OUR KITH ABROAD.
>
> It was our pleasure in the issue of 17th to record chronologically the scholastic career of Mr James Arthur Harley, a son of Antigua, who this year took the degree of B.A., with honours in Semitic languages; and won the Cambridge University Scholarship $200,00 and the Pierre Jay Prize for the best essay on 'Japanese Shintoism' worth $100. It is now our pleasure to note that Mr Harley left New York on 20th inst, for Oxford, to read for Honours in Theology. He is a proud record.[214]

Unlike the Caribbean and Americas, the small island of Britain is not traditionally associated with a longstanding black presence. But a significant black presence here dates back to at least 1555, when seamen returned to English ports with Africans.[215] In 1596, Queen Elizabeth I issued an 'open letter' to the Lord Mayor of London, his aldermen and mayors and sheriffs of other towns expressing her displeasure that there were too many 'Blackamoors in the realm' and ordering that they be

---

214 *The Antigua Standard*, 28 September 1907.
215 Nigel File and Chris Powell, *Black Settlers in Britain 1555-1958*, London: Heinemann, 1981, p. 5.

deported. She complained again in 1601 about the significant number of 'Negars and Blackamoors, who had crept into the realm', and defamed them as 'infidels, having no understanding of Christ or his Gospel'.[216]

The black community continued to grow and develop, especially in the port cities of Liverpool, Bristol, Cardiff and London. Francis Barber, a Jamaican brought to England in 1750, ran a school with his wife at Burntwood, near Lichfield.[217] Olaudah Equiano, an anti-slavery campaigner, travelled widely throughout the English towns and cities of Birmingham, Bristol, Hull, Devizes and Sheffield.[218] Ignatius Sancho was brought to England as an enslaved person from Grenada, and he and his wife, a black West Indian woman, ran a grocer's shop in Charles Street, Westminster. Sancho produced plays and poetry and worked on music. After his death in 1780, five editions of his book of letters were published.

By the eighteenth century, many blacks were in England; about 20,000 in London, it was estimated.[219] The displeasure voiced by Queen Elizabeth continued in the pages of newspapers such as *The Morning Post*.

> When the late Mr Dunning was some years ago reasoning against making this country a refuge for all the blacks who chose to come here, he observed, 'that the numerous dingy-coloured faces which crowded our streets, must have their origin in our wives being terrified when pregnant, by the numerous Africans who were to be seen in all parts of the town, and if the legislature did not take some method to prevent the introduction of any more, he would venture to prophesy, that London

---

216 Ibid, p. 6.
217 Ibid, p. 2.
218 Ibid, p. 2.
219 Ibid, p. 5.

would, in another century, have the appearance of an Ethiopian colony.[220]

A very popular member, it is said, intends to bring in a bill to prevent blacks being brought into the Kingdom. There is such a law in France and a very excellent one it is. When so many of our young men and women are out of employment, and, literally speaking, are starving in the streets, it is abominable that aliens, and more particularly black aliens, should be suffered to eat the bread of idleness in Gentlemen's houses.[221]

The arrival of ex-enslaved Black Loyalists from the American War of Independence reignited the issue of race as many of them, unable to find work, were forced onto the streets as beggars and vagrants. Several initiatives were proffered by the Committee for the Relief of the Black Poor in the form of food and clothing, but the Committee's solution to the 'problem' was to repatriate blacks to Africa. A plan presented to the Committee by the naturalist Henry Smeathman was to establish a settlement on the west coast of Africa in Sierra Leone with promised money from the government.[222]

The eldest son of Queen Victoria, King Edward VII, was monarch and ruler of the British Empire when Harley arrived in England in mid-October 1907. The black community had developed significantly throughout Britain. London especially had a sizeable black and mixed-race population made up of a working and middle class, which contained distinguished members such as Samuel Coleridge-Taylor, the son of an African father from Sierra Leone and an English mother. Coleridge-Taylor was born in 1875 in Holborn and lived most

220 *The Morning Post*, 1 December 1786.
221 *The Morning Post*, 29 December 1786.
222 File and Powell, p. 34.

of his life in Croydon. A talented composer, he was noted for his work, *The Song of Hiawatha*. Dr Ernest Goffe came to London from Jamaica in 1889 to study medicine at University College Hospital. He and his wife became general practitioners in Kingston-upon-Thames after working in London hospitals.

Harley travelled to Oxford, a city founded in the ninth century and renowned around the world for its university. King Henry VIII refounded one of its most famous colleges, Christ Church, as part of his reorganization of the Church of England. The city's skyline was dominated by the spires of the Church of St Mary the Virgin, the Radcliffe Camera and All Souls College, where Christopher Codrington III's wealth, amassed from the forced labour of enslaved people in Antigua and Barbados, secured his legacy: the Codrington Library, endowed with his collection of over 12,000 books and £10,000.

The city of Oxford was entirely different in look and feel to Cambridge, Massachusetts, and Harvard University. The university then consisted of some twenty colleges,[223] situated within the city, each with its own identity, style, history and - depending on founders and benefactors - its level of wealth. The university had no precise date for its foundation, but there was a consensus that teaching of some form existed by 1096, developing rapidly after Henry II banned English students from attending the University of Paris.

Christian Frederick Cole, born in 1852, was the first black student to graduate from the University of Oxford. Cole attended the oldest European-style school in West Africa, Fourah Bay College, known as the Athens of West Africa, because of its strong curriculum in Greek and Latin. His father

---

223 The figure of twenty colleges does not include St Edmund Hall and Keble College, for instance, both in existence in 1909 but which then had different status and are now full colleges of the University. In total, there are now thirty-nine collages, some postgraduate only. Bodleian Libraries, Keeper of the Archives.

died in 1872 and his uncle assumed his guardianship. Cole enrolled at University College on 19 April 1873, aged twenty-one, as a non-collegiate student to read for an Honours degree in Classical Moderations (Classics). The subject of his degree was deemed one of the most difficult, and Cecil Rhodes himself was turned down by University College when he applied to read Classics, eventually studying at Oriel College.

As a non-collegiate student, Cole did not receive the privileges extended to a member of the college which included lodgings and meals. His fees and living expenses were supported by his uncle. Cole's presence inevitably attracted comment. Florence Ward, sister of William Ward, best friend of the Irish playwright Oscar Wilde (1854-1900), came up to Oxford a year after Cole. Her entry relating to the annual Sunday show, *Promenade in the Broad Walk Christ Church*, on 18 June 1876 noted: 'I spied the Nigger Coal, hair as curly and skin as black as Coal.' The *Oxford Chronicle* of 29 June 1878 recorded that, before the Encaenia procession entered, 'Some amusement was caused by "Three Cheers for Christian Cole", a gentleman of color, of University College, who had entered the Theatre a few moments previously and was standing in the area.' The nickname of Old King Cole was attributed to him by Colonel Thomas Higginbottom.

As a member of Oxford Union Debating society, Cole debated on numerous subjects including arguing in favour of the death penalty. He achieved his degree in Classical Moderations, which permitted him to become a full member of the college in 1877. He incurred a significant debt of £200 in his last year of study because his customary remittance from his uncle had stopped, and he refrained from asking his friends for assistance until increasing embarrassment forced him to do so. To supplement his income, Cole, a talented musician, taught music to undergraduates as well as tutoring for Responsions,

Christian Frederick Cole, the University of Oxford's first black student.
The Caricature, dated 1878, is the only known image of Cole.
(Bodleian Library, Oxford)

the first of three examinations once required for an academic degree at the university, as well as preparing students for the divinity exam, which they had to pass to graduate. However, this extra work proved precarious and an inadequate source of income. He eventually sought assistance from the Master of University College, George Granville Bradley. Bradley produced a circular requesting aid to relieve Cole stating, 'taking into account the absence of extravagance in his expenditure, that the exceptional nature of Mr Cole deserves and calls for the sympathy of and assistance of those in Oxford in which he lived with so much credit to himself.' University College alumnus Herbert John Gladstone (1854-1930) also added his support to the circular. Despite Bradley's and Gladstone's help, Cole was still in a difficult financial position and decided to return to Sierra Leone.

While in Sierra Leone it appeared that Cole became politically conscious and developed an in interest in Pan-Africanism through his association with Edward Wilmot Blyden, the father of Pan-Africanism. Cole delivered a series of lectures in Freetown. One talk was entitled 'The Wall Case: Can anything good come out of Sierra Leone? Being a letter addressed to Letter Derby. Her majesty Secretary of State for the Colonies on one or two of the burning questions of West Africa of the hour'. Cole's friends in Sierra Leone raised funds to enable his return to England to realize a career in the law. On 1 September 1879, aged twenty-eight, Cole became the first black African member of the Honourable Society of the Inner Temple. During his time at the Inner Temple, he published a slim pamphlet of two poems titled 'Reflections on the Zulu War, and What men say about negros. By a Negro, B.A., of University College'.

Cole, now thirty-two, was called to the bar in the Easter term of 1883 and the following year became the first black

African to practise law in the English High Court, more widely known as the Old Bailey and now the Central Criminal Court. There are no records of any chambers that Cole was attached to. Unable to find regular work in England, though, Cole moved to East Africa and secured a role as a barrister to the Consular Court in Zanzibar. His success was short-lived, however, and a year after arriving he contracted smallpox and died on 7 December 1885, at the age of thirty-three.

*

Harley had made an application to Manchester College for special student status while still at the Theological Seminary in Massachusetts. He attended the General Committee meeting of Manchester College on 14 October 1907,[224] when his application was read for admission to the second Theological Year as a Regular Student. He had his letters and testimonials in support[225] and stated to the twenty-one members of the General Committee that he was a British subject born in the West Indies.[226] The committee resolved to admit him as a Special Student for a year and approved a grant of £50 from the Webb Fund.

The Webb Fund was set up by Annie Theresa Webb to enable students for the ministry to 'take advantage to the full of that Oxford offers of culture as well as ordinary instructions'.[227] The daughter of Thomas Webb of Clapham Park, London, Annie Webb married George Webb, a schools superintendent in 1864. Mrs Webb was a worker at the mothers' meetings at Rhyl Street Mission in Kentish Town and Bell Street Mission

---

224 Harris Manchester College, minutes of the committee, 14 October 1907, University of Oxford.
225 Ibid.
226 Ibid.
227 A. Webb to Manchester College, Harris Manchester College Archives.

in Marylebone, London, and a staunch supporter of her Unitarian church, the Essex Church, Palace Gardens Terrace, Kensington.[228] She endowed £100, paid annually in August, to the Fund to enable additional grants to be given in such cases as the committee saw fit.[229] Harley received half of the Webb Fund allocation, a substantial subsidy for a year.

Harley's reasons to study at Manchester College perhaps now became more explicit; broadening his religious knowledge could have been a factor, but the lure of the Webb Fund was an attractive motivator. He had risked venturing to England without sufficient funds to support his further studies and speculated with his application to Manchester College. There was no guarantee he would be awarded any funds from the College, and certainly not such a substantial amount. The award was a testament to Harley's gifts of oratory and recognition of his skills and abilities.

Harley was now a student at Manchester College, formerly known as the Manchester Academy, founded in 1786 by English Presbyterians. It provided an opportunity for Nonconformists to take degrees, previously denied to them by Oxford and Cambridge because of the religious test and confession of faith requirement. The college relocated from Manchester to London before finally settling in the heart of the educational Establishment - Oxford - in 1889.[230] It had temporary premises at 90 High Street before purchasing land from Merton College to build the neo-Gothic stone edifice at the lower end of the wider Mansfield Street. With close proximity to the city centre, Mansfield Street nonetheless offered quiet respite away from its hustle and bustle.

---

228 *The Inquirer*, 29 September 1929.
229 Harris Manchester College Archives.
230 J.H. Parker and Richard Ennis, *Manchester College: A Short History 1786-1990*, Oxford: Manchester College, 1990.

Manchester College existed for the purpose of promoting the study of Religion, Theology and Philosophy, without insisting on the adoption of particular doctrines. It had established strong international links and attracted students from Hungary because of ties with the Unitarian Church of Transylvania. Indian and Japanese students were also prominent at the college due to links with India and the Brahmo Samaj - the reforming theistic movement founded in the early nineteenth century by Ram Mohun.[231]

Inscribed over the main college entrance is the motto, 'to truth, to liberty, to religion', the words of Thomas Barnes, the college's first Principal from his opening address in 1786. According to the minister and philosopher Lawrence Pearsall Jacks[232]: 'the erection of that building in Oxford is an impertinence. Even the architecture is obtrusively Unitarian; solid but cold.'[233]

Harley was at liberty to select the classes he wanted to attend as a Special Student. He had access to the Tate Library and junior common room and could enjoy all the privileges of the College. He was expected to be present at the 8.45 am daily prayers and take his turn in conducting them, at the Divine Service on Sunday, the Wednesday 6.15 pm students' services and the meetings of the Discussions Society, a requirement of a Special Student and in line with regulations affecting theological students.[234] He had to wear his gown at chapel

---

231 Ibid, p. 19.
232 Lawrence Pearsall Jacks (1860-1955), or L.P. Jacks, as he was always known, was probably the most widely known Unitarian minister in both Britain and North America between 1914 and 1940. He was an educator, a prolific writer and an interpreter of modern philosophy. In 1903 Jacks was appointed Professor at Manchester College and Principal in 1915 until he retired in 1931. Alan Ruston, *The Dictionary of Unitarian and Universalist Biography*, an on-line resource of the Unitarian Universalist History & Heritage Society.
233 Parker and Ennis, *Manchester College*, p. 18.
234 Manchester College Special Student's regulations.

services, dinners and lectures. An accomplished musician, Harley had the opportunity to use the chapel organ with the consent of the Organist and the Principal if the practice took place between 2 and 5 pm. Students were not allowed to marry during the period of their course.

Meanwhile, Alain Locke had arrived in Plymouth on 24 September 1907, sailing on the *Kaiser Wilhelm* with his close companion Carl Downes.[235] Locke's Rhodes Scholarship provided for the costs of study at Oxford, but it was no guarantee of admission. Applications were handled and sent out to individual colleges by Francis J. Wylie, Secretary of the Rhodes Fund in Oxford. Locke wrote to Wylie in May 1907, while at Harvard, to say that five Oxford colleges had rejected him: Magdalen, Balliol, Merton, Brasenose and Christ Church. Seemingly unperturbed, he wrote again to Wylie to state he would reapply, and if still rejected, would accept provisional status at any of the smaller colleges. In August, Wylie replied to Locke that Balliol had accepted only one of the twenty-four foreign students who had applied. New College had recently adopted a policy of accepting no more Rhodes Scholars whatsoever. He suggested Hertford College. But unbeknown to Locke, Wylie had been working diligently to rescind his Rhodes award. He had researched Locke's birth certificate, finding that the name on the certificate was Arthur, and that it falsely read 'white'. He organized a meeting to re-evaluate Locke's January 1907 exam and supported those white students who were threatening to refuse to reside at their colleges if Locke were admitted. Yet Wylie even wrote to Locke at the same time supplying advice on how to manage the personal and racial slights he was receiving. He told Locke that 'you have this question on interest which is racial and not merely personal.

---

235 Downes was the son of a wealthy art critic for the *Boston Transcript*. Downes matriculated and spent a year at Merton College.

Those interests will no doubt give your work here a special zest. It may also sometimes bring its difficulties.'[236]

Locke finally matriculated at Hertford College, one of Oxford's poorer colleges. The college stands on the junction of Catte Street and New College Lane opposite the entrance to the Bodleian Library. A small college, it now has a landmark bridge, reminiscent of the Bridge of Sighs in Venice, linking its old and new quadrangles and completed in 1914. Locke had elegant rooms in the New Buildings, equipped with a long sofa, writing desk, sideboard, two window seats, a hanging electric light chandelier and a large oak table. He also had a scout, whom he described as a 'near-servant', who served breakfast in his room 'with a linen cloth and steel bone cutlery', which Locke had to purchase.[237]

At Oxford, Locke attempted to escape the racial identity thrust upon him in the United States. He wrote to his mother, 'I am not a race problem. I am Alain LeRoy Locke.'[238] His eyes would soon be opened as to how others perceived him. Horace Kallen, for intance, who wrote a reference for Harley, was a 'friend' of Locke's while at Harvard. Kallen came to Oxford because of his Sheldon Travelling Fellowship. But Locke may have been surprised, if not disgusted, by the racist views Kallen expressed in writing about him in a letter to his former professor and mentor, Barrett Wendall, the President of Harvard University:

> You will perhaps remember little Locke, the yellow boy who took Comp Lit 1 when you first gave it as English 42

---

236 Leonard Harris and Charles Molesworth, *Alain L. Locke: The Biography of a Philosopher*, Chicago IL: University of Chicago Press, 2010, p. 66.

237 Jack C. Zoeller, 'Alain Locke at Oxford: Race and the Rhodes Scholarships', *The American Oxonian*, Spring 2007, p. 210.

238 Jacoby Adeshei Carter and Leonard Harris, *Philosophic Values and World Citizenship: Locke to Obama and Beyond*, Lanham MD: Lexington Books, 2010, p. 168.

… He is here as a Rhodes Scholar, and some people have been in America officious and mean-spirited enough to draw the 'color-line' for the benefit of Englishmen. The boy earned his scholarship in an open competition. He has said nothing to me himself. Others have depreciated his being here. But he is here, one of America's scholars, and a Harvard man. He finds himself suddenly shut out of things, unhappy, and doesn't know how or why.

As you know I have neither respect nor liking for his race - but individually, they have to be taken each on his own merit and value, and if a Negro was worthy, this boy is.[239]

Kallen's views were not representative of his fellow students, for the latter were even more racially offensive. But Kallen had known Locke since his Harvard days, interacting with him educationally and socially on numerous occasions, and yet still referred to his contemporary with the dismissive racial trope 'boy'. Kallen's diary presented a harsher tone and he observed that Locke seemed 'darker than at home', though he preferred his manner to that of Harley, remarking: 'What is disagreeable black in Harley crops out much more readily than it does in Locke.'[240] He also described Harley as 'an egregious ass'.[241]

Kallen failed to acknowledge, or could not accept, that Harley, a much older man, had acquired the same Ivy League education as he had, and was not intimidated or overawed by his peers or his circumstances. Kallen could not process the fact that Harley was his educational equal, and in Harley's eyes, also his equal in status.

---

239 Horace Kallen to Barrett Wendell, 22 October 1907, Wendell Papers, Houghton Library, Harvard University, bMS 1907.1, series A, folder 2, item 733.
240 Carter and Harris, *Philosophic Values*, p. 168.
241 Kallen's diary, 18 and 23 October 1907.

The Cosmopolitan Club at Oxford. Back row - Pixley Seme, third from
left; Alain LeRoy Locke, third from right. (Howard University)

Locke studied Philosophy, Greek, and Literae Humaniores.
He joined the French Club and along with the black South
African Pixley Seme and his friends the Scotsman Percy J.
Philips, the Ceylonese Lionel de Fonseka and others, founded
the Oxford Cosmopolitan Club. A social group of international
students, the club's charter stated that its purpose was 'to
promote mutual knowledge and sympathy between members
of different nationalities residing in Oxford.' Locke noted that
it attracted men of 'remarkable refinement and culture' from all
over the world.[242] The club met every second Tuesday during
each term and held debates. It also produced its journal - the
Oxford Cosmopolitan - dedicated to 'removing many narrow
national and racial prejudice by coming into contact with new
ideas and ways of thought'; the first issue appeared in June
1908.[243]

242 Weinfeld, p. 189.
243 Harris and Molesworth, p. 66.

Shortly after Locke's arrival at Oxford, the American Club in St Giles Street hosted its annual Thanksgiving dinner to honour American Rhodes Scholars: a dinner to which Locke was not invited. Kallen wrote of the incident:

I was there at the time … he was penalized. There were among the Rhodes Scholars at Oxford, gentlemen from Dixie, who could not possibly afford to associate with Negroes. They could not possibly attend the Thanksgiving dinner celebrated by Americans if a Negro was to be there. So although students from elsewhere in the United States outnumbered the gentlemen of Dixie, Locke was not invited; and one or two other peers authentically Americans, refused in consequence to attend.[244]

Kallen, who was among those who refused to attend, invited his 'friend' as a guest to tea in lieu of the Thanksgiving dinner; again, though, his racial intolerance is evident. He wrote to his professor: 'Tho' it is personally repugnant to me to eat with him, but then, Locke is a Harvard man and such he has a definite claim on me.'[245] Kallen's indignation was not so much at the racist treatment Locke received from his fellow Americans; respect, he believed, should have been afforded to him because he was a Harvard man and a Rhodes Scholar.

Harley was one of twelve students in 1907 at Manchester College, his cohorts made up of first-, second- and third-year students. They included, in the first year: Thomas McKenzie Falconer, Edward Stanley Russell. E.H. Pickering; in the second: Sasadhar Haldar, Bertram Lister, Raymond V. Holt; and in the third Richard. J. Hall and Mortimer Rowe.

---

244 Rudolph Alexander Kofi Cain, *Alain LeRoy Locke*, p. 2
245 Ibid, p. 102.

Harley's fellow students at Manchester College, Oxford, c 1907.
(Private collection)

Thomas McKenzie Falconer had graduated from Durham University with a Bachelor of Letters degree. He had also received funds from the Webb Fund. He studied at Manchester for two sessions and held chaplaincies at Dudley and Glasgow. His longest chaplaincy was at Bank Street Chapel, Bolton, for over twenty-three years.[246] Edward Stanley Russell spent three years as a co-minister at Ullet Road Church, Liverpool. He enlisted in the Liverpool Regiment and soon became a corporal and then a sergeant. He received a commission from the Herefordshire Regiment, which earned him a Military Cross. Russell became the first Unitarian minister to be killed in action, in November 1917.

Sasadhar Haldar, an Indian orphan from Calcutta, passed the entrance exam of the Calcutta University in 1893 but struggled to get through examinations until 1897. He was sent over from India by the leaders of the Brahmo Samaj.[247]

246 unitarianhistory.org.uk.
247 *Christian Life*, 12 December 1908.

Haldar claimed that 'the attitudes of most English men whom he met wounded [him] deeply.' He spent two years at Manchester College before attending Dresden University to benefit from western methods of analyzing Hindu philosophy. He died while still at the university.[248] Bertram Lister served as an assistant at Bank Street, Bolton, and at Hackney. He was appointed Secretary of the Sunday Schools Association in 1927. Raymond V. Holt arrived at Manchester with a first-class degree in History; he spent three years at the college. Awarded a Hibbert Scholarship, he attended Marburg University and returned to Manchester College in 1921 on a Daniel Jones Fellowship.[249] He was appointed a tutor in Christian History and remained there until his appointed as Principal in 1944. He died, aged seventy-two in March 1957.[250]

Richard. J. Hall, a third-year student, came from Belfast and spent several years at Oxford. In 1910 Hall became a minister in Auckland, New Zealand, and then in Johannesburg. He returned to Swansea Unitarian Chapel in 1922 and married Mary Carpenter, the niece of Joseph Estlin Carpenter, Principal of Manchester College. He died aged forty-nine.[251] Mortimer Rowe read geology at Lincoln College before entering Manchester College. He held ministries at Preston 1908-1913, Norwich 1913-1919 and Chowbent, Lancashire, 1920-1928. He became Secretary of the British and Foreign Unitarian Association in 1929 and died in 1964.[252]

---

248 *The Inquirer*, 24 October 1908.
249 Dr Daniel Jones (1771-1810) was a student of Charles Wellbeloved at Manchester College, York. He was originally the pastor of a Particular Baptist church in Swansea, but changed his Calvinist and Trinitarian views and became a Unitarian. He was chosen unanimously by the congregation at the Conigre Church in Trowbridge to be their minister. Jones willed money for the purposes of Manchester College in Oxford. (E Starr, ed., *A Baptist Bibliography*, New York, 1957.
250 *The Inquirer*, 30 March 1957.
251 *The Inquirer*, 10 January 1931.
252 *The Inquirer*, 22 August 1964.

Harley's pursuit of his academic career continued when on 2 November 1907 he matriculated at Jesus College[253] as a Commoner, without a scholarship, to read for a degree in Theology. At the time it was not unusual for a student to attend more than one Oxford college at the same time, and now Harley's ambitions extended beyond Manchester College. It would later be suspected that he had used Manchester and his membership of that college as a means to make entrance into a more prestigious institution easier. In any case, the Theology degree would fit nicely into his long-term strategy of a life in the Anglican Church.

Jesus College was founded at the request of Dr Hugh Price, a Welsh clergyman and the treasurer of St David's Cathedral, who wanted a college to educate young Welsh men. The college received its first royal charter on 27 June 1571 as 'Jesus College in the University of Oxford of Queen Elizabeth's Foundation'. Jesus soon became known as the Welsh College, and the motif of the Welsh dragon can be seen around the college, as in the cradle of the wrought-iron gate, where a tiny Welsh dragon reading a book can be found.

The Principal, Sir John Rhys' lodgings were located directly next door to the chapel on the right side of the quad. The dining hall linked the first and second quadrangles, the hall glorious in its size and grandeur with the dragon motif reprised on the wooden panelling above the entrance door. Students sat snugly next to each other on the large wooden benches for their meals while the Fellows ate at the reserved High Table. As a non-resident, Harley did not take his meals at the college. He had secured lodgings outside at 22 Gloucester Street.[254]

Turl Street, so-called because of the turnstile that used to be at the bottom of the street, is home to three colleges: Jesus,

---

253 *Oxford University Gazette,* 1907-1908, p. 137.
254 Harley to Locke, Moorland-Spingarn Research Center.

Exeter and Lincoln. Halfway along, the narrow street frames the tower and spire of All Saints Church (now Lincoln's library), as it almost steps out into the middle of the street. The small, cobbled Brasenose Lane provides access to Radcliffe Square, where standing majestically in the middle of the square is the domed-roof circular building of the Radcliffe Camera. The gates of All Souls College are situated in an easterly direction from the Radcliffe Camera and to the north is the Bodleian Library.

Turl Street leads out to Broad Street, where Trinity and Balliol Colleges are located, and here is the site of one of Oxford's cruellest moments in history. A cross in the road marks the burning in 1555 of three Anglican Bishops: Hugh Latimer, Bishop of Worcester, Nicholas Ridley, Chaplain to King Henry VIII and Bishop of London, and Thomas Cranmer, Archbishop of Canterbury, collectively accused of heresy and known as the 'Oxford Martyrs'.

Four roads, Cornmarket Street, St Aldates, the High Street and Queen Street, converge at Carfax, a crossroads with a large, stone-built tower. A diverse array of retailers

Aerial view of the High Street, Oxford, 1907.
(Library of Congress, Washington DC)

occupied Cornmarket, Queen Street and the High Street. The latter's stores sold goods ranging from the groceries at M. Underhill & Sons, porcelain and glasses at S. King & Son, while Standen & Co. were tailors and robe makers - the tailor of choice for Locke. He ordered a single-breasted Chesterfield jacket lined in black satin, an exclusive velvet collar at seven shillings and sixpence and a black dress Shetland dinner jacket for three pounds thirteen shillings. He also enjoyed the fine food from Frank Cooper, the wine merchant at 84 High Street, ordering Camembert, Claret, Green Chartreuse, Mocha coffee, figs, a Genoa cake and three bottles of Mosel.[255] All these shops, including Grimbly Hughes of Cornmarket Street and Elliston & Cavell, the largest department store in the city situated in Magdalen Street, offered expensive goods to the wealthier among the local population. These stores extended students very generous credit terms on the assumption that their families would subsequently settle any outstanding debts.[256]

The High Street, not a directly straight road, had a slight curve, leading down to the grandeur of the Examinations Schools, University College and The Queen's College. The booksellers of Slatter & Rose, the milliners, dressmakers and fancy repository of Misses French were further along the High Street. Interspersed between the retailers was the University's oldest Church, St Mary the Virgin, where the Oxford Martyrs were tried before their execution. Towards the end of the High Street is the substantial gift presented by Henry Danvers, Earl of Danby, in 1632, for use by the University: the Botanic Garden. Magdalen Bridge and Magdalen College complete the eastern end of the High Street.

---

255 Harris and Molesworth, p. 60.
256 Zoeller, 'Alain Locke at Oxford'.

Two of Harley's contemporaries at Jesus were Thomas Edward Lawrence (1888-1935) and Pixley Seme. Lawrence, a short, skinny Welsh man with deep brown eyes, studied History. He received the moniker of Lawrence of Arabia because of his role as a British Army officer in uniting the Arab tribes in their quest against the Turks during World War I. Though Harley did not know it, his path had previously crossed, tangentially, with Seme's, a small, dark-skinned Zulu from South Africa, in the US. Seme had not been able to match Harley's success in passing the Yale entrance examination in 1902 and he went to Columbia University instead. He matriculated at Jesus College a year before Harley in 1906 to read Law, having acquired the assistance of missionaries to gain his place at Oxford. Seme wrote to Booker T. Washington on 29 January 1907: 'I am the Zulu, who graduated from Columbia last spring. I am studying Law here. Oxford is full of inspiration. Your older son ought to be here. Pixley Ka Isaka Seme'.

At Oxford, Seme went riding with Locke, who kept his favourite pony, Prince, at the Clarendon Hotel Stables, where his riding fees for two months came to £4.[257] Seme was a member and treasurer of the Cosmopolitan Club and also founded a club for African students. A keen debater, he joined the Oxford Union. Seme had lodgings in Beaumont Street, where he hired a piano and took up pipe-smoking. Locke followed his friend, decamping from his lodgings at Hertford College (much to the pleasure of the College administration) to also take up one of the most expensive student lodgings in Oxford at 20 Beaumont Street.[258] The smart and sophisticated Randolph Hotel, the Ashmolean Museum and the Oxford Playhouse Theatre are all situated in Beaumont Street. Locke also rented a piano and took French lessons from a private tutor,

---

257 Ibid.
258 Harris and Molesworth, p. 60.

the daughter of a Sorbonne professor.[259] Seme spent more time in London than in Oxford, often listening to debates in the House of Commons.

Not content with studying at Jesus College and Manchester College, Harley now enrolled for the Diploma of Anthropology at the Pitt Rivers Museum. What was Harley's motivation for undertaking the Diploma? He already had an intensive workload.

From the Greek root *Anthropos* (man), anthropology is the study of humans and human behaviour. Harley's reasoning for undertaking the Diploma of Anthropology may have been to gain a deeper understanding of man as a species, enabling him to become a better communicator and listener by understanding human science. The Diploma may also have provided Harley with an opportunity to consider his own identity and the factors that shaped him. Traditional religion appeared in any case to be under siege at the turn of the twentieth century, with questions ranging from the position of the Church on Charles Darwin and his evolutionary theories to the very truth of Scripture itself. Evolution was seen by some as simply a further insight into the way in which God worked in nature.[260] Harley may have wanted to explore further and test such theories.

Harley arrived at the Pitt Rivers Museum seven years after the death of its founder, Lieutenant-General Augustus Henry Lane-Fox Pitt Rivers, on 4 May 1900. A Yorkshire man from a wealthy landowner family, the appendage of Pitt Rivers was added to his name as a requirement of his inheritance from his great uncle. In 1880 he inherited the 27,000-acre Dorset estate Cranborne Chase, and it was here that Pitt Rivers amassed a

---

259 Ibid, p. 60.
260 Kevin Christopher Fielden, 'The Church of England in the First World War', East Tennessee State University, Electronic Theses and Dissertations, 1080, 2005, p. 23.

collection of some 20,000 archaeological and ethnological artefacts, many collected duribg his career abroad as a military officer. His collection was exhibited at the Bethnal Green branch of the South Kensington Museum, and the limited space at the museum was Pitt Rivers' impetus for offering the collection to the University Museum in Oxford with two stipulations: that a museum was purpose-built to house his collection solely, and that a lecturer in Anthropology be appointed. The museum was designed by the son of the architect who had undertaken the design and building of the University of Oxford Museum, on the comer of South Parks Road opposite Keble College. Fully opened in 1891, the Pitt Rivers Museum was an annexe, accessed through the Oxford University Museum.

Like a labyrinth, the museum is laid out over two gallery floors filled with glass cases, crammed full of exotic and usual

Pitt Rivers Museum, Oxford, with totem pole. (Pitt Rivers Museum)

artefacts collected and donated by anthropologists. An unusual sight was the impressive forty-five-foot totem pole displayed on the ground floor, brought back from Queen Charlotte Island, British Columbia, by Edward Burnett Tylor.

Pitt Rivers' second stipulation endowed Burnett Tylor with the position of lecturer in Anthropology, the first in Britain. Tall and imposing, his Quaker religion had, ironically, prevented him from attending the University of Oxford, and instead he entered his family's brass foundry business. A bout of tuberculosis cut short his time in the firm and precipitated a trip to Mexico, Cuba and the US to recuperate. During his travels Tylor discovered his interest in anthropology and so-called primitive societies. His first book, *Anahuac*, was published upon his return from Mexico in 1861. In 1865, he followed this with *Researches into the Early History of Mankind and the Development of Civilization*, which made him a leading figure in anthropology. Six years later, in 1871, he produced his best-known publication *Primitive Culture: Researches into the Development of Mythology, Philosophy, Religion, Language, Art, and Custom*. The book explored his central theme and concept: the relation of primitive cultures to modern populations. Culture, he wrote, is 'that complex whole which includes knowledge, belief, art, morals, law, custom, and any other capabilities and habits acquired by man as a member of society'.

In that same year, he was elected Fellow of the Royal Society and awarded an honorary degree by Oxford.[261] Attention received from the press and two public lectures he delivered on anthropology in 1882 resulted in Tylor being chosen as the new Keeper of the Oxford University Museum of Natural History. In 1883, he was appointed to the first anthropological academic

---

261 Edward Burnett Tylor, Pitt Rivers Museum Archives.

post in the United Kingdom as Reader in Anthropology.[262] The curator of Pitt Rivers Museum was Henry Balfour, a recent zoology graduate, elected in 1891.

Balfour was tasked with the packing up of the Pitt Rivers collection at South Kensington and unpacking, labelling and displaying it in Oxford. Pitt Rivers, however, was now losing enthusiasm for the museum after its construction and taking a greater interest in his new museum in Farnham, Dorset. In 1883, he became the Inspector of Ancient Monuments following the Ancient Monuments Act of 1882. In this role he travelled extensively throughout Britain recording, advising, collecting and recommending sites for scheduling.

Tylor, Balfour and Robert Marett were the three men associated with Oxford's early Anthropology Diploma's development and teaching.[263] Robert Ranulph Marett (1866-1943) was a classical scholar, a tutor in philosophy at Exeter College and a social anthropologist. His interest developed from his work for Oxford University's Green Moral Philosophy Scholarship, which in 1893 was awarded for an essay on the 'ethics of savage races'. His success in securing the scholarship brought him to the attention of Tylor.[264] His position as Reader in Anthropology required him to deliver eighteen lectures a year, but these only attracted small audiences. The concept of developing a postgraduate qualification in anthropology was first mooted and discussed in 1902, and Tylor and Balfour were instrumental in instigating the Diploma, while Marett is credited with steering through its progress, largely, it was said, because he 'belonged',[265] was an accepted figure and would not 'tread on anyone's toes'. To enable the establishment of a new

---

262 Ibid.
263 Peter Riviere (ed), *A History of Oxford Anthropology*, Oxford: Berghahn, 2009, p. 43.
264 Ibid, p. 44.
265 Ibid, p. 44.

postgraduate qualification, Marett had to make considerable compromises; the study of anthropology at the University would limit itself to the study of past and present 'savagery'. On 23 May 1905, a statute setting up 'a committee for the organisation of the advanced study of Anthropology, and to establish a Diploma in Anthropology to be granted after examination' was promulgated.[266] The Committee for Anthropology came into existence on 1 October, its first meeting held on 27 October.[267] In 1907, the introduction of the Certificate in Anthropology required a candidate to have been engaged in the study of physical anthropology or cultural anthropology (ethnology either with archaeology and technology or with sociology) for three months. The regulations allowed a candidate to earn a Diploma by accumulating all three Certificates over a number of years.

Harley, Barbara Freire-Marreco and Francis Howe Seymour Knowles became the first three students enrolled for the Diploma in Michaelmas Term 1907, Freire-Marreco and Harley becoming history makers in the process: she as the first woman to take the Diploma, and Harley as the first black man. Freire-Marreco was of Portuguese extraction, and her area of study for the Diploma was 'Notes on the hair and eye colour of 591 children of school age in Surrey',[268] Knowles was a member of the British aristocracy, Fifth Baronet of the Baronetcy of Lovell Hill in Berkshire. He read Law at Oriel College before embarking on the Anthropology Diploma.

The first Diploma in Anthropology, which took five years to come to fruition, was thus not undertaken by students who fitted the prevalent Oxford type - white, male and elite. The choice of these three students from different backgrounds,

266 Ibid, p. 44.
267 Ibid, p. 45.
268 Barbara Freire-Marreco, Pitt Rivers Museum Archives.

culture, ethnicity, gender and class to become the first Diploma students may have been deliberate, and in some way a social experiment. Tylor, Balfour and Marett all had an interest in primitive cultures and races. A practice in Victorian museums, adopted at the Pitt Rivers Museum, was the displaying of objects of one type gathered from around the world to illustrate differences and similarities. Harley, Knowles and Freire-Marreco may unwittingly have been the objects on display and studied; their similarities and differences scrutinized to determine where each of them stood on the hierarchical ladder of cultural development.

Harley's simultaneous study for his theology degree at Jesus College, his Diploma in Anthropology at the Pitt Rivers and religious study at Manchester College, not to mention his membership of the Church Social Union, ensured that he had a full workload. In Michaelmas Term he juggled theology lectures in Divinity, Hebrew, Pastoral Theology, Holy Scripture and Septuagint[269] with Manchester College lectures about the development of the early Church according to the Book of Acts; the life and teaching of Jesus Christ according to the first three Gospels; the history of early Buddhism[270] and then a departure with the anthropology lectures. The elements of Physical Anthropology included: the comparative study of the principal anatomical characters which (a) determine the zoological position of a man amongst the Anthropomorpha and (b) distinguish the chief races of man from each other together with measuring and recording such characters. Lectures were given on elementary craniometry, the structure of special sense-organs and skin. Harley's anthropology lectures were deemed acceptable in terms of theories and teaching: now they would

---

269 Sydney Herbert Mellone, *Liberty and Religion: The First Century of the British and Foreign Unitarian Association*, London: Lyndsey Press, 1925, p. 107.
270 Michaelmas Term lectures, Harris Manchester College, University of Oxford.

be considered extremely racist. The Physical Anthropology component of the course promulgated an ideology that black people, and 'the exotic other', were intellectually inferior, a concept underpinned by elements within Darwinism and evolutionary theory.

Most of Harley's theology lectures were held in the jewel in Oxford University's crown - Christ Church, in the ancient Cathedral Chapter House.[271] His Hebrew lectures were held at Wadham College and Anthropology lectures at the Pitt Rivers Museum and Exeter College. Harley also had the opportunity to attend additional lectures at the cost of a £1 per lecture on History of the Jews after the Exile, The Life of Christ, Introduction to the Literature of the New Testament, Jesus Christ according to St Mark, Dogmatic and Symbolic theology, Post-Augustinian Theology and Ecclesiastical History Ante-Nicene.[272]

Harley's curriculum at Manchester College included practical ministry work, a requirement to ensure students for the ministry learned first-hand about the problems and issues facing the poor and disadvantaged. The College had links with the Mansford Street Mission in Bethnal Green, East London. Most of Harley's weekends during November and December 1907 were spent at the Mission in Bethnal Green.[273]

In 1703, Bethnal Green was almost entirely rural, providing open country for market gardens. It became a borough in 1899[274] and was soon one of London's poorest areas, situated in the heart of London in what is now the Borough of Tower Hamlets. It stood in stark contrast to the architectural elegance and academic gentility of Oxford. A visiting priest wrote:

---

271 *Oxford University Gazette*, 27 April 1908.
272 Ibid.
273 Harris Manchester College report, University of Oxford.
274 Bethnal Green Gardens, *Conservation Area Report*, London Borough of Tower Hamlets, 2009, p. 4.

'Bethnal Green! A howling wilderness; drunkenness in the back streets; fights in the squares; starvation in the alleys; pauperism rampant; religion nil.'[275]

As industries expanded, an overflow of immigrants from Spitalfields and Shoreditch arrived in the area. It was already characterized by its history of migration, with refugees from the seventeenth-century Huguenots to East European Jews, Poles and Africans, all of whom added to its diversity and vibrancy. Bethnal Green was close to Wapping and the aptly named Tobacco Docks, where the growth of the cigar and cigarette making industry provided work. The industries of silk and lace making were the domain of Huguenot weavers. Men and women were also employed in the brewing and tanning industries. Yet extreme poverty, primarily caused by overcrowding, could be seen, smelt, heard, felt and touched; from the rotting fruit and vegetables strewn on the streets churned together with excrement from pigs and the horses pulling the trolley buses and Hanson cabs, to the stench and noise emanating from the overcrowded tenement buildings and terrace houses filled with families and their children in insanitary conditions. Cramped and tiny rooms, with water for numerous houses provided occasionally by a single tap, were ideal breeding conditions for infection and disease like whooping cough, scarlet fever, diphtheria, measles, smallpox, bronchitis and tuberculosis.[276] Most people (76 per cent in 1901 and 79 per cent in 1911) lived in tenements of fewer than five rooms and nearly a third of those in two rooms.[277] Bethnal Green was an area where the head of the household, either a skilled or semi-skilled artisan

---

275 www.eastlondonhistory.co.uk
276 Sarah Wise, *The Blackest Streets: The Life and Death of a Victorian Slum*, London: Vantage, 2008. P. 10.
277 'Bethnal Green: Building and Social Conditions from 1876 to 1914', *A History of the County of Middlesex*, vol. 11, Stepney, Bethnal Green. Originally published by Victoria County History, London, 1998, pp. 126-132.

or labourer, eked out a living through piecework or whatever work could be acquired on that day. The women, weak from numerous births and poor nutrition, worked as laundresses, weavers, or, like Harley's mother, seamstresses, as did their older children to help bring in an additional wage to support the family. Waterloo Road was a location many of the residents feared to go; it is where the workhouse was situated. In Charles Dickens' novel *Our Mutual Friend*, the child-minder Betty Higden, says:

> Kill me sooner than take me there. Throw this pretty child under cart-horses feet and a loaded wagon, sooner than take him there. Come to us and find us all a-dying and set a light to us all where we lie and let us blaze away with the house into a heap of cinders sooner than move a corpse of us there!

The impetus for the formation of workhouses was the implementation of the 1834 Poor Law Amendment Act. Previously, each parish had to look after its own poor. The Bethnal Green Workhouse came into operation in August 1842 renamed the Waterloo Road Workhouse, it closed in 1935.[278] Families were separated upon arrival at the workhouse, women and children in one area and the men occupying another. The poor were given clothes and food - usually a watery soup - in exchange for several hours of manual labour. Men broke rocks, made rope, chopped wood and ground corn, while the women carried out domestic jobs of cleaning, helping out in the kitchens and laundry.[279]

For many, especially the disabled, elderly, and unmarried mothers, it was the last resort; the stigma and shame scared many people from entering it, perhaps one of the main

---

278 Peter Higginbotham, www.workshouses.org.uk
279 Ibid.

aims behind their creation. The grim tales about the horrific conditions behind the dark forbidding walls of the institution filled many East End residents with dread, most preferring to survive on the streets either through begging or petty crime.

The concept of the city mission was first proposed at the Unitarian Association's Annual General Meeting in June 1830.[280] The founding principles were derived from the earlier work of Joseph Tuckerman (1778-1840), a Boston Unitarian minister, founder of the Benevolent Fraternity of Unitarian Churches, and known as the Father of American social work. A Harvard graduate, Tuckerman took to the neighbourhoods of Boston, particularly the dock area, to implement the moral principles of liberal Unitarian Christianity: the perfectibility of human beings; the moral responsibility of the privileged to address and solve civic problems; the creation of all persons in the image of God; and love of others as the highest expression of Christian life. 'There is no human being, however depraved, who is yet totally depraved,' he wrote, 'no one for whom moral efforts are not to be made as long as God shall uphold him in being.' He met young children sent out to steal and prostitute themselves, as well as the starving, widowed and elderly invalids. Tuckerman's ministry-at-large included public advocacy for an extraordinary array of social and political reforms. He considered alcoholism a disease, not a moral failing; he promoted as treatment education and the regulation of excess, rather than punishment. He urged employment of school officials - the forerunners of truant officers - to ensure children's school attendance. He urged that delinquent children should not be dealt with by the courts, but on farms and in vocational training schools, to be designed and established to meet their needs. He lobbied for the reform of prisons and for the inclusion of educational programmes in

---

280 Mellone, *op. cit.*

penal institutions. Tuckerman created a detailed record of his ministry, the problems he sought to address and the results of his work. Excerpts were printed in 1874 as *Joseph Tuckerman on the Elevation of the Poor. The Principles and Results of the Ministry-at-Large in Boston*, a summation of his work written at the end of his ministry in 1838.[281]

Harley wrote:

> I spent my Christmas vacation at the mission.[282] I also spent three Sundays at the Barton Street Chapel Unitarian Church in Gloucester, and I made the twenty-one miles' journey to the market town of Banbury on two Sundays to preach at their Unitarian church.[283] Locke came to hear me preach both in Banbury and in Gloucester.[284] I also undertook mission work in Oxford.[285] I spent one Sunday at St Ebbs Mission.[286]

Away from the manicured lawns of the college quads and Fellows' Gardens, Oxford also had its pockets of poverty and deprivation; and St Ebbes was such an area, home to the poorest of Oxford's residents. Rows of cheap houses were built for college servants and workers employed at the wharves, on the railway, at the University Press, the gasworks or the breweries.[287]

In February 1908 Harley gave the Pitt Rivers Museum some glass flakes 'used as razors from his home island of Antigua, along with the bottle from which they had been struck'.[288] It

---

281 Unitarian Universalist History & Heritage Society website, accessed 12 January 2017.
282 Harris Manchester College report, University of Oxford.
283 Harris Manchester College, report, 1907, University of Oxford.
284 Harris and Molesworth, p. 60.
285 Ibid, Harris Manchester College.
286 Ibid, Harris Manchester.
287 Oxford Museum.
288 Pitt Rivers Museum Archives.

is highly unlikely, due to his parlous financial position, that Harley had returned to Antigua; he already had the glass flakes, scrapers, and bottle in his possession. As with his Christmas vacation, Harley spent the Easter vacation in Taunton, Somerset, at the St Mary's Unitarian Church and back at St Ebbes. During Hilary Term Harley took a series of lectures and on 4 May 1908 received the Certificate of Examination in Physical Anthropology, Ethnology and Sociology, which meant that the work he had undertaken was proportionate to the time allotted to the subject for him to present as a Candidate for Examination for the Diploma in Anthropology. For the archaeology component of the Diploma, Harley decided to excavate flint scrapers from Wookey Hole Caves.

Situated in Somerset in the Mendips Hills, Wookey Hole presents an awe-inspiring sight. The caves were home to the earliest men who lived in the valley some 50,000 years ago, hunting bears and rhinoceros with stone weapons. When the

Bernard Lens, *The Entrance to Wookey Hole, Somerset*, 1719.
(Wikimedia Commons)

Celtic people of the Iron Age moved into Britain, the caves provided a haven and comfortable place to live. By the fifteenth century, only bones and broken pottery remained.

When Harley carried out his fieldwork in 1908, excavating at Hyaena Den Caves, the caves were still largely unexplored. They were discovered accidentally by the cutting of a mill sluice in 1852.[289] The caves remained naturally dark, as no electricity was available, with electric lighting only arriving from 1922. Torches had to be taken in, candles were used to illuminate the caves, or local guides lit paraffin thrown against the walls. Although Harley conducted his research in 1908, the archaeologist Henry Balch is credited as the first person to excavate the caves in 1912.

While in Somerset, Harley took the opportunity to preach at the St Mary's in Taunton in May 1908.[290] From his expedition to Wookey Hole, he donated another small collection to the Pitt Rivers Museum, a small collection of archaeological material consisting of a selection of flints, pottery sherds, animal bones and teeth which he had collected on the spot.[291]

At the meeting of Manchester College General Committee on Friday 26 June 1908, it was resolved that Harley should be admitted as a Special Student for a second year. He also received a warning that he had to apply himself more diligently to his studies and that the continuance of his grant was dependent on him doing so.[292] His intensive workload in undertaking three courses, each with its own demanding curriculum, and the addition of mission work for Manchester College, inevitably took a toll on Harley and his work. It also was now jeopardizing his vital financial support.

He nonetheless found time to entertain. 'Mrs Locke was in

---

289 The Hyaena Den (Wookey Hole) University of Bristol, 1971, pp. 245-47.
290 *Taunton Courier and Western Advertiser*, 27 May 1908.
291 Pitt Rivers Museum Archives.
292 Minutes of the meeting, Manchester College, 26 June 1908.

Oxford in the July of 1908 visiting her son, Alain; I wrote to invite both of them to tea on Sunday.' Locke's mother found Harley 'particularly cultured', observing that the Antiguan behaved in a manner as 'refined as any man with his training should be' but nonetheless possessed of a 'fighting West Indian temperament'.[293] While at Harvard Locke had written to his mother:

> [Harley] is outspoken like all of them [West Indians] and doesn't hesitate to sling mud and sarcasm when he gets good and ready. He is no doubt naturally gifted in speaking and like all of them is alert and ambitious - but I hope I shan't lead you to idealize him, for if he ever gets crucifixion and hands, you your bread and wine a la Phillips you [will be] disillusioned [sic].[294]

Harley withdrew from Manchester College in November that year, as he was 'getting into hot water with his Anglican friends'.[295] Quite what this means, we cannot be sure, but it seems that the appeal of Unitarianism had abated, especially after financial support was no longer forthcoming. On 28 January 1909, the Oxford Anthropological Society was launched, and Harley became a member. Its founding meeting was held in the Old Bursary of Exeter College with over two dozen people. The Society's objectives were 'to promote interest in all its branches by lectures, the reading of papers, discussion and the exhibition of specimens'. Meetings were held in the University Museum, the Ashmolean Museum, the Pitt Rivers Museum and Barnett House; the Society's annual subscription was initially half-a-crown. The lecture given at it first full meeting on 5 February was entitled 'Archaeological work on the Zambezi', and the

---

293 Mary Locke to Alain Locke, undated, ALP 164, Box 46 folder 49.
294 Alain Locke to Mary Locke, undated, probably autumn 1905, ALP 164, Box 46 folder 49.
295 Yale Yearbook entry, 1911.

second was about the Andaman Islands and was entitled 'A pre-totemic religion'. Also, in that year Marett spoke on Andrew Lang's theory of 'savage supreme beings'. By the end of Hillary Term, the Society was attracting over one hundred members.

In March 1909, Locke received an invitation to attend a luncheon reception held by the American Ambassador William Whitelaw Reid at Dorchester House, London, as one of the American Rhodes Scholars. The Southern Rhodes Scholars requested that he not attend. Locke arrived at the reception just before it had started and was the first to leave. He noted, 'they were sore I came but sorer still that I should be the first to leave.'[296]

Harley registered in May 1909 to take the Diploma in Anthropology; the cost of the Diploma was £2,10s. His examination took place on 16 June and over the following two days, consisting of our three-hour papers on Physical Anthropology, Ethnology, Sociology and Technology.[297] On the morning of Thursday 18 June, he had to undertake a practical and oral examination lasting three hours. Alfred Cort Haddon, MA SCD Fellow of Christ's College Cambridge, had been duly nominated to serve as examiner for the Diploma in Anthropology in 1908 and 1909.[298] However, Harley was eventually examined by Arthur Thomson, Henry Balfour and Marett. On the day of the practical examination, a photograph was taken with the tutor Henry Balfour in the Upper Gallery of the Museum to document and mark the

Harley's Diploma of Anthropology certificate, 16 June 1909. (Private collection)

---

296 Harris and Molesworth, p. 60.
297 *Oxford University Gazette*, 24 April 1908.
298 *Oxford University Gazette*, 17 March 1908.

occasion of the first three students on the Diploma Course: Harley, Freire-Marreco and Knowles. Harley satisfied the examiners,[299] and was awarded his Diploma on 16 June 1909 signed by Edward Burnett Tylor.[300]

Harley's papers provide no insight into what he thought about the subjects covered in the Diploma course, or how he thought he was perceived as a student undertaking it. Harley would have been pragmatic about the situation, seeing the achievement of the Diploma as the prize at the end of the study. No matter how pragmatic and stoical he was, however, the lectures, discussions and nature of the debates during this period must have had some intellectual and psychological impact on him.

Two of the three first Diploma students, Knowles and Freire-Marreco, continued in anthropology. Knowles carried on teaching and research in physical anthropology and was appointed Assistant to Professor Arthur Thomson while Freire-Marreco, who received a distinction in 1909,[301] stayed on at first to work at the Museum as a volunteer, compiling card catalogues and publishing her paper as an article in *Man*. Towards the end of Harley's last year at Oxford, she secured a research fellowship at Somerville College; her research work was centred on 'the nature of the authority of chiefs and kings in primitive society'. Tylor retired the same year that Harley completed his Oxford sojourn, having also obtained in 1909 a Class II BA in Theology at Jesus College.

Seme became the first Zulu ever to graduate from the University when he gained a BA in Civil Law in June 1909. Seme passed his first Bar examinations and the following year was called to the Bar at the Middle Temple, London.

Harley had survived in a medieval city steeped in history,

299 Hertford College, Minutes of the Governing Body, 1874-1929, p. 362.
300 *Oxford University Gazette*, 22 June 1909.
301 Pitt Rivers Museum Archives.

The first three Diploma of Anthropology students with (standing centre) Henry Balfour. From left to right, Francis Knowles, Barbara Freire-Marreco, Harley. (Pitt Rivers Museum)

traditions, customs, and privilege. He would be leaving Oxford with what could be interpreted as proof of success; he had a degree in Theology and a Diploma in Anthropology. His eighteen months spent at Manchester College had resulted in him receiving the Webb Fund Award, which he undoubtedly used, in part at least, to fund his theological degree and study for his Diploma at Pitt Rivers. Armed with an array of qualifications, Harley was now starting on the next step of his journey.

12. An Edwardian Curate

'The word "curate" refers to the "cure of souls" or "care" of souls.'

Glossary of Anglican Clergy Titles

After eleven years of study, Harley was equipped with degrees in Law, Semitic Languages and Theology as well as a Diploma in Anthropology. Theoretically, he had the world at his feet and could choose one of the professional fields pertaining to his degrees or to enter academia. But Harley was now in his mid-thirties, in a country where racism of every sort was prevalent, albeit not as dangerously as in America. Academia would have presented many obstacles, as would the legal establishment, where class and race were determining factors in professional advancement. His years of studying he thus saw as preparation for the realization of his childhood dream and desire: to be a minister in the Protestant Episcopal Church, and this was the course he pursued.

Harley entered an institution at the beginning of the Edwardian era that was firmly ruled by the values, ideology and practices of the Victorian period - the Church of England. The clergy identified with the landed gentry and educated classes, and were often viewed, and revered, as a gentleman clergy.[302] Victorian churchmen and pastoral theologians placed considerable emphasis on the educational and social background of the clergy. The eighteenth- and nineteenth-century priest was usually a graduate of English or Irish universities, a gentleman aspiring to an essentially rural lifestyle and the status

---

302 Kelsey Sterling, 'The Education of the Anglican Clergy 1830-1914', PhD. thesis, University of Leicester, 1982.

of a traditional profession.[303] A man entering the Anglican Priesthood should possess two basic requirements: a spiritually and morally elevated character and a gentlemanly social status identified by a university education.[304] The clerical profession maintained a distinct demarcation between the social classes, and its identification as a gentleman clergy was paramount. Like needed to attract like; a gentlemanly clergy was assumed to be independently wealthy, and a university graduate of refined good taste and cultural accomplishments would probably be more affluent than most of his parishioners.[305] The elite could not be expected to unburden their souls to a minister who was a social inferior; therefore their clergyman had to be of a class with whom the landed gentry was socially and intellectually compatible.[306] The function of the Church was to place a civilizing influence in the form of an educated gentleman in every parish in the kingdom.[307]

Against this background, Harley applied for a curacy position in the small town of Shepshed, Leicestershire, at the Church of St Botolph. The detailed application contained questions about his education, degrees and the state of his health in the past three years, including what course of theological reading - Holy Scriptures and Christian Fathers - he had followed. He was also asked questions about the history of the Church and the Church of England; the book of Common Prayer, its Doctrine and Discipline.[308] Harley provided the following references for his application: Rev David James, Sir John Rhys and Rev Walter Lock.

---

303 Ibid.
304 Brian Heeney, 'On Being a Mid-Victorian Clergyman', *Journal of Religious History*, 7, 1973, p. 219.
305 Ibid, p. 217.
306 Ibid.
307 Kevin Christopher Fielden, 'The Church of England in the First World War', East Tennessee State University, Electronic Theses and Dissertations. Paper 1080, 2005.
308 Candidate for Deacon's Orders application, Harley's personal archive.

Rev James appeared to be either a friend or associate of Harley. Born on 15 August 1875, the second son of David James, a farmer, he came from Aberystwyth. He matriculated at Jesus College in October 1901 and only read for a Pass Degree, taking his BA in 1906.[309] In 1909 he was a Curate in Llangeler, North Carmarthenshire, Wales.[310] Sir John Rhys was the Principal of Jesus College. Rev Walter Lock was the Sub-Warden of Keble College, Fellow of Magdalen College and also Dean Ireland's Professor of the Exegesis of Holy Scripture.

Harley was applying for Deacon's Orders, as he wrote: 'The Lord Bishop of Peterborough sent me to his examining chaplain for three days at Jesus College, Cambridge University, to be examined for the diaconate.'[311] During the examination, Harley had to give an account of himself. He was aware that as a colonial British West Indian, with time spent in America and his year's 'excursion' at Manchester College, the panel wanted reassurance that his form of Anglicanism aligned to the British way rather than American Episcopal teaching. The examining panel of three wanted evidence that his teaching was in line with the Church's instruction of the Scripture. Harley wrote:

> The chaplain, the Dean of College, was quite satisfied with my papers. My invitation to have lunch with Lord Bishop and Lady Mary Glenn at Peterborough Palace I took as a sign of acceptance of Holy Orders.[312] I was licenced to the Curacy of Shepshed on September 19th, 1909.[313] My Licence signed by the Bishop of Peterborough, C. Petersburg.

---

309 Oxford University Calendar 1909.
310 *Crockford's Clerical Dictionary* 1929 edition.
311 Yale Alumni Yearbook, Harley's personal archive 1911.
312 Ibid.
313 Extract from events of the year 1909, Harley's personal archive.

Harley's Licence stated:

> The Bishop will revoke the License, and will not
> countersign the Testimonials of any Curate who accepts
> a smaller Stipend than the sum assigned in the License,
> or who undertakes the duty of another Curacy without
> the Bishop's sanction; who resigns the Curacy to which
> he is licensed without giving the Bishop notice of his
> intention.

Harley publicly and openly made his Declaration before
Edward Cary in the presence of the congregation assembled by
Divine Permission of the Bishop of Peterborough at St Peter's
Church, Leicester, on Sunday morning, 26 September 1909.[314]

> I, James Arthur Harley B.A do solemnly make the
> following Declaration:
>   I assent to the Thirty-Nine Articles of Religion and
> the Book of Common Prayer, and of the Ordering of
> Bishops, Priests, and Deacons. I believe the Doctrine
> of the Church of England, as therein set forth, to be
> agreeable to the Word of God, and in Public Prayer and
> Administration of the Sacraments. I will use the Form
> in the said Book prescribed, and none other, except so
> far as shall be ordered by lawful Authority.

That evening, Harley preached his first sermon to a crowded
congregation in the Parish Church. His text was Isaiah 6:8:
'Also I heard the voice of the Lord saying, Whom shall I send,
and who will go for us? Then said I, Here am I; send me.'[315]
    Harley was now a Deacon in the Church of England; his
role, assistant to the Vicar, the Rev William Henry Franklin

---

314 Licence Certificate, Harley's personal archive.
315 Ibid, 1909 extract, Harley's personal archive.

Hepworth MA. He would receive a yearly stipend of £130 paid quarterly. He was required to live in the said Parish and resided at the vicarage.[316] Harley's Harvard degree was verified by the editor of *Crockford's Clerical Directory*.[317]

The son of Rev R. Hepworth of Cheltenham, Rev William Hepworth was born in Tewkesbury in 1832.[318] He was ordained in 1855 and priested a year later. He became Vicar of Shepshed in 1875.[319] Rev Hepworth had suffered a series of tragedies; his wife died in 1883, and six years later his second daughter Helen also died. Hepworth was aged seventy-seven when the thirty-four-year-old Harley arrived at

Harley in his Deacon's clerical gown, c 1909. (Private collection)

St Botolph's. Hepworth was a tall, well-built, no-nonsense-looking man with a full beard and moustache. His presence had been established in the parish for thirty years and he was solidly supportive of the Church's Victorian ideology. An unbending Conservative, he held with Dickens' view that 'the freedom of the subject and the liberty of the individual are among the first and proudest boasts of the true-hearted Englishmen.'[320]

---

316 Ibid.
317 Letter from *Crockford's* editor to Harvard University, 28 December 1909, Harvard University Archives.
318 Trefor Griffiths, *Henry Freeman's Shepshed Almanacs 1915-1920*, Shepshed Local History Society, 1998, p. 5.
319 Ibid.
320 Ibid, p. 142.

As a gentleman-cleric, Hepworth acquired and maintained an elevated social position and standing within the community. However, he was not very active in local affairs.[321] His position afforded him a benefice[322] of 141 acres of glebe.[323] Like Harley, Hepworth was an alumnus of Jesus College, but in his case Jesus, Cambridge, and Magdalene College. Hepworth's son, Rev Charles Leonard Hepworth, an alumnus of Lincoln College, Oxford, was appointed curate at All Saints Parish Church in the larger town of Loughborough on the same day Harley was ordained.[324]

It was expected that a curate would spend a year in his first parish to develop the requisite skills and qualities needed to take on the responsibilities of a parish before applying for a licence to be ordained a priest. The town of Shepshed, five miles north-west of Loughborough on the northern edge of Charnwood Forest, was 119 miles from London, with a station on the Loughborough and Nuneaton branch of the London and North Western Railway. The small town had a population of 5,293 in 1901.[325]

'A hill where sheep graze' was believed to be the origin of the name Shepshed. The town could trace its origins back to the Domesday Book with an early spelling of 'Scepeshefde'.[326] It grew up from its wool trade; sheep grazed on the land which belonged to the Cistercian Abbey at Garendon, about six miles from Shepshed. The sheep fleeces were sold to Bradford wool merchants, and the Abbey had permission to export the wool to Flanders. As one of the oldest seats of hosiery manufacture,

321 Ibid, p. 142.
322 Forbears genealogy portal.
323 Land granted to clergymen.
324 Harley's personal archive.
325 *Shepshed Conservation Area Character Appraisal*, Charnwood Borough Council. 2007.
326 Ibid.

the wool industry provided employment for most of the town's people.[327] The principal employers were the Shepshed Lace Manufacturing Company, which began in 1905 when William Price sent his eldest son Harold to Barmen, Germany, for a year to study the methods of making lace and the building of machinery.[328] Harold Price, aged nineteen, returned to Shepshed in 1906 with twelve Barmen machines he purchased in Germany and set up the company.[329] Initially housed above a cycle shop, the firm soon expanded, and in 1909, Harold built a small factory in Sullington Road.

Standing proudly on high ground, as though built on top of a gigantic mound, is St Botolph's Church, where Harley served.[330] Located in the centre of Shepshed and providing a focal point and distinctive landmark, St Botolph's and its tower could be seen above the surrounding buildings from a number of streets. A large medieval seven-foot stone wall encloses the church and access is via a steep and narrow winding lane leading from the town's central Bull Ring up Church Street. Church Path across the front of the church is also medieval in character.[331]

Three small stone steps brought parishioners to the medieval arched stone porch entrance. The interior of St Botolph's Church may have reminded Harley of what Antiguans called 'big church' or 'high church' - the Anglican Cathedral of St John the Divine, in Church Lane, St John's. St Botolph's imposing stone pillars, its carved arches and polished wooden pews with ornate carvings made it an impressive building. The church had numerous memorials to noted Shepshed residents:

327 Ibid.
328 *Fifty Years of Lace: The Shepshed Lace Manufacturing Company Ltd*, Loughborough: Reprint, n.d., p. 5.
329 Ibid, p. 9.
330 *Shepshed Conservation Area Character Appraisal*, 2007.
331 Ibid.

Charles Philips Esq of Love Layrin in Essex, commemorated by a polished marble memorial adjacent to the altar; Joseph Merriman, Doctor of Divinity DD, born at Shepshed, 9 January 9 1834, the first headmaster of Cranleigh School, 1866-1892, and Rector of Freshwater, 1892-1805, died 27 January 27 1905.

Harley wrote: 'The church was packed when I preached.'[332] A black Edwardian curate in a semi-rural town, his presence certainly caused some raised eyebrows and resulted in him being viewed as a curio. Rev Hepworth and the parishioners, upon hearing about his educational qualifications and achievements, may have concluded that he could only be a white man. For his part, Harley may have liked to be a fly on the wall in his parishioners' homes, to eavesdrop on their conversations. Yet the church was consistently packed, even after his novelty value had waned, and people were still coming to listen to his sermons - much to the disdain of some who considered the church packed with 'scum' when he preached.[333] Harley's sermons were described as eloquent and inspiring.[334] He inaugurated a men's service, which was later taken up by every church in England.[335] Miss Jessie Cooke noted; 'Never before had so many men been brought together at the little ancient parish church then when he officiated.'[336] Harley also started a men's Bible class and an English class for the special study of Shakespeare, and urged parishioners to consider the 'true meaning of life and its possibilities for them'.[337] Harley shared his experiences, knowledge and quest for social justice with his flock. He wanted all of them to participate fully in every aspect

---

332 Yale Alumni Yearbook.
333 Harley's personal archive.
334 Jessie Cooke to Harvard, Harvard University Archives.
335 Ibid.
336 Ibid.
337 Ibid.

St Botolph's Church, Shepshed, Leicestershire.
(Phil McIver/Creative Commons)

of the church and become involved with the initiatives he instigated; not just turn out for the obligatory Sunday service.

Harley's style did not conform to the Victorian Church that Rev Hepworth held dear. The Church had prided itself on maintaining a class distinction between the people of its parishes and the clergy. The clergy did not offer sufficiently practical answers to working-class needs to allow them to break down barriers between the classes. Anglican clergymen were not successful agents of social reconciliation because they were incapable of learning from their social inferiors, and they attempted to impose inappropriate middle-class solutions on working-class problems.[338] Rev Hepworth's pastoral care may have been reserved for the March-Phillipps De Lisle family, the landed gentry who had occupied Garendon Hall since 1684, when Sir Ambrose Phillipps, a successful London lawyer and King's Sergeant to James II, purchased the Hall for £28,000.

---

338 Sterling, *op. cit.*

The De Lisle's family presence is obvious at St. Botolph's. In 1893, a stained-glass window was placed to the late Rev Charles March-Phillipps De Lisle, a former vicar of the parish, the church plate includes a chalice, presented by Mary, wife of Sir Ambrose Phillipps kt. in 1687; and a paten, presented by Rev Charles March-Phillipps De Lisle MA, vicar in 1868. Rev Hepworth's social position and standing had to be upheld with the utmost authority in administering to Everard March-Phillipps De Lisle, the current heir to the lineage.

Harley's methods and sermons predictably brought him into conflict with Rev Hepworth; but he had won around the congregation, so much so that the Sunday school teachers signed a petition about the unjust treatment he received after a Sunday school event on St Andrew's Day.

To the Reverend Hepworth

Sir,

We the undersigned, teachers in St Botolph's Sunday School, wish to protest most strongly against the unjust censure passed upon the Rev. J.A. Harley, in our presence on the evening of St Andrews. Day, for courageously doing what he felt to be his duty. Signed Ernest Martin, Ethel Spacy, John Knight, Hannah Crooks, Ernst Urwin, Leonard Lakins, Thomas Kirby, and Wilfred Coup.[339]

The 'teachers' were a collection of volunteers of different ages and trades. Ernest Martin, 26, was a sole sewer in a boot factory; John Knight, 25, was a shoe factory finisher;[340] Hannah Crooks, 19, a machinist in the boot trade;[341] Thomas Kirby,

---

339 Harley's personal archive.
340 Census records 1911, Leicestershire Records Office.
341 Ibid.

58, a framework knitter;[342] and Wilfred Coup, 17, a hosiery apprentice.[343] There are no substantial details about the unjust treatment Harley received.

This action further alienated Rev Hepworth, and after six months Harley decided to resign, first obtaining the Bishop of Peterborough's sanction. His efforts did not go unnoticed, however, and there was support for him from the *Leicester Chronicle* newspaper:

> During the past few weeks [he] had pursued a vigorous policy and has made various efforts to resuscitate church work in all its branches, and large congregations have been attracted to the church to listen to his straight talks and outspoken sermons. His two visits to the Sunday Morning Men's Adult School and the helpful address he gave were a true sign of his broadmindedness, and the regret at his departure is very genuine.[344]

Shortly after Harley left Shepshed, Rev Hepworth resigned. There is no explanation for his resignation, but whatever the reason, a new vicar, Mr Clark, was appointed soon afterwards, and the parishioners petitioned Rev Clark on Harley's behalf.[345]

Despite the petition requesting Harley's reinstatement owing to the excellent work he had done, especially among the men, their appeal was fruitless. Harley decided it was best to leave the parish.[346] The parishioners presented him with a framed testimonial and a purse of £30 in gold.[347] The grateful parishioners also saw in him a future 'Bishop Harley'.[348]

---

342 Ibid.
343 Ibid.
344 *Leicester Chronicle*, 30 July 1910.
345 Kent to Bishop of Peterborough.
346 Ibid.
347 Yale Alumni Yearbook 1911.
348 Ibid.

For all the popularity he had gained, the experience of his first curacy may have had a discouraging effect on his outlook after the culmination of years of expectation in wanting to be a minister. The ending of Harley's short-lived curacy in Shepshed coincided with the country losing a monarch; the death of King Edward VII on 6 May 1910. The sixty-eight-year-old king had reigned for nine years. His death also marked the end of the Edwardian era.

Harley now had to focus on securing another position. An advertisement in the *Church Times* for an assistant curate's position at Marshside, Kent, provided his next employment.[349] Harley applied for the position knowing that he might stand a much better opportunity of securing a curacy in a rural parish, where competition was likely to be less intense. Harley took the train from London, and the journey took him out of the smoked-filled industrial air, the landscape of chimney tops changing as the train thundered into the brightness of the Kent countryside. Alighting at the Grove Ferry and Upstreet Station, he was immediately hit by the pungent smell from the adjacent lavender farm. Harley was now in East Kent, home of hops, windmills and oast houses - features of its beer brewing landscape. Gangs of pickers worked the land picking hops and paid per bushel. Harley arrived in East Kent in May 1910 during the threading phase of the hop growing season, a delicate process in which workers had to thread the vines up strings to encourage growth.

Harley made the mile-long journey from the train station to meet Rev Kent at his home - The Farm, a vast and imposing house situated in the little village of Upstreet. Reginald Arthur Kent was the vicar in charge of the parish and Harley's new employer. He had attended Worcester College, Oxford, and Ely

---

349 Harley to Archbishop of Canterbury, 10 May 1910, Canterbury Cathedral Archives.

Theology College and was curate at Lincoln Church from 1902 to 1904 before taking up his relatively recent position as the Vicar of St Mary the Virgin's Church in the parish of Chislet in 1909.[350] Rev Kent was also a recently married man. He married Agnes Lillian Rashleigh two months before Harley's arrival, on 30 March, at Canterbury Cathedral.[351] His wife came from a large family, the sixth child of William Boys Rashleigh and Frances Portia King. Her father was a farmer of considerable wealth, farming 320 acres in Farningham, Kent, and employing fourteen men and seven boys. Agnes had married exceptionally late in life at the age of thirty-seven; one possibility is that this may have been her second marriage.

Harley's position was created to replace the previous vicar, Rev Stickling.[352] The parish he had chosen, Chislet, was a scattered, rural parish consisting of five small villages and hamlets: Chislet itself, Highstead, Boyden Gate, Upstreet and Marshside, situated between Canterbury and the Isle of Thanet. A colliery would open in 1914 as part of the Kent Coalfield, but when Harley arrived, the place was still remote and undeveloped. The name Marshside was derived from the marshland that over the years had been breaking away from the mainland. The flat open fields and water inlets of the Chislet marshes indicated the end of the Wantsum Channel, formerly a strait separating the Isle of Thanet from the mainland until silted up. The atmosphere and surroundings of the fog-bound marshes gave the area an eerie feeling, and then fog horns from ships venturing up the channel could be heard across the bleak landscape.

The hamlet of Boyden Gate had a public house, the Gate Inn, situated on the main road from Chislet. The public house doubled

---

350 *Crockford's Clerical Directory*, p. 763.
351 Canterbury Cathedral Archives.
352 Letter to Archbishop of Canterbury.

as the local bakery shop and sold everyday provisions, bread, milk and eggs. The focal point of the community and the centre of the village was the church and a small schoolhouse in Chitty Lane. Most of the community were poor and uneducated agricultural labourers on low wages living in small cottages tied to the land. Their life was physical and arduous, working fifteen-hour days. The women were homemakers with large families living in very cramped conditions, ideal for the spread of disease among them and their children. Money and luxuries were not prevalent in this community; every penny was accounted for and spent wisely.

Harley was the curate based at St John's Church, a small clapperboard house situated in Church Lane, Marshside. The church, built in 1879, was lined with neat wooden pews facing the front and altar. A wooden crucifix at the top of the church made clear the purpose of the building. The 360-degree view outside the church provided Harley with a vista of flat arable

St Mary's Church, Chislet, Kent. (Nilfanion/Wikimedia Commons)

fields as far as the eye could see, with the spire of St Nicholas Abbey at Wade on the horizon. Harley's primary duties were to visit the parishioners throughout the parish.

Rev Kent was based at the larger and much older St Mary the Virgin Church, on the main road in the village of Chislet. Situated next to the church was Chislet Court Farm, an 800-acre mixed dairy and hop farm, with three large oast houses managed by the Spanton family but owned by the church. Kent also held services in the mission room, an outbuilding behind Grove Court, Upstreet.

Rev Kent was initially pleased with Harley's appointment describing him to the Archbishop of Canterbury as a 'very able man and exceptionally keen with a strong wish to work in a parish where hard work is needed.'[353] He also knew that it was difficult to get a good and enthusiastic curate in rural places and difficult even to get one at all. Kent wrote to the Archbishop to inform him that would give Harley a six weeks' trial, and if he was satisfactory, which he saw no problem with, he would then apply for Harley's licence.[354]

The winds blowing in from the coast came straight across the flat farmland making the very rural hamlet of Marshside much colder than the city of Oxford, and the watery trenches at the side of the land contributed to the damp cold in the atmosphere. Harley lived at Mill House,[355] a small cottage adjacent to the Chislet windmill. The windmill was a prominent feature of the landscape with its four spring sails. Unlike the stone-built mills at Betty's Hope in Antigua, the Chislet windmill was a three-storey black smock mill on a low brick base constructed from corrugated iron with a plain roof winded by a fantail driving three pairs of millstones.

353 Kent to Archbishop Davidson, 4 May 1910, Canterbury Cathedral Archives.
354 Kent to Archbishop Davidson, 10 May 1910, Canterbury Cathedral Archives.
355 Kent to Archbishop Davidson, 4 May 1910, Canterbury Cathedral Archives.

Harley's small cottage stood in Brook Lane, on the road to Reculver, isolated from any close neighbours and with a panoramic view of vast open fields in every direction he looked. The surrounding county offered many attractions, such as the Twin Sisters at Reculver, the name given to the imposing towers of the twelfth-century former monastic church and Roman fort. There were many huts lined up like soldiers on the beach of the bustling seaside town of Herne Bay, where residents and day-trippers enjoyed sea bathing or promenading along its pier jostling with nursery maids and children enjoying the warmer weather and healthy climate. Margate was popular with locals and hop pickers coming up from London on the train, as was the predominately fishing town of Whitstable. Eight miles from Marshside is the city of Canterbury, home to Canterbury Cathedral, a beacon for Anglicans.

Rev Kent's pleasure in Harley's appointment was short-lived. The Archbishop questioned the facts surrounding his appointment, requesting further information as a discrepency had surfaced. Harley's entry in *Crockford's Clerical Directory* referred to him only being in Deacon's Orders.[356] This presented a problem; being in Deacon's Order's would be quite contrary (in the clerical language used) to His Grace's rule to receive Harley into the diocese to (or 'intending to') Priest's Orders unless it was at the distinct request (as contrasted with the mere sanction) of the Bishop who ordained him to the Diaconate. Kent replied to the Archbishop stating that he knew of the irregularity of Harley changing diocese during his Diaconate. He concluded that as Harley had sought the sanction of the Bishop of Peterborough, this would be satisfactory in accepting him for the position.[357] The Archbishop instructed Kent not to make any firm arrangements

---

356 Archbishop Davidson to Kent, 9 May 1910, Canterbury Cathedral Archives.
357 Kent to Archbishop Davidson, 13 May 1910, Canterbury Cathedral Archives.

with Harley until the facts that he supplied could be checked with the Bishop of Peterborough.[358] The Bishop of Peterborough responded to the Archbishop's letter:

May 14th, 1910
Dear Mr Sheppard,

You wrote to me about Mr Harley; I ordained him a Deacon in September 1909. I think Shepshed. He is by birth a West Indian graduate of Washington (America) – one year at Yale, B.A. at Harvard – and then some time at Episcopal Training Massachusetts. Then came to England and took a B.A. at Jesus College, Oxford, August 1909. So, he is a man of good education – but he is also a West Indian in characteristics – very excitable and rather difficult to order, but I hold nothing against his moral character and makes a good strong vicar. He would do well.

The old vicar resigned, and his incumbent (wisely) declined to keep on Mr Harley, I admire him to try and get work on a new front, and I thought that in another diocese it would be easier for him, and I communicated this fact to the Bishop in the Diocese he sought to work in. In any case, I have advised a prolonged Diaconate for him. If with this knowledge of the circumstances the Archbishop advises me to let Harley find work in the Peterborough Diocese, and to ordain him, priest, after a prolonged Diaconate, I will be of course act on such advice.

Yours sincerely,
G.C. Petersburg.

---

358 Archbishop Davidson to Kent, 13 May 1910, Canterbury Cathedral Archives.

Kent communicated to Harley the Archbishop's decision of a 'prolonged Diaconate'. Harley had now been in the parish for three weeks, but Rev Kent felt he had not seen enough of him to form an adequate opinion.[359] He acknowledged Harley's good qualities and abilities but was doubtful in some ways relating to discipline and loyalty, and given the circumstances he wanted a further period of probation to be able to assess him properly. Kent also informed the Archbishop of Harley's displeasure at an imposed prolonged trial period.[360] The Archbishop made it very clear, writing to Kent:

> The very fact that Mr Harley fails to realise the anomalous position in which he stands makes me more than ever sure that it is wise that there should be a delay before he is licensed. Mr Harley's work in the Peterborough Diocese (St Botolph's Church, Leicester) was very far from being smooth or free from difficulty. It is not for us to attempt to assign the relative amount of fault which there may have been on the part of different people, but it is quite clear with these facts before me (and the Bishop of Peterborough) has emphasised them. If Mr Harley is loyally prepared to accept the conditions I have laid down and to work for a full month from this time before being licensed, I should prepare his licence at the end of that time on your definite request.

In addition to a further month's trial from 29 May to demonstrate his reliability, Harley also had to take and pass two examinations, the first in November and the next in April or May 1911; if all went well, he would be ordained Priest in Trinity 1911.[361]

---

359 Kent to Archbishop Davidson, 25 May 1910, Canterbury Cathedral Archives.
360 Kent to Archbishop Davidson, 24 May 1910, Canterbury Cathedral Archives.
361 Kent to Archbishop Davidson, 29 May 1910, Canterbury Cathedral Archives.

On 8 June 1910, seven weeks after the agreement to the prolonged trial, Rev Kent informed Harley that he should find another parish; he emphasized the need for a priest to work the scattered parish adequately instead of a curate. He said that if Harley were to continue in the Diocese for another year, his own work would increase and become enormously stressful.[362] He went on to explain that he was one and a half miles from Chislet and two and a half miles from Marshside church. Some Sundays he had to take five services and a Sunday school class, meaning he had to leave at 5.00 am to get to Marshside for 6.30 am service, and then get to Chislet for the 8.30 am service. A whole year of this routine would be too great a strain upon him, and a priest curate would simply create more work. Kent explained that he thought Harley would be much better suited to a parish with a large population, with three or four curates and a good strong rector. He concluded by saying that although Harley was an able man, he needed a guiding hand and practical experience in the conduct of services.[363]

Harley's interpretation was very different from that of Rev Kent. He saw this explanation as a move to get rid of him. After all the time spent in America as a lay preacher and as a curate in Shepshed, he did not accept that he still needed practical experience in the conduct of services. The timing, moreover, was not good for Harley; he was now thirty-seven, still only a curate, an assistant with no real permanent position. The prize of obtaining his licence seemed to be slipping even further from his fingers.

*

---

362 Kent to Harley, 8 June 1910, Canterbury Cathedral Archives.
363 Ibid.

News reached Harley at this time that Locke had faced a catastrophe during his final term at Oxford. His lavish spending resulted in substantial obligations to local creditors[364] - his liabilities totalled £600.[365] Despite the overt racism Locke encountered, he still laboured under the impression that the privileges enjoyed by his white counterparts would be extended to him. He was brought up on charges in the Vice-Chancellor's Court related to his outstanding commitments to local creditors. White students were given the time to settle their debts, but not Locke. His case was referred to Hertford College's Governing Body, which concluded that Locke had no means of satisfying these claims and instead, on 31 May 1910, Hertford College instructed Locke to leave the university and gave him four days to leave the college. His landlady also seized his property. If he wanted to be considered for a degree, he had to send in his thesis by October.[366] Locke travelled to Berlin, completed his thesis and submitted it before the October deadline - only to have it marked unsatisfactory and sent back in a cheap envelope.

*

During the many trials and tribulations encountered by Harley in England, Josephine Lawson seems to disappear from view, but she remained in the background, corresponding with Harley. And suddenly, in the summer of 1910, she reappears. Josephine departed New York and sailed into the port of Southampton on the *Adriatic*, one of the many ships operated by the White Star Line company.[367] She was the unworldly young girl who had

---

364 Zoeller, *op. cit.*
365 Colin Grafton to AL, MSRC, 164-190, Folder 32 (26 July 1910). Grafton responded to Locke's inquiry: 're: - Personal Loan of £600/700... I shall be pleased to arrange this Loan.'
366 Zoeller, *op. cit.*
367 Passenger arrival records.

her head turned by the charismatic stranger, enchanted by his tales and his ability to paint pictures with words, illustrating his childhood, the difficulties that brought him to Washington, and ultimately to her. When Harley left for Yale and Josephine for Oberlin, their relationship continued via an exchange of letters.

Josephine had invested eight years in a relationship which had undoubtedly grown and deepened into love and a shared connection based on an idealistic dream of starting a new life together in a new country. Protected from Jim Crow by her parents, the last couple of years as a teacher may have jolted Josephine into the harsh realities of what the average African American faced. Harley's letters artfully constructed imagery which complemented Josephine's knowledge about England, knowledge she had obtained from the classics: Shakespeare, Jane Austen and Dickens - books she had read or used to teach her English lessons and employed as foundations to complete her picture of a genteel new life. She may have romanticized about sipping tea and playing croquet on an English lawn. After all, this was a world that she was to some degree familiar with; her thoughts and daydreams were not entirely fanciful but expectations about life in England drawn from tales from the Washington black elite and from her mother returning from sojourns in Europe where suffocating racism was not so prevalent. Josephine thus made a momentous choice, a brave decision to carve her own way in life, to marry whom she wanted, to forge her own identify and gain her own independence and travel unchaperoned on her journey. She knew her decision would change her life forever.

Josephine arrived in England on 9 June 1910. Her place of residence was initially in Oxford, at 19 Friars Entry,[368] a narrow pedestrian passageway located in the middle of the city linking

---

368 Harleys' marriage certificate, national records.

Gloucester Street to Magdalen Street. The passageway is thought to be named after the Carmelite friars who lived in the area; they used it to go to and from the chapel at the Church of St Mary Magdalen.

The familiar atmosphere of the university town of Oxford may have put her at ease and made her feel comfortable in the esteemed seat of learning. The University and city contained a number of black students and residents from the Commonwealth, America and Africa. The city's population, however, was not comparable to the numerous black students at Howard University or the mixed population of Washington DC. Josephine remained in Oxford to prepare for their marriage.

Matters between Rev Kent and Harley finally culminated in disagreement. Kent requested that he leave, writing to the Archbishop to inform him that Harley would be leaving the parish on 23 June 1910. The vicar would be seeking a suitable curate, an active man who could get about visiting in all weathers in the parish – 'one who does not mind distance and is manly' – as 'visiting was the chief work to be done here before any real spiritual progress'.[369] Nine days before his planned marriage, this was not news that Harley welcomed. The actions of Kent then became bewildering as he made an astonishing U-turn. From effectively sacking Harley he wrote to the Archbishop again to apologize.

Dear Grace,

I fear you may find me changeable and troublesome, but I want to do what is best for Mr Harley and the parish. Moreover, after praying, I have sought the guidance of the Holy Ghost and desire has come to me to keep Mr Harley here longer if possible.

---

369 Kent to Archbishop Davidson, 29 May 1910, Canterbury Cathedral Archives.

From the damning indictment of Harley's behaviour, Kent's retraction is amazing. He continues: 'He is without a doubt far and away above the average curate in abilities and powers. He is proven in teaching. The people all like him and want him to stay'.[370]

It now appears that Harley not only visited all the people throughout the parish but drew all the community to church. Travelling across the cold, bleak landscape, he repeatedly visited the same parishioners, who came to accept and appreciate him. These were people who may have never ventured further afield than the next village; the sight of a black man standing at their doorstep, announcing himself as the new curate, would have been alarming for many of them. But Harley repeatedly carried out this thankless task in order for the community to voice their approval of him. He had proven himself to his parishioners, his skills in preaching and pastoral care recognized by them as being useful in their lives. Far from the Holy Ghost visiting Rev Kent, the people of Marshside may have visited him, just like in Shepshed, and insisted that Harley remain as the curate.

Rev Kent started to lobby the Archbishop for Harley to be priested before the following Trinity, stating that he needed an exceptional man for the parish to restore its spiritual life.[371] Harley wrote:

> It was decided that we would both visit the Archbishop of Canterbury, on Wednesday 22nd June, at his London residence - Lambeth Palace. Reverend Kent's motives are for the Archbishop to 'get the measure of me' and to request that I be priested before Trinity 1911. We departed on the 9.30 am train from Canterbury and arrived in London Victoria at 12.00.[372]

370 Kent to Archbishop Davidson, 21 June 1910, Canterbury Cathedral Archives.
371 Ibid.
372 Ibid.

Kent and Harley entered the imposing Morton's Tower gatehouse of Lambeth Palace. Steeped in eight hundred years of history and located on the South Bank of the River Thames opposite the Houses of Parliament, the Palace is the official London residence of the Archbishop of Canterbury. Archbishop Randall Davidson, the first Baron of Lambeth, was a heavy-set sixty-two-year-old man. He had an esteemed pedigree, appointed Knight Commander of the Royal Victoria Order (KCVO) in 1902, Privy Counsellor and a Knight Grand Cross (GCVO) of the Royal Victorian,1904. A shooting accident as a young man

Rev Randall Davidson, Archbishop of Canterbury, c 1908. (Wikimedia Commons)

put paid to a scholarship at Oxford, but he matriculated as a Commoner at Trinity College in 1867.[373] Davidson had only been in the Church of England's highest office for seven years; previously he had worked as a curate in Dartford in north-east Kent[374] and presided over Winchester as its Bishop.

The Archbishop saw Kent and Harley together.[375] Rev Kent assured the Archbishop of his wish to retain him and, if possible, for Harley to be ordained priest at an earlier date than Trinity 1911.[376] This was arguably for Kent's convenience, of

---

373 G.K.A. Bell, *Randall Davidson, Archbishop of Canterbury*, Oxford: Oxford University Press, vol. 1, 1935, p. 21.
374 Ibid.
375 Interview with Archbishop Davidson, Rev Kent and Harley, 22 June 1910, Canterbury Cathedral Archives.
376 Ibid.

course, as Harley was unable to give the Eucharist - and hence share services such as Holy Communion until priested. The Archbishop made it plain that this was impossible. The issues that had arisen in Shepshed were discussed, and Harley gave a full explanation of them.

The Archbishop then saw Kent by himself where he spoke candidly about Harley, noting that 'he has a hot West Indian temper'. He also acknowledged and regarded him as a man of real power and an admirable preacher. His impending marriage was also raised at the meeting. It was resolved that Kent had to instruct Harley that he must first marry, provide evidence of the wedding and bring his wife to live in the parish before he applied for Harley's licence. Harley then met with the Archbishop on his own. The Archbishop explained that he must have from the Bishop of Peterborough all information from before Harley went to Peterborough Diocese. The Archbishop then instructed Kent to write to him when he made up his mind with regard to what he proposed.[377] Harley's fate, therefore, lay entirely in the hands of Rev Kent. It was clear that he was eager for Harley to be made a priest sooner rather than later, and that he seemed contented with his work in bringing people to the church, describing him as an admirable preacher.[378]

With his marriage looming, Harley took the opportunity - perhaps unwisely given the circumstances - to ask for a raise in his stipend. The request was met with what appears to be a confrontation with Kent. Whatever transpired, Harley left the parish and promised to return on Sunday, with the veiled threat that unless his request was accepted he would not be returning. He voiced his displeasure with some passion to the churchwarden.[379]

---

377 Ibid.
378 Ibid.
379 Kent to Archbishop Davidson, 29 June 1910, Canterbury Cathedral Archives.

Harley's fresh contretemps over his stipend precipitated yet another letter from Rev Kent to the Archbishop:

> I have done my best for him - his temper gets the better of him. Where Mr Harley is I do not know as he has not come near me or told me of his movements. It is most unfortunate for my work in the parish and I must look about for another curate. Perhaps your Grace may be able to assist me. I fear Harley's temper and behaviour will be a great drawback to him in his career. When your Grace comes to Canterbury I will see you about it all as I have kept Mr. Harley's letter.

Harley had meanwhile travelled to Oxford for his marriage to Josephine; she had now been in England for a month. On one of the biggest days of her life Josephine was alone in a strange country: no father to proudly walk her down the aisle; no mother to plump her dress and fuss over her; no Washington black elite bridesmaids, giggling and merrymaking as she got ready. Their marriage took place on Friday 1 July 1910 at St Giles Register Office. The licence cost 10s 6d, and Harley had to pay the clerk 5s. Mr Frank James Adam and Ms Sarah Francis were their witnesses.[380] The 'Week in Society' news section of the *Washington Bee* newspaper later included a notice of their marriage:

> Miss Josephine Lawson, daughter of Prof. Lawson, was married in Oxford, England to Prof. James Harley of Antigua, B.W.I.[381]

Three days after his marriage, while still in Oxford, Harley wrote to the Archbishop. He told him that he carried the

---

380 Harleys' certificate of marriage.
381 *The Washington Bee*, 10 September 1910.

memory of the kindness with which he received him in audience and that the Vicar of Chislet had found it best to dispense with his services. Harley begged his 'kindly advice on whether he should look to Lord Bishop of Peterborough or continue to be guided by his Grace in seeking work further in the church'.[382]

The couple only enjoyed each other's company for four days before Harley returned to Marshside, leaving Josephine in Oxford. No job, a new wife to support and expenses to meet; this was not an ideal way for Harley to start married life. Perhaps Josephine advised Harley to apologize to Rev Kent, return to Chislet and ask for his position back. Harley had done good work at Marshside and had earnestly tended to his parishioners. His temper may have got the better of him, but Kent was aware that he was getting married. Proof of his nuptials had been requested, and an increase in his stipend would have been greatly appreciated.

Harley went to see Rev Kent upon his return to Marshside, explaining that he had written very hastily before and apologizing for his letter and actions.[383] Kent accepted his apology. He wrote to the Archbishop for guidance:

> I am willing, in view of his abilities, and for the sake of Marshside where he did bring people to church - to try him again if you consent of course. I am greatly in need of a curate and do much want to get a capable and brotherly man -keen and loyal.
>
> Awaiting your reply
> R.A. Kent

---

382 Harley to Archbishop Davidson, 4 July 1910, Canterbury Cathedral Archives.
383 Kent to Archbishop, 21 July 1910, Canterbury Cathedral Archives.

The Archbishop replied on 22 July:

> I cannot rightly judge what you ought to do and if you desire that he should work with you I do not want to stand definitely in the way provided the necessary conditions can be complied with, but after all these conditions have passed, these conditions would have to be served. Of course, he must show you that he is now married and that his wife must come with him, that would be a necessarily primary. On the other hand, I could not regard a man, who has behaved in this way, in a position which justifies me at present in licensing him, and that makes it perhaps hard for him to obtain the necessary accommodation for himself and his wife while his tenure of curate is uncertain. That difficulty, however, is due to no fault or your or mine but is the outcome of his own action. If he really satisfies you that he is willing to come, on probation, and work without a licence, bringing his wife, with him, I will on your request let him do so. But I am doubtful whether I could ordain a man, who has shown his total lack of balance, discretion, and sobriety of mind, to the Priesthood, until he has been working for a full year in the Diocese as a Deacon with a completely satisfactory record, besides passing his necessary examinations. I should have thought that he returns to the Diocese where he was ordained Deacon and endeavour to win back the confidence he evidently forfeited. You are quite at liberty to show him this letter, for it is right that he should understand how gravely I view the matter and how inconsistent such a course as he has followed is in the case of a man preparing for Priesthood.

Harley had no option other than to buckle down and accept the conditions stipulated by the Archbishop. He re-evaluated his position and settled down to the work of the parish, working in harmony with Rev Kent. They made progress in the parish.[384] Harley noted: 'One of the major tasks I took on at Chislet was the painting of the church with my hands, and I collected enough to have it thoroughly furnished and restored.'[385] Rev Kent wrote to update the Archbishop:

> If Mr Harley were to leave me now after the work he has done, and the affection in which he is held in by the people, it would leave me terribly crippled, as it would be almost impossible to get a man to take his place in the efficient way shown by him.

He went on to explain that he recognized the justice and fairness of the agreement made at Lambeth Palace and that he might consider an appeal if Harley worked steadily for six months for him to be considered for Priesthood by Trinity 1911. Kent felt that 'we would be able to do splendid work in the coming winter, reawakening the spiritual life among the people'.[386] It was reiterated very strongly to Harley from the Archbishop that Josephine had to join him in Marshside before he could entertain any further thoughts about his licence.[387]

---

384 Kent to Archbishop Davidson, 30 July 1910, Canterbury Cathedral Archives.
385 Yale Alumni Yearbook 1911.
386 Kent to Archbishop Davidson, 30 July 1910.
387 Archbishop Davidson to Kent, 2 August 1910, Canterbury Cathedral Archives.

13. Josephine Arrives in Marshside

'Wherever you go, go with all your heart.'

Confucius

Josephine arrived from Oxford in late August, leaving the bustling city environment to 'settle' in Marshside and undertake her position as the curate's wife in deepest rural England. Marshside may have been eight miles from Canterbury and the spiritual home of Anglicans, but for Josephine this new life was a million miles from anything she had been acquainted with in America. She had grown up in an environment of luxury, privilege and protection. Isolated, confused, resentful and displaced emotions very probably swirled within her when she saw Marshside for the first time, and the reality of exactly what she had come to dawned on her.

Women in Edwardian rural England knew their place. The legislation introduced in the 1830s defined women as a group requiring special protection, reinforcing a belief in the domestic sphere as the focus of women's roles.[388]

The women of England in 1910, like the restricted waist-pinching corsets they wore, were confined. 'Let women be what God intended, a helpmate for man, but with totally different duties and vocations.' The words uttered by Queen Victoria added further justification for men to compound this stereotypical view of women. Women were not equals and far from being treated as such; their role was to cook, clean, bear and raise children and have no opinion, political or otherwise.

---

388 Nicola Verdon, *Rural Women Workers in Nineteenth Century England: Gender, Work and Wages*. Woodbridge: Boydell Press. 2002, p. 15.

The women's suffrage movement was in its infancy, and its stronghold was in London and the major cities, not in a small backwater like Marshside and Chislet.

The black, educated and articulate woman, perceived as an oddity for her visible qualities, stood out like a flashing light. Yet Josephine was also invisible - her thoughts, opinions, and ideas neither sought out nor wanted.

Standing on its own and surrounded by fields, the little mill house looked out on open arable land. The views were a far cry from Josephine's home in the 'romantic' district of Washington's LeDroit Park. The music, chatter, colour and vibrancy of the U Street Corridor were replaced with dark, lowering fog pierced by the ships' foghorns from the Wantsum Channel. In Oxford, Josephine stepped out into Friars Entry and immediately into the city, interacting with people, admiring the beauty of the various colleges, strolling down the High Street and window-shopping. In Marshside she lived in a small cottage with austere Unitarian furniture and heating provided by an open fire, for which fetching scuttles of coal and cleaning the grate were daily chores. There was no inside toilet; several houses were meant to share an outside toilet, but luckily for the couple, they did not have the indignity of sharing the toilet with other families.

Josephine had to get used to a new way of life: sights, sounds, smells and tastes. The restaurants frequented by the Washington black elite were now dim and distant memories. Collard greens, rice and beans, sweet potatoes, spices and seasoning now gave way to English cooking influenced by Puritan roots and shunning strong flavours and complex sauces associated with European (Catholic) nations. Most dishes, such as bread and cheese, roasted and stewed meats, meat and game pies, boiled vegetables and broths, freshwater and saltwater fish, had ancient origins and recipes in *The Forme of Cury*, a fourteenth-century cookbook dating from the Royal Court of Richard II. Her new diet consisted of boiled potatoes, root vegetables and local delicacies that she could not pronounce or stomach. She may have been quite perturbed but relieved when she discovered that toad in the hole was not a frog-based dish, but sausages in batter. There was no shared sense of cultural references, sense of humour, language or sayings. She had to attune herself to the local dialect and become accustomed to deciphering a new language and turn of phrase. In England, she was exposed and vulnerable.

There was a small village school in Chitty Lane teaching only boys, and it would have taken a brisk twenty-minute walk to reach it from the little cottage. Josephine's skills and expertise as a professional teacher could have provided a valuable resource for the school, but this was not the norm. She was probably more qualified than her English counterparts, but the idea would not have entered the minds of the school's governing body. What would have been more detrimental and offensive to the school's reputation: her being a woman, being black or being American?

She was no longer imparting knowledge, facts and figures to craft, mould and develop the minds of young people in her charge; instead, Josephine settled into her new life as a curate's wife. She became accustomed to an unfamiliar curriculum, one of domesticity. Washdays involved the early morning start of getting the tin bath out of the washhouse and fetching water from the standpipe before beginning the laborious process of washing clothes in cold water. She had to rub each item vigorously up and down the washboard with the aid of harsh carbolic soap to coax the dirt from the fabric, the soap cracking and blistering the skin of her smooth teacher's hands. The effort of taking the wet clothes and feeding them through the double rollers of the mangle to remove as much water as possible before they were hung on the makeshift clothes line in the garden was a process that would take nearly the whole day to complete. Josephine's new curriculum also included shopping and household chores. Milk was fetched in a jug from a nearby farm; a man would deliver provisions such as meat, bread and groceries by horse and cart. During the periods in between deliveries,

The Gate Inn, Boyden Gate, 1906. (Courtesy Rory Kehoe)

Josephine had to make her way to the village of Boyden Gate to the Gate Inn, carrying her wicker shopping basket, heavy even before any items were placed into it.

While Harley visited the parishioners and worked hard at developing the church, Josephine's loneliness was amplified in the quietness of the little cottage. Her days of soirees, parties, conversing and intellectualizing in Washington must have seemed remote. The local housewives barely offered the intellectual stimulation she had been used to, that is, if she saw anybody in the first place. And few dared converse with her. She may have been offered polite pleasantries as the curate's wife when she ventured down to the village instead of being completely ostracized, but doors were not readily open for her to 'pop in' and to partake in the English custom of a 'cuppa tea'.

14. The Appeal

'When God approves of your life, even your enemies will end up shaking your hand.'

Proverbs 16:7

The Archbishop of Canterbury responded to Rev Kent's appeal on 6 August 1910:

Dear Mr. Kent,

I have talked over fully with the Bishop of Dover the question of Mr Harley and his position at Chislet. I am clear that after all that has passed, I must not be under any obligation to accept Mr Harley as a candidate for Priest Order's till he shall have worked for a year in the Diocese to the complete satisfaction both of you and me. At the same time if Mr Harley prefers to come up for examination next November and pass the first part of the examination for Priest Order's I am willing that he should do so and that he should then come up in the following May for the second part of the examination, and if at that time everything seemed to have worked so well that we felt justified in modifying the plan I have proposed, it would be possible that he might be ordained Priest at Trinity. But I do not wish to hold out any definite hope of this. Mr Harley must understand that to receive a man at all who is in Deacon's order is contrary to our ordinary rule.[389] In this case, the difficulties are increased by the strange way in which he

---

389 Ordinary rule referred to the Church not ordaining a man who was only in Deacon's Orders.

has behaved. He now has an opportunity of showing by quiet diligence and general sobriety of action that he is entitled to our full confidence. I hope this will show Mr Harley my real wish to be helpful to him so far as I can consistently meet his wishes without complete violation of our rules, and I very earnestly trust that the work which you and he together can do in Chislet may have the abundant blessing of Almighty God.

Harley noted:

I had a full and frank interview with the Archbishop's secretary, four days after his response to Reverend Kent's appeal. I explained that my grievance was that leaving Chislet through a misunderstanding I was being punished by not receiving a licence and having my ordination postponed and that if I had behaved scandalously, it would have been better in some way. I did not see how I could remain at Chislet still a Deacon if not ordained by next Trinity. The Archbishop was willing to make one small compromise, allowing me to take the examination in November 1910 and May 1911 instead of May 1911 and November 1911.[390]

The Archbishop's secretary, George Bell, observed that Harley would need a strong vicar to control his actions and a vicar ready to put up with self-aeration of the most pronounced kind. However, he was judged to be full of energy and deserving.[391]

Harley's yearning to continually inform others of how well he was doing resulted in him writing letters to former alumni, professors and colleagues, each line of his letters celebrating

---

390 Interview between Archbishop's secretary and Harley, 10 August 1910, Canterbury Cathedral Archives.

391 Ibid.

his achievements. The bespectacled little mulatto with the big dreams *had* achieved an English education in its premier seat of learning and he was now residing in the home of the British Empire, had luncheon with the Bishop of Peterborough and his lady wife, and was now a curate pursuing his ambition to become a priest. Harley's letters were a master class in the art of smoke and mirrors, carefully crafted illusions projected an image of how successful he had become. He had continued to correspond with his professors and staff at Harvard. In October he wrote to the secretary, Edgar Wells, who passed his letter on to Byron Hurlbut, Dean of Harvard, who replied rather archly:

> Dear Edgar,
>
> Many thanks for the sight of Harley's letter. I wonder when he is going back to help his race in the West Indies. That's what he wanted the very best education for. I am glad that he is done well, but somehow, I cannot even now feel that I should want him for my spiritual adviser.

Horace Kallen, a student at Oxford with Harley and one of his referees for Manchester College, discussed Harley with Hurlbut resulting in the Dean writing to a Brother Wilson.

> October 22, 1910
> Dear Brother Willson,
>
> In the course of a talk which I had with H.M. Kallen this morning I gained some more information about our friend Harley which will, I think, amuse you. Kallen said that Harley's career in England was much like what it was in America. He borrowed money rather extensively for a man in his position; obtained admission to Manchester College by uncertain means (Kallen said 'false pretences'), and then on the strength of having

got into Manchester College and secured a scholarship there went to Jesus College. Did I tell you that Edgar Wells sent me a letter from him the other day! He is now a curate in England. Meanwhile, those unhappy fellows of his down in the West Indies, to whom he was to bring light after he secured the very best education, still languish in spiritual darkness.[392]

Across the Atlantic, Kallen and his Harvard professors reveled in their disparaging opinions of Harley. As an idealistic young man, it may have been an ambition for Harley to return to Antigua to start his own church, but he never returned. Several factors may have derailed his dream: the reality and practicalities of life in England, the finances required to return to Antigua, his responsibilities as a married man, navigating the impact of colonial racism. But ultimately, he had outgrown Antigua and what the country could now offer him. Go back to what? The small island where everyone knew each other. No matter how many degrees Harley had achieved, and however prestigious the colleges he had obtained them from, he was still the mulatto son of the seamstress who had left to make his fame and fortune. A highly educated man would return only to have to succumb to the grinding poverty and limited opportunities on the island. England was now Harley's home.

In November, Kent wrote once again to the Archbishop stating that he regretted asking for Harley to be licensed because of his behaviour and attitude towards him and reiterating that he would be better off in a parish with more than one curate.[393] The Archbishop responded with a very detailed letter which left no room for misunderstanding about his position.

---

392 Byron Hurlbut to Brother Wilson, 22 October 1910, Harvard University Archive.
393 Kent to Archbishop Davidson, November 1910, Canterbury Cathedral Archives.

Dear Mr Harley,

I have today been asking Mr Kent how matters stand in the parish with regards to yourself. It is clear to me that Mr Kent is increasingly convinced that this is not the right parish, perhaps not the right (sort of) parish for you. You are older than a man in Deacon's Orders. You clearly have difficulty in working happily and loyally in a subordinate position. And in the conditions of a rural parish like Chislet. After what Mr Kent has told me I am not surprised to learn that he feels that he ought not to nominate you for formal licence, and nothing could be gained in your interest by you working on indefinitely upon the present voluntary arrangement. I was always doubtful to the wisdom of you coming back after some previous rupture with the vicar, and I now feel that you will, be more likely to work happily if you are in a larger parish, say some Midland town or similar place, with colleagues and friends more abundant.

Mr Kent is clearly anxious not to put you to unnecessary inconvenience, but it cannot be for your own happiness or usefulness to work on longer at Chislet without obtaining formal status or licence and these it is clear will not be obtained for you there.

You should now arrange with Mr Kent as to your date of leaving, as to your mutual convenience. I shall be ready if all goes well to recommend you to some other Bishop, in whose Diocese you may find an opportunity or more suitable work, of course, my powers of recommending you must depend absolutely on the manner in which you wind up your work in Chislet. If you work on quietly and usefully until the time comes for going. I shall be able to testify to that point in your favour. If, on the other hand, difficulties are allowed to arise, or if you seem to be forming a faction in the parish, or if, in short, your departure becomes the occasion of unrest, for in which you appear to be in anyway responsible. I should be in honour bound to state those facts to any Bishop. I shall also be able to testify to your recent examinations results, such as they were, and to my readiness, had all gone smoothly, and well, to admit you into Diocese, and after adequate examination as a curate for Priest Orders. I hope nothing to occur which can interfere with my powers of so commending you.[394]

Quite what Harley drew from the phrase 'difficulty in working happily and loyally in a subordinate position'[395] is hard to know. It may well have conjured up thoughts of being back in America and being 'a Negro': happy, smiling, appeasing everyone rather than standing tall and proud as a black man. Harley must have thought he had adequately demonstrated his loyalty to Rev Kent, the Archbishop and his parishioners; toiling on their behalf, now only to be told that he would be better off in another parish. The undertones of a threat, warning him that he must not be the cause of any unrest in the parish, serve to suggest that Harley had the confidence and support of the parishioners.

With five weeks remaining to complete his notice, he wrote to the Archbishop in January to notify him about a series of dilemmas that he now faced. Harley thanked him for the kindness he had shown on his behalf when the Vicar of Windsor had approached him. The Archbishop of Canterbury had been Dean of Windsor and had played an integral part in the funeral arrangements of Queen Victoria. The Vicar of Windsor, acting

---

394 Archbishop Davidson to Harley, 5 December 1910, Canterbury Cathedral Archives.
395 Yale alumni record, 1911.

on the Archbishop's recommendation, interviewed Harley for a position there. He was satisfied with Harley, it seems, in all respects, apart from the question of income. The position required a substantial private income, which he had largely used up. Harley's note to the Archbishop further stated:

> Mr. Hampton of Dover might employ me as a priest by Easter, but Diocese custom defies my ordination until June. I might have gained the post, but only I am not a priest; while I shall not be a priest until I have a post. At any rate the noble act of kindness your Grace has shown to me will help me complete events.[396]

Yet what Harley did not know as he was trying desperately to secure another curacy after the prized jewel of the post at Windsor slipped beyond reach because of financial constraints, was that a communication containing outrageous, slanderous and heinous statements was crossing the Atlantic. It was a development that would make his current predicament seem almost trivial.

---

396 Harley to Archbishop Davidson, 23 January 1910, Canterbury Cathedral Archives.

15. A Damning Allegation

*'You cannot rectify every real or alleged wrong immediate.
Time must enter into the picture.'*

Arthur Goldberg

The Rev C. Ernest Smith, DD, BCL, Rector of St Thomas Church, Washington, wrote to the Archbishop of Canterbury on 20 February 1911 to inform him that he had received a visit from a Mrs Rosetta Lawson, Josephine's mother, who proceeded to tell the following story.

Her daughter, Josephine, until a few months ago was a member of the choir of St Luke's Church (colored) in the city. A man named Harley was the choirmaster and won the girl's love - although he was many years older than her. Harley left and went to Oxford. 'A few months afterwards he was ordained, and then he sent for the girl and eight months ago they were married in England. He is now, a curate in your Grace's dioceses though a *mulatto*.'

> Since the wedding, the bride has been brutally treated by her husband if the statements made by her are true and I have no reason to doubt her. Her mother hearing of the sad plight of her daughter has come seeking my counsel. She says that the husband cashes any money she sends to her daughter. The mother is afraid to write to the daughter for fear that her husband could do her bodily harm and from the way he treated the unborn infant and the language he used there seems to much reason to think he would such kill her. I do know who the rector of Chislet is, or I would write to him to ask him to take up the matter and see that his conduct will

be duly punished and brought to your Grace's notice. But not knowing his name and fearing that if I sent a letter to him officially, the curate might open it. I am writing to you to request your help.

Rev Smith goes on to state that Mrs Lawson had given him 'paper good for passage from London to Philadelphia; post office order for her daughter to cash and pay other expenses on the journey', two letters written by her daughter[397] which will show her condition and position and a letter for her daughter, all of which he has sent to the Archbishop. He urges the Archbishop to have 'some person take up this matter at once'. It was important apparently that Josephine be given the passage receipt, and the post office order and letters endorsed and that she be guarded so that she could leave the village before harm was done to her. And on no account must anything intended for Josephine be sent to Harley. Rev Smith concludes by appealing to 'the duty we all owe to this poor woman alone in a strange land away from her kith and kin, and secondly, the duty one owes the Church to unmask, expose and shun a frightful hypocrite.'[398]

Rosetta's testimony contained several damning allegations about Harley's behaviour and his treatment towards her daughter. The depths of her contempt for Harley is evident; she is outraged that the Church of England ordained a mulatto. Yet so much more is unexpected and is at no stage hinted at in other documents that trace Harley's day-to-day life. There are enormous questions. In what way did Harley, a man of God, treat an unborn

ROSETTA COAKLEY LAWSON
1856 - 1936

---

397 Despite numerous attempts to locate Josephine's letters, they remained lost.
398 Rev C. Ernest Smith to Archbishop Davidson, 20 February 1911, Lambeth Palace Archives.

infant? We learn now that Josephine had given birth to a son, Arthur, who died under mysterious circumstances.[399]

Mrs Lawson followed up her visit with a letter to Rev Smith:

National Women's Christian Temperance Union
Mrs Rosetta E. Lawson
National Organiser and Lecturer Washington D.C.
2011 Vermont Avenue

Reverend C. Ernest Smith. DD
Dear Sir,

I am sending you the enclosed money orders and letters for my daughter. I cannot express to you your kindness and interest in this matter. The customs of England are so different from those in America that I have no suggestions to offer as to the means of sending Josephine's purse? All I beg of you is to make it very plain to the Archbishop that no mail can reach my daughter if addressed to the Mill House, Chislet, Canterbury, without being read firstly by the man to whom she is married and that Law asking that the utmost caution in reaching her be observed as I believe his objective in adopting the little girl was to have her report on what might transpire in his absence.

Josephine is a graduate of Oberlin College, Class of 1907, and has the highest endorsement from Dean Miller, President Regis and Ethics there. That she should have thrown away her opportunities on one so unworthy is indeed a mystery to me. When this matter has been open to Josephine, please ask for her the assurance of the protection of the Church, as I believe, if she is left at his mercy, a moment when the matter has reached him, no act will be to mean for him to do to

---

399 Makiel Talley related this family history to me.

thwart her homecoming. Please ask for the return of the letters I herein enclose.

Very respectfully and gratefully yours
Rosetta E. Lawson
P.S. Rev Smith,
    I have only one fear that is that this may not reach the Archbishop before the end of Feb and later than that the man may be outside the command of the Church.

Who was the little girl Rosetta spoke of? Was she a neighbour's child whose role was to keep Josephine company while Harley worked in the parish or, as Rosetta seemed to allege, a spy for Harley who would feed him information about who Josephine had spoken to and interacted with? Was the 'adoption' proper and legal? Or was adopting merely a term Rosetta loosely used to indicate the little girl's presence in the house? To Rosetta, Josephine had the world at her feet as an educated, professional young woman, with the opportunity of marrying a black elite bachelor, maybe one of the Cooks' sons. Instead, she chose an 'old' West Indian mulatto man who had wrenched her away from her family, friends and all that she knew. But Josephine had chosen; she chose to reap the dividends from her eight-year investment, and opted for a new country, adventure, love. She had chosen Harley.

    Harley was probably ignorant of any of these communications between Mrs Lawson, Rev Smith and the Archbishop, or was he? Did he have an inkling about what was going on, was he genuine in his sentiment in his letters to the Archbishop and his former Dean at Harvard, or was it a ruse to ingratiate himself?

The Mill House
Chislet,
Canterbury
Feb 21, 1911

His Grace,
The Lord Archbishop of Canterbury,
My Lord Archbishop,

My duties here at Chislet Parish terminate on the first
Sunday in Lent. Meanwhile, I have seen the Rector of
the Parish of St. Leonard, Deal, and he has offered me
the curacy, now vacant, in his parish. I expect to begin
work on the first Sunday after Easter. I beg, therefore,
to ask your Grace, to accept this expression of my deep
sense of obligation towards your Grace for so graciously
remembering one who is among the humblest of the
myriad of church ministers place under the authority
of your Grace.

I have the honour to be
Your Grace's grateful servant.
J. Arthur Harley

The Mill House
Chislet,
Canterbury
Feb 21, 1911

Dear Mr. Hulbert,

Mr Patterson has been pleased to appoint me to the
vacant curacy of his parish at Deal, so I have hastened to
let you know without delay. My duties begin there after
the first Sunday after Easter, while I leave her on the first
Sunday in Lent. If I can be of any use during Lent in
the matter of supply, I shall be glad. Again thanking you
for your kindness to me.

After the Archbishop received Smith's letter - a letter so
detrimental to Harley's character and an alarming revelation of

what Josephine's mother feared he was capable of - the Harleys were summoned at once to Lambeth Palace to meet with the Archbishop and his wife, Edith.

16. The Archbishop Intercedes

'She assures us very positively (and this in the most private conversation with my wife) that she is not in the least afraid of her husband, that on the whole, they get on quite well, although he has fits of temper, and that if she goes home for a visit if would be with the wish to return to him before long.'

3rd March 1911
Dear Mr. Harley,

I have seen your letter to Mr Hertalet (sic), and I should like upon you giving up work at Chislet to see both you and Mrs Harley. This had better be at once. I write to ask whether you can both come here on Monday next March 6th, at 2.30pm. If Mrs Harley, as is possible, would find it too fatiguing to go up and down on the same day we could arrange for her sleeping in London. If Monday is impossible for you or Mrs. Harley, I could arrange another day, but I attach great importance to seeing you both. I will be responsible for the cost of the journey to London and back. As I am very busy on Monday and have to fit in different arrangements, I shall be grateful if you let me know on the enclosed telegraph form whether I may expect you and Mrs Harley at the hour I have named.
I am
Very truly,

The meeting took place, and what materialized is reported in the Archbishop's response to Rev Smith's letter:

8th March 1911
My Dear Dr Smith,

I have to thank you for your letter of Feb 20th and papers for Mrs Harley, the coloured wife of the West Indian curate in this Diocese. I have had a great deal to do with Mr Harley, although I have not seen his wife. The difficulties are not small when a man of West Indian blood tries to take up clerical work in this country!

I did not feel that I could rightly transmit to Mrs Harley without the knowledge of her husband, the letters you had sent, and I have felt it better not to show even to Mr Harley the letter which she had written to her mother and which was sent to me through you. These letters I, therefore, return herewith. On receiving your letter, I sent for Mr and Mrs Harley and talked over everything fully with them both, having first talked to Mrs Harley privately, as you will see from Mrs Davidson's letter [the Archbishop's wife] to Mrs Lawson, which please read before sending it on. My wife has also gone into everything very fully and confidently with Mrs Harley. We both advised that she should take advantage of her mother's proposal and should go home to her mother for a time. I doubt however whether she will do this: indeed, I think she will not. She assures us very positively (and this in the most private conversation with my wife) that she is not in the least afraid of her husband, that on the whole, they get on quite well, although he has fits of temper, and that if she goes home for a visit if would be with the wish to return to him before long. He is going, if all being well, to a new curacy at Deal where the surroundings will be less remote and rural than they have been at Chislet, and this would be good. Perhaps you will explain to Mrs Lawson how the matter stands. You will, I sure will agree, that it will never do for me, as Bishop of the Diocese, to open communications with the wife behind the husband's back, unless matters were so outrageously wrong that this was necessary for her protection; and she is perfectly clear that there is not the smallest difficulty or danger of that sort. Mrs Harley will now communicate directly with her mother as to whether she is going to cross the Atlantic. In any case, both Mr and Mrs Harley are both aware that we are both cognizant of the difficulties which have arisen, and Mrs Harley can communicate with us directly at a moment's notice should she so desire.

Except for what is said by Mrs Harley in her private letters to her mother, there is nothing definitely alleged, far less proved, against Mr Harley's character, and as I cannot use those private letters, and the two seem at present to be quite happy together, I can only hope that the outrageous conduct and language alluded to, if they were accurately reported, were due to some uncontrollable fit of temper and are not recurrent. Of course, if I have any real evidence of anything of the sort that I can use it, I shall deal with him with the utmost sternness. I think you will feel that I have done all that I can properly do in the matter, for the present at least. They will now be in the midst of friends to whom we command her and would tell us if anything seemed seriously amiss.

17. Within Touching Distance

'All great achievements require time.'

Maya Angelou

Before Harley began his new position at St Leonard's Church in Deal, the Rector, Robert Patterson, had a full and frank conversation with him on 15 March 1911. Harley wrote to inform the Archbishop on 31 March that he had been over to Deal to see the parish, take a house and prepare for Josephine coming there after Easter. Rev Patterson was very thankful to the Archbishop for mentioning Harley and thought that if he did not quarrel with him, he would be a great help.[400]

The Harleys took what appears to be a recuperative break in Somerset at the beginning of April.[401] They stayed as boarders at the home of Mr Frederick Arthur Young and his wife Ada, and their three children, Ethel Ada, Frederick Arthur and Ernest in Easton, near Wells in Somerset. Mr Young worked as a papermaker at the paper mills at Wookey Hole.[402] Harley was familiar with the Somerset area as he had undertaken missionary work in Taunton as part of his course at Manchester College and excavated flints scrapers at the caves for the archaeological component for his Diploma of Anthropology. Harley returned to take up his new position in Deal, leaving Josephine in Somerset.

The town of Deal is approximately twenty miles from Chislet but far removed in its look and feel from the rural isolation of Marshside and Chislet. The town had a cosmopolitan feel, its

---

400 Rev Patterson to Archbishop Davidson, 15 March 1911, Lambeth Palace Archives.
401 1911 census.
402 1911 census.

diversity of nationalities attributed to the fact that it was one of the first ports of call for ships sailing from East and West Indies and trade destinations before docking in London. Josephine, when she eventually joined Harley, would no longer look so out of place. The three parishes of St Leonard's - St George's, St Andrew's and a triangle of Upper, Middle and Lower Deal - made up the town.

The original village, Upper Deal, stands on a hill above Middle Deal. The town's rich history encompassed a well-known tale that it was one of the possible sites for the landing place of Julius Caesar in 55 BC and there is plentiful evidence of its past as a haunt for smugglers. 'There are said to be in the town of Deal, not less than two hundred young men and sea-faring people, who are known to have no visible way of getting a living but by the infamous trade of smuggling. This smuggling has converted those employed, first from honest, industrious fishermen to lazy, drunken and profligate smugglers.'[403]

Boatbuilding and fishing later formed the town's primary industries. Lined up along the seafront the fishermen's boats sold their morning catch on the wharf. Unlike the small clapperboard church at Marshside. St Leonard's, the original church of Deal, is a large stone building dating back to 1180 and dedicated to St Leonard of Limoges, a sixth-century French abbot, the patron saint of the sick and prisoners. A mile from the town centre, the church dominates the corner of London Road and Manor Road. Located along Manor Road was the Tormore School 'for young gentlemen' and opposite the church stood the Court House. Along the London Road was a parade of shops, a bakery, butcher, ironmonger and the Red Admiral public house.

---

403 Smugglers' Britain http://www.smuggling.co.uk

St Leonard's Church, Deal, Kent, 1906. (KentOnline)

Rev Patterson lived at the rectory next door to the church. There was also a small cottage, usually allocated to the curate, but the Harleys did not receive this privilege and took a house, as tenants, in Middle Road, Upper Deal. The congregation of wealthy parishioners demanded when their time came that they should be buried in the cemetery at St Leonard's Church rather than suffering the indignity of being transported down 'coffin way', the name given to Church Path. This narrow passageway ran from St Leonard's down to the overflow cemetery. Standing at the furthest corner of the churchyard at its highest point, a raised mount offered Harley a view of the sea and Deal Castle.

On 10 June 1911, the day before Harley was finally able to be priested, the Archbishop had a long and frank talk with him and impressed upon his views on his duties and obligations. The ordination followed:

By the Tenor, of these Present **We, RANDALL THOMAS**, by Divine Providence **Archbishop of Canterbury**, Primate of all England and Metropolitan, do make it known unto all men, that On Sunday the Eleventh day of June, in the year of our Lord One thousand nine hundred and eleven, **We**, the Archbishop before mentioned, solemnly administering Holy Orders under the protection of the Almighty, in our Cathedral and Metropolitical Church of Christ, Canterbury, did admit our beloved in Christ *James Arthur Harley of Jesus College, Oxford B.A.* (of whose virtuous and pious life and conversation, and competent learning and knowledge in the Holy Scriptures, we were well assured) into the Holy Order of **Priesthood**, according to the manner and form prescribed and used by the Church of England; and him the said James Arthur Harley did then and there rightly and Canonically ordain **Priest**, He having first in our presence made and subscribe such Declaration, and taken and subscribed such Oath as are by Law in such case required. **In Testimony** Whereof We have caused our Archiepiscopal Seal to be affixed to these presents. **Dated** the day and year above written, and in the ninth year of **translation**.

After all his education, training, trials and tribulations, the realization of his childhood vocation finally manifested itself to him when he was ordained a priest on 11 June 1911 at Canterbury Cathedral. Josephine, however, was still in Somerset, accepting her 'confinement',[404] and not by his side to share in his dream and achievement. It is unclear what Josephine's confinement related to: possibly a pregnancy, or a physical or mental health issue. Harley, it would appear, began

---

404 Archbishop Davidson to Patterson, 10 June 1911, Lambeth Palace Archives.

working without any repercussions from previous incidents and confrontations and is recorded as having officiated at several marriage ceremonies.[405] Josephine in due course joined him in Deal and was placed under the guidance of Mrs Patterson, the rector's wife.[406]

By mid-1911, Harley was curate-in-charge of St John the Baptist in the small Medway village of Wateringbury, near Maidstone.[407] His service on the theme of icebergs and their danger was reported in the local paper, *The Deal Mercury*, after the sinking of RMS *Titanic* on 15 April 1912.[408]

*

Harley may have entered a relatively stable period in his career after his many confrontations and crises. But the same could not be said of Josephine, and her unhappiness could not be ignored any longer. She had made a considerable decision and act of commitment in coming to England. She had endured the tedium and isolation of life in Marshside, far from friends and cultural stimulation. Now, after meeting with the Archbishop, and with a move to a less rural parish in prospect, her mind seemed to be made up. Perhaps the idea of 'being in the care' of Rev Patterson's wife was too unpalatable. In any case, rather than embracing what was an improvement in her life in England, Josephine finally made the decision, with considerable inner strength and courage, to leave Harley. This decision, not taken lightly, weighed up the positive and negative consequences. The positives meant returning home to the safety and support of her family, resuming her teaching career, regaining her identity, self-worth, self-esteem and the ability to become financially

---

405 Canterbury Cathedral Archives.
406 Archbishop Davidson to Patterson, *op. cit.*
407 *Whitstable Times & Herne Bay Herald*, 29 July 1911, p. 2.
408 *The Deal Mercury*, 20 April 1912.

secure. The negatives, however, would be significant: it was no trivial matter to be leaving a priest - to the outside world, and in the eyes of the community, a man of God; a good man who provided their spiritual guidance.

Josephine's experience of Harley was different from that of his parishioners; behind closed doors he was a man prone to fits of temper over his constant battles with the Church and his single-minded ambition to be a priest and a person of good standing. Her dream of being the wife of a learned scholar and priest in England was also shattered by the stark reality of an unforgiving rural existence and, quite possibly, the loss of a precious child. No longer would she be seen as the curate's wife: but would be shunned as a woman who left her husband. In walking out on him, she was abandoning her husband, the Church and her briefly adopted country.

Leaving her husband meant she would have nothing, no money except what her mother had sent her and what she managed to conceal from him. But by leaving Harley, Josephine asserted and regained her control. It could not be helped if it indicated to the community that Harley had failed to assert his position as head of the household. And so Josephine returned to America sometime in 1912 and resumed her career as a teacher at the Bluefield Colored Institute, West Virginia. There is more to her story, told in Chapter 22.

18. A Black Canary

'We hear war called murder. It is not: it is suicide.'
Ramsay McDonald, 1924

After Josephine returned to America, Harley settled into life in Deal, presiding over weddings, christenings and burials.[409] There is no indication as to what he felt about Josephine's departure. Life, on the surface at least, carried on more or less uneventfully until 28 June 1914, ordinarily an insignificant date, but the day the Archduke Franz Ferdinand of Austria was shot and mortally wounded by the nineteen-year-old Bosnian Gavrilo Princip, a member of the Serbian nationalist Black Hand group. His single act in Sarajevo caused reverberations through Europe. Hostilities escalated quickly: Britain declared war on Germany at 11 pm on 4 August 1914. Twenty-five days later, over 800 men responded to an advertisement that appeared in the *Kentish Gazette*.[410]

> A call to all men of Kent - Your country asks for soldiers, you the successors of the men of Kent, who were never vanquished in all the centuries past, must respond to the call. A new battalion of the Buffs is being formed. Join at once. Every man who joins will earn the honour for himself, the gratitude of his friends and the thanks of his country.

Both clergy and laity took it for granted that the Church of England should aid the war effort by whatever means possible.

---

409 Canterbury Cathedral Archives.
410 *Kentish Gazette,* 29 August 1914, *In Their Own Words: Kent Voices of the First World War*, Kent History and Library Centre exhibition, 2015.

The responsibilities included explaining the causes and meaning of the war, maintaining morale on the home front, and reminding the public that the primary obligation of young men was to enlist.[411]

Men enlisting in the military were presented with an opportunity for adventure: factory workers and farm labourers might at first have viewed the war as an escape from the mundane humdrumness of their daily existence. Before the true horror of the conflict was widely known, some may have envisaged an 'all boys adventure', but the primary motive for enlisting was to serve King and Country, and to avoid the stain of being identified as a coward.

African and Caribbean men did not turn a deaf ear to the call of duty but valiantly and unquestioningly answered the call of War from Kitchener. But the War Office's enthusiasm in their regard was lukewarm; it did not want black men in its Army. The War Office relented after the personal intervention of King George V. On 3 November 1915, the British West Indies Regiment (BWIR) was established by Royal Warrant. The West Indies also contributed men through the West India Regiment (WIR), consisting mainly of black African soldiers. This Regiment had existed since 1795.

Troops were recruited from the Caribbean using posters, films and rallies. The BWIR consisted of eleven battalions, with 15,600 men. The majority, two-thirds, came from Jamaica, the remaining men from Barbados, the Bahamas, British Guiana, British Honduras, the Leeward Islands (including Antigua), Grenada, St Lucia, St Vincent and Trinidad & Tobago.

The men of the BWIR did not have the opportunity to fight as equals alongside their white counterparts. Instead, their participation was limited to labour duties and supporting roles

---

411 Fielden, p. 39.

digging trenches, building roads and gun emplacements, acting as stretcher-bearers, and loading ships and trains.

It soon became evident that the war was not to be a short-lived affair, over by Christmas, as everyone expected. The first German bomb on British soil fell on Dover on 24 December 1914, smashing the windows of St James' Rectory.[412] Bombs began to 'rain' from the skies at the beginning of January 1915 after Kaiser Wilhelm authorized aerial bombardment; the Kentish towns suffered as they lay along the route aircrafts followed into London.

The Race to the Sea, the campaign to reach the English Channel by advancing into France, the Battle of the Marne, the Battle of the Aisne, the first and second Battles of Ypres had all taken place with huge loss of life and with the German resorting to the use of chlorine gas. In May 1915, nine months after the war began, Harley posed several challenging questions to his Deal parishioners via his editorials in the Deal parish magazine.

> Are we downhearted? No. Why? A *Times* writer suggested conceit and inertia. A nation is known by the songs it sings. Germany has an unholy hymn of hate. We have a holy one. Theirs is the key to German psychology. Ours is the nurse of national apathy. Theirs they translate into ghastliness daily. Ours we chant every Sunday in cathedrals, churches and chapels. It runs thus:
>
> As it was in the beginning, is now, and ever shall be, the world without end. Amen.
>
> Why will not single men enlist? Why are scientific men scantily utilised in this our hour of trial? Why are drunken men recorded as badly repairing warships?

---

412 *In Their Own Words.*

Why are we still snailing along after nine Heroic months? Can we lose in this awful struggle?

Can Zeppelins grind London institutions to powder? Can a secret submarine onslaught concocted by Germans in Germany, abetted by Germans in Britain, smite us unceasingly with shuddering calamity? Our two million fighting men say no. Our twenty million hordes of Louthood and Bobbydom deny it. Also, they ought to know, see, and they are exploding with enthusiasm - of football and horseracing specimen. And England will never snatch victory in Berlin without 'ten million' more.[413]

Harley wrote his editorial on 3 May. Four days later, the Cunard passenger ship *Lusitania* was torpedoed by a German U-boat, with 1,198 souls, including 124 American citizens, losing their lives. Was it a prediction or a common-sense view of the way the war was progressing? The sentiments in Harley's article did not turn him into a jingoistic recruiting sergeant. Clergymen were expected to present the war as a struggle of good versus evil to their parishioners. Arthur Winnington-Ingram, the Bishop of London, was one of the most outspoken and patriotic proponents of the war. In a much-repeated quote, the Bishop, after a year of war, called for the men of England to be 'branded in a great crusade - we cannot deny it - to kill Germans; to kill them, not for the sake of killing, but to save the world; to kill the good as well as the bad; to kill the young as well as the old, to kill those who have shown kindness to our wounded as well as those fiends who crucified the Canadian sergeant, who superintended the Armenian massacres, who sank the Lusitania - and to kill them lest the civilisation of the world should itself be killed.' The Bishop gave the war a further

---

413 Ibid.

crusading touch by adding, 'As I have said a thousand times, I look upon it as a war for purity, I look upon everyone who dies in it as a martyr.'[414] Winnington-Ingram was unabashedly jingoistic where Harley was not.

The sinking of the *Lusitania* began the piling of pressure upon President Woodrow Wilson to support the Allied war effort. Harley continued to be unapologetic in his rhetoric about British apathy, lack of initiative and the treatment and methods the Germans were deploying - all dispatched to local residents in the *All Deal* parish magazine:

My dear Friends

As time advances, more and more of the things so urgently needed to prosecute this War against a nation steeped in science, are being put in rapid motion, as you will see upon reflection. When we have had all the things we want, there will still be the need to have things to do.

It is to the National Register,[415] therefore, that we will turn at a distant date with the hope of finding outlets for our war-stirred, patriotic energy. I speak of the nation as a whole. There is cause for satisfaction in all this, insomuch that we might ordinarily rest at that. But this is no commonplace war. And in nothing whatsoever have we shown the slightest indication of the initiative.

Here then is the place where we ought to ponder.

There are ways and means of conducting the War,

---

414 Fielden, p. 35.
415 The National Registration Act 1915 was passed on 15 July 1915. The act required that all men and women, between the ages of 15 and 65, register at their residential location on 15 August 1915. The scheme was essentially a census to get a up to date list of those men (and women) who might be useful to the war effort.

ways and means of organizing ourselves, ways and means of putting forth all our energy that must appeal to each one of us from time to time. Now the danger does not lie in our ignorance, our indifference, or our inertia. We are capable of comparison unblushingly with the other greatest and best nationalities, so far as these points are concerned. Even in the matter of initiative, we sometimes hold our own. It is because of a leading characteristic that we lag behind in promptitude. The ideas are here; the will is here; the means to, and the grip.

Is there any reason we should not do a thing seeing that others are doing it also? There is a reason, but not the usual reason advanced, nor should we worry to stoop to gas - why? The usual reason alleged is either that we are not Germans or else that we are too rich, or even that we are too gentlemanly. This sort of allegation ambles along enough when there is music from the pipes of peace in our ears. But we are in the midst of War's alarms. And the only reason, the sole, the single solitary reason why we should not do these things which are admittedly judicious in themselves, is because we have at our disposal a way which he who runs may read better.

Such a way, such a better way, can never result from humdrum imitation. What appears from this chain of reasoning? What emerges from the obscurity of our usually unscrutinized thought? We must somehow throw aside our national slowness and move rapidly and dash in this War. Who will take the initiative? Nobody. The greatest of all politics that ever lived, if bouncing from department to department counts for aught, has lately ordered us to pay half-pennies no more but to put pennies stamps on everything we post. At once, a lot of idiots begin to point out how many people will suffer; how many firms will lose should such a tax eventuate. Let us take the initiative in suffering through our pockets so that some more of the best of our men might live, and not die through the prolongation of the War.

We need a better way. Hence, we have called the best brains together to invent and contrive for the Navy. This is really the point that is painful. For when the War is over, there will be no further need for their services. At present, even their high intentions look down upon their slumbering acts, for much that they have advanced has been laid upon the table indefinitely. And, to the point, they were only convened when the music was martial.

This is far from taking the initiative. This is not even a better way. For the points in my mind are two. We must hereafter be sensible enough to create and take the initiative. That is first. And the second is this: we must be sure that our way is best not merely a better than our dear former way, but our new way must be a better way by far or near than the scientific way of the enemy. The lack of initiative keeps us covering ourselves with contempt in the national whining about compelling cowards to defend themselves. The lack of a way that is better than the way of the enemy kept us and in part, still keeps us from having sufficient shells. Fear of displeasing our masters the people would be a salutary thing were our masters the people able to decide what is best. But in many a case, our masters are heard singing the good old rollicking song, let us eat (at home) and drink (at the pub) for tomorrow (or sometimes) we die. Life means more than that. It is time that fears were eliminated. It is time that we realized some courage and let the votes and the intrigues of peace times alone. Ah most noble modern God, social and political intrigue, thou dealest urgently with those who serve thee not in the time of peace. Go for a change to the Polar Region or undertake lovingly to hibernate during the present horrible rampage of thy pet offspring of the Rhine. We will all find something to do during the winter to help War to its proper close.

Ever yours
J. Arthur Harley.[416]

Harley used his sermons as propaganda, 'an essential tool during the war and one in which the Church was a willing participant'.[417] With each passing day, the war introduced new and barbarous methods such as chlorine and mustard gas poisoning. Men were no longer willingly reporting to form long queues outside recruiting stations. The stories about the realities of fighting on the Western Front had begun to permeate the myth of fighting for King and Country. Instead, the horrors of the trenches - maggots, flies, rats, hair and body lice, trench foot, acquired from standing in the damp, muddy ground, the decomposing bodies of fellow soldiers strewn around no man's land surrounding the trenches, the loss of 70,000 lives attributed to the Gallipoli fiasco - all contributed to men being reluctant to go into war.

Clergymen were convinced of the righteousness of the British cause and the civic responsibilities they saw as an integral part of the Christian life. There was hardly a bishop or Church dignitary who did not participate in some way in the recruiting drives. Lord Derby, the head of the Parliamentary

---

416 Harley's personal archive.
417 Fielden, p. 42.

Harley in the pulpit at St Leonard's Church. (Private collection)

Recruiting Committee, had requested that the Church encourage recruitment from the pulpit.[418] Pastors and Church leaders used several different recruitment approaches. Pastors trying to motivate parishioners to enlist would often stress duty or equate fighting for England with fighting for Christ. Others railed against cowardice. The Master of St Catharine's College Cambridge said of those who were able to volunteer but would not, 'It is a pity that we cannot brand that sort of man "Made in fear of Germany". Would to God, we had known when they were born that they would eat our bread and grow and live amongst us, trusted and approved, and yet cowards. We need not have prayed and worked for them.'[419] Harley would later return to Shepshed and tried hard to persuade young men to join the colours between screenings of Charlie Chaplin at the Picture Place on Britannia Street.[420]

To counter the recruitment problem, the government introduced the Military Service Act, passed into law on 27 January 1916, to conscript men between eighteen and forty-one. The official position regarding clergy was that they should not take up arms in the military. Ordained ministers were not to enlist and fight in the trenches, a position held throughout the history of the Church of England. However, they could and were encouraged to serve as chaplains and in other non-combatant roles.[421]

Harley, at forty-three, was too old by two years to enlist and prohibited as an ordained man. Undeterred, he decided to serve the Mother Country on the home front and contribute as a munitions worker. At the beginning of December 1916, Harley became the 545th man to complete the preliminary

---

418 Fielden, p. 44.
419 Ibid, p. 44.
420 Russell Fisher, *Soldiers of Shepshed Remembered 1914-1919*, Market Harborough: Matador, 2008, p. 48.
421 Fielden, p. 39.

training in munitions manufacture offered by the University of London, King's College campus, in the Strand, London.[422] The introductory training course had emerged out of the previous year's shell crises. There were sufficient guns to fight with on the Western Front but slow manufacturing of munitions and, incomprehensibly, not enough shells; by mid-1915, guns were restricted to only using four or five shells a day. The War Department looked for ways to increase munitions production and output. David Lloyd George, Chancellor of the Exchequer in the Conservative government, was appointed as minister for the newly created Ministry of Munitions.

One proposal the government put forward was utilizing the Engineering workshops and laboratories of universities to ascertain if they could usefully be employed for war purposes.[423] King's College Principal, Sir Frederick Donaldson, wrote on 16 May 1915 to the Industrial Reserve to suggest the government munitions committee send a representative to inspect the Engineering workshop.[424] The Industrial Reserve told him soon afterwards that King's College workshops could be used for training unskilled or part-skilled men in munitions work. and offered to send suitable volunteers. H. Glaser of Linotype visited the college on 4 June to inspect the workshop and offered some useful suggestions on the type of training.[425] The scheme was approved on 8 June. The college decided, after careful consideration, that it was unwise to attempt the manufacture of munitions and requested plant equipment for the teaching of the course and to utilize the capacity of the

---

422 Munitions preliminary certificate, King's College, 1915, Harley's personal archive.
423 Report on King's College munitions training scheme, Liddell Hart Centre for Military Archives, King's College, University of London.
424 Ibid.
425 Ibid.

National Advisory Committee munitions recruitment poster.
(Library of Congress, Washington DC)

workshop to its fullest.[426] The Industrial Reserve authorized a sum not exceeding £153 for machinery.[427]

The preliminary training scheme would be open to any men, with preference given to those with previous mechanical training or a good education who could be efficient as skilled or part skilled workers. Special classes were held daily (except Saturdays) in the Mechanical Engineering Department to train in the use of the machine and other tools.[428] The workshop contained four screw-cutting lathes, one centring lathe, two drilling machines, one shaping, one plaining, one slotting and one horizon milling machine. There was a fee of two shillings and six pence per week for each class or five shilling per week for two classes.[429] Harley had to provide approved tools, which cost five shillings.[430] Although there was increasing demand in munitions factories for men with preliminary training, such employment was not guaranteed.[431]

Harley may have made the daily commute from Deal to London for the duration of the course, but a more likely scenario is that he stayed in London at the King's College Theological Hostel at 42-43 Mecklenburgh Square. Harley completed 105 hours on 29 December, which included chipping and filling; making limit gauges; use of micrometres and callipers, lathe work: plain turning and finishing; screw cutting V and square threads, and successfully completed the course.[432] Eighteen men went to Shoreditch Training School; four to Twickenham,

---

426 Memo, 14 June 1915, Liddell Hart Centre for Military Archives, King's College, London.
427 Ibid, 24 June 1915.
428 Application form for preliminary training course, 3 September 1915, Liddell Hart Archives.
429 Ibid.
430 Ibid.
431 Ibid.
432 Preliminary munitions training certificate, King's College, London, Harley's personal archive.

one to Allen's Bedford, and three to work elsewhere. Harley was one of the 'elsewhere'.[433]

Harley had been a frequent visitor to Shepshed during the war, returning to deliver sermons and lectures about the German threat.[434] One of the perils he may have warned of became a reality for Loughborough on 31 January 1916, when the town's lights attracted a Zeppelin pilot's attention. The Zeppelin dropped two bombs at the Technical College on Green Close Lane, and two further bombs were dropped at the Herbert Morris steelwork factory in Empress Road, killing ten people. Loughborough did not then have a blackout as did Derby, Nottingham and Leicester.[435]

Harley completed further munitions training at Goldsmiths' College, another campus of London University. What followed is less clearcut, as there are several uncertainties about the subsequent period of Harley's life after his training. It is known is that he did not stay in Deal but returned to Shepshed to start munitions work. Less clear is whether he remained a priest. By the time of his return, the Shepshed Lace Manufacturing factory had been placed at the disposal of the government, and the engineering section turned over to the manufacturing of eighteen-pound high explosive shells.[436] On 6 November 1915, the first delivery of one hundred shells for the British Army was on view at the Roman Catholic School.[437]

Harley worked at the requisitioned factory in Sullington Road, where his small cottage, no. 55, was located. Sullington Road owes its name to the Latin word *solus*, meaning sun, and legend has it that a path, the oldest in England, ran from Sullington Road to a place of worship to the Goddess Solina in

---

433 College Report of December 1916, Liddell Hart Archives, King's College, University of London.
434 Harley's personal archive.
435 *World War One at Home*, Imperial War Museum.
436 *Fifty Years of Lace*, p. 10.
437 Ibid, p. 10.

Charnwood Forest.[438] Harley's cottage was flanked either side by the two unmarried Cooke sisters.[439] Lucy Cooke, the older of the two, aged twenty-nine,[440] was the Head of the Infants Department[441] and Jessie Anne Cooke, twenty-seven, was the Senior Mistress and Deputy Head at Hall Croft Primary School. Jessie had joined the staff of Hall Croft Primary from Church Gate School in Loughborough on 1 March 1920. Harley and Jessie shared a love of Shakespeare, and the three of them also had debates over religion lasting into the small hours of the night.[442] Harley enthralled the sisters with stories about his time at Yale, speaking highly of the college and making Jessie fall in love with Yale as much as with her college.[443] After Josephine's return to America, there is no evidence that Harley entered a relationship with either of the Cooke sisters or another woman, but his friendship with Jessie Cooke lasted for over thirty years. Harley had met her when he was a curate at St Botolph's Church and reconnected when he returned to Shepshed. The depth of feeling and the high regard in which she held Harley suggests a platonic relationship resembling hero-worship.

Harley's job as a munitions worker was challenging, with twelve-hour shifts starting at 6 am with no breaks and only an hour for lunch and to recharge before the afternoon shift began. At forty-three, Harley was a man unafraid of rolling up his sleeves and getting stuck into hard work. Munitions work was

---

438 *In Search of Sheepshead: A Walk around Historic Shepshed*, Shepshed Local History Society, 1985.

439 Oral history related by Michael Wortley, Shepshed local historian.

440 1911 census records.

441 G.H. Mallory, *The First 100 Years: The Founding of the Old Shepshed British School and its Subsequent History. 1875-1975*, www.crbcshepshed.org.uk/britishschool

442 Wortley.

443 Letter to Secretary of Yale alumni from Ms Cooke, November 1943, Yale University alumni records class of 1902 call number 830 Box 199 folder 19.

gruelling and took place in a noisy, dirty and dangerous factory. The noise from the heavy machinery operating day and night and the commands shouted across the factory floor prevented the usually loquacious Harley from engaging in conversation. The production of shells required lifting the seventy-two-pound shell cases,[444] loading them onto the lathe machine which rotated the cases at high speed to shape them, and drilling the top end to fill them with the high explosive of Trinitrotoluene - TNT. Workers responsible for filling the shells suffered the effects of TNT poisoning, which turned their faces, lips, hands and fingers yellow. They became known as canaries, and Harley became a black canary. The use and storage of many explosives at the plant also made it a dangerous place to work. Strict codes had to be adhered to avoid accidental explosions. Metal-tipped shoes could cause sparks, igniting the TNT, and instead clogs had to be worn. Harley had left behind the serenity of the church environment to become an insignificant cog, albeit a trained and well-paid semi-skilled cog, in an enormous wheel working to assist the war effort.

Two years after the U-boat torpedoed the *Lusitania*, the US declared war on Germany. President Woodrow Wilson addressed a special meeting of Congress on 2 April 1917, and four days later signed the declaration which sanctioned the induction of millions of men into the armed forces. The war continued for a further two years. The ceasefire that took place on the eleventh day of the eleventh month at the eleventh hour tentatively signalled the end of the Great War, and the signing of the Versailles Treaty on 28 June 1919 finally marked the end of the conflict. The Great War had lasted fifty-eight months, or four years and ten months or 1,825 days.

Whether counted in days, weeks, months or years, nearly

---

444 First World War Permanent Exhibition, Imperial War Museum, London.

every country was touched by devastating tragedy and horrific losses. Nine million soldiers lost their lives; many more were wounded and there were close to ten million civilian casualties.[445] Of the BWIR 185 were killed in action, and 1,071 had died of sickness. The war had also witnessed the fall of the imperial dynasties of Germany, Austria-Hungary, Russia and the Ottoman Empire; the world had changed forever.

---

445 *WWI: A Complete History of the Great War*, Igloo Books, 2014.

19. The General Strike

'The General Strike has taught the working class more in four days than years of talking could have done.'

Arthur Balfour

England was in turmoil after the Great War. The demography of towns, cities and villages had changed dramatically. African and Asian servicemen from the Diaspora who had answered Kitchener's call settled in the country. The returning service people encountered unemployment, poverty and, in some cases, a new ethnic mix in their communities. The *Liverpool Echo* newspaper described the concentration of black enclaves in Liverpool, South Wales and London as 'distinct foreign colonies', viewed as 'the pollution of a healthy community by undesirables'.[446] The same paper said that the black population of Liverpool had grown by 'leaps and bounds' during the war and estimated it at 4,000 to 5,000.[447] *The Times* reported the blacks were 'largely West Indians' and put their number at about 5,000.[448] The *Daily Express* estimated 2,000.[449] The *South Wales Echo* estimated that in Cardiff there were 1,200 unemployed 'Coloured seamen', including Arabs, Somalis, West Africans and West Indians.[450] In the largest town in Wales there was a population of 'some hundreds of Brazilian negroes, many of whom have been living on unemployment benefit'.[451]

The impact of sizeable black populations and conflict with returning servicemen resulted in race riots in the latter part of

446 *Liverpool Echo*, 6 June 1919.
447 Ibid.
448 *The Times*, 10 June 1919.
449 *Daily Express*, 12 June 1919.
450 *South Wales Echo*, 10 July 1919.
451 *Liverpool Echo*, 12 June 1919.

1919 in Liverpool, Newport, Luton and Cardiff. There was also rising unrest among women who had stepped into the breach to undertake a man's job in industry. They had acquired newfound freedom and demanded that they keep their work and called for the implementation of women's universal suffrage to take place at a faster pace.

After the war, Harley was initially something of a recluse, living day to day in Shepshed and working at the Shepshed Lace Factory. This period of his life remains relatively undocumented. Yet he resurfaced and entered an entirely new phase at the age of forty-four. He became active in local politics as a member of the Labour Party and an organizer of the Loughborough Divisional Labour Party.[452]

Britain faced economic depression; it had incurred significant debts. The coal, shipbuilding and steel industries had all contracted, and one industry facing the post-war fallout was coal mining. One in ten of the male labour force in Britain was employed in the coal industry, making mining the largest and most important industry and the Miners' Federation of Great Britain a significant force in the trade union movement. The outdated industry had failed to modernize; workers were still using pickaxes and machines cut only a fifth of the coal. The mine owners' approach to the problem was not to modernize but have the workers absorb underinvestment through reduced wages and increased working hours. Snibston Colliery near Coalville was Leicestershire's chief coal mine, the town of Coalville built to house the miners. The Snibston Colliery had flourished as recently as 1915, when a second shaft was sunk and named the Stephenson Shaft after Robert Stephenson, who constructed the Leicester and Swannington Railway. Mine owners tried again in 1925 to cut wages and increase hours.

---

452 *Nottingham Evening Post*, 10 June 1926.

The miners' problems escalated further in the same year when on 28 April the government decided to tie the value of the pound to the amount of gold in the Bank of England - a policy known as the Gold Standard; this reduced exports, especially coal. The Gold Standard impacted the production of British coal and prices plummeted with private mine owners introducing pay cuts. In March 1926, Stanley Baldwin's government brokered the Samuel Commission, which recommended closure of uneconomic pits and a 10 per cent cut in wages.[453] Negotiations broke down owing to the refusal of the miners' leaders to commit themselves to the Commission's recommendations in the *Report on the British Coal Industry*.[454] Meetings between the government, mine owners and miners' organizations could reach no compromise, igniting the General Strike. The Trade Union Congress (TUC), the Secretary of Mines (the Right Hon George Richard Lane Fox, a relative of Augustus Lane-Fox Pitt Rivers - founder of the Pitt Rivers Museum), the Chancellor of the Exchequer, Winston Churchill, and members of Baldwin's Cabinet had begun negotiations to avoid the strike.[455] They collapsed after print workers refused to publish an edition of the *Daily Mail* newspaper attacking the miners as a revolutionary movement. The strike went ahead.

On 3 May 1926, the TUC called for the General Strike to begin. On the first full day of action, an estimated one and a half million people came out on strike. To support the coal miners, workers from railways, road transport and docks, people working in the printing, gas, electricity, building, iron, steel and chemical

---

453 Peter Catterall, 'Churchill and the General Strike, 1926', in Richard Toye (ed), *Winston Churchill: Politics, Strategy and Statecraft*, London: Bloomsbury, 2017.

454 Minutes of the Cabinet meeting, 2 May 1926, Cabinet\23\52 National Archives.

455 Minutes of the Cabinet meeting, 14 July 1926 Cabinet\23\52 National Archives.

industries all stayed off work. Over the following two days, one million coal miners had been locked out of their mines.

The coal strike caused considerable hardship and suffering in the districts around Shepshed. Factories were on short time, and the quarry was closed for an extended period.[456] Harley turned his attention to the coal miners, their families' campaigning and fundraising by producing and selling one penny poems. One such poem read:

A Winter's Soul poem for coal miners

Hush! There's a hungry babe asleep
In the cot at home in Orton Cole;
Soft let me sink into the deep:
Jesus, mercy on a miner's soul.

I dream this night. It would be my last:
That dread, immortal drums would roll:
My lamp of life seems fading fast:
Jesus, mercy on a miners' soul.

Dear Mother, sister, wife and child,
Our name are written on the scroll.
Wormwood and gall! I am pit-beguiled
Jesus, mercy on a miner's soul.

Coal-dust to dust, my soul is white:
My manhood gleaming as the pole
Help mates! Disaster! Endless night!
God have mercy on a miner's soul.

Shepshed June 1926

---

456 Henry Freeman, *The Shepshed Almanac for the Year 1927*. Freeman Press, 1927.

The proceeds went to the aid of Leicestershire coal miners' children.[457]

The distress experienced by Shepshed miners had been partially relieved by money raised by donations, collections and concerts, including Harley's efforts in selling his poetry, but his token penny poems could not contribute sufficient funds. The strike had bought many to their knees, including those who had fought for King and Country. Harley accompanied forty miners to the Loughborough workhouse to advocate and apply for aid. Grown men, humbled by their circumstances, were met by disdain and disgust from Board members. 'Five shillings dispensed, not the usual ten shillings earned - sixpence for each child.' The Chairman reportedly relished his closing remarks; the money had to be paid back as it was only a loan. One member of the Board left the meeting as a protest against granting the same amount of aid to each family member irrespective of the number of children.[458]

The strike was halted nine days after it began; not a single concession was made to the miners. The end of November signalled the return of most miners to the pits, working longer hours for less pay; others remained unemployed for many years. A year later, Baldwin's government passed the 1927 Trades Disputes Act, which banned sympathy strikes and mass picketing.

---

457 Harley's personal archive.
458 *Nottingham Evening Post*, 10 June 1926.

20. The Stormy Petrel

'Between the clouds and the sea proudly soars the stormy petrel, as a streak of black lightning.'
Maxim Gorky, 'Song of the Stormy Petrel', 1901

Harley stood as an independent councillor for Shepshed after his brief association with the Labour Party. There is no evidence as to why he left the Labour Party, but it is fair to assume that his strong sense of self-importance ruled out what he would have seen as capitulating to others. The party machinery constraining him to operate within the confines of a hierarchal system and curtailing his activities may well have been the reason for his departure. Harley would have autonomy as an independent councillor; he did not need to answer to anyone for his behaviour. Conversely, Harley could see that as long as he remained in the Labour Party he would never be nominated to stand as a councillor.

Harley in top hat and tailcoat, date unknown. (Private collection)

Harley's extensive education encompassing his qualification as a lawyer, his talents as an orator, his role as a priest, his practical experiences of working in the slums of Washington, Boston and London, his deep-rooted commitment to social justice and his ability to connect and communicate with a range of people, from the crème de la crème to the lower echelons of society, were all skills which made him an ideal candidate to implement real change. Another motivating factor that may have influenced Harley's political intentions was his significant time in America. The country had actively sought and engaged in methods to deny the black population their right to vote. The Fifteenth Amendment was adopted in 1870 and in theory guaranteed protection from racial discrimination for all African Americans, even if the Amendment only extended to men. Yet methods were still employed to prevent black political participation ranging from disenfranchisement, secret ballots, literacy and understanding tests, the so-called Grandfather Clause to violence and intimidation. The secret ballot was a process whereby the voter's privacy was protected to avoid intimidation at the polls, but secret ballots operated as literacy tests, requiring voters to choose from the numerous names and offices printed on the official ballot, a task many blacks and poor whites could not perform. The literacy and understanding tests applied to an applicant understanding any section of the state constitution read to them or giving a reasonable interpretation. The Grandfather Clause, which Harley's father-in-law had campaigned against, required an applicant's grandfather to have a property in the state they wanted to vote in. These methods denied registration to many blacks and were factors which may have contributed to Harley's decision to formalize his commitment to local politics in England.

In 1927, Baldwin's government was still in power, with opposition from Ramsay MacDonald's Labour Party and David Lloyd George leading the Liberal Party. Harley had now lived in Shepshed for eight years and quickly met the residency qualification of residing in the district for twelve months before the election. He was elected for three years as an Independent to the Shepshed Urban District Council on Saturday 2 April 1927, polling 1,003 out of the 1,962 votes cast.[459]

Shepshed had first been constituted as an Urban Sanitary District Council in 1887, when the first election of nine representatives to serve on the Board occurred.[460] In December 1894, the local Board ceased to exist and the Local Government Act created Urban District Councils with responsibilities for council housing and repairs, refuse collections, street cleaning, parks and planning. The Urban District Council membership was increased to twelve representatives. Rev Hepworth, the Vicar of St Botolph's Church, where Harley held his first curacy, failed twice to be elected to the Council in 1894 and 1896.[461]

Harley was elected with the following councillors: Frederick Clench (Labour), Charles Grain (Labour) and John Lacey (Liberal). Harley's fellow councillors were William Martin, Chairman, who also served as a Justice of the Peace during his tenure. The Vice-Chairman was George William Blood, a Conservative and construction business owner. Roland George Heyward was a Methodist. William Pallett, a Conservative, retired the previous year after twenty-six years of service as assistant master at the Church of England Schools.[462] Ambrose King had served with the Royal Engineers,[463] John Gilbert

---

459 Freeman, *Shepshed Almanac for the Year 1927*.
460 Henry Freeman, *The Shepshed Almanac for the Year 1915*, Freeman Press 1915.
461 Ibid.
462 Freeman, *Shepshed Almanac for the Year 1927*.
463 Fisher, p. 21.

Foston, a shopkeeper in Field Road, was Inspector of Nuisances - a position created to address public health issues (known as nuisances) that were in breach of the law, i.e., inadequate sanitary conditions, smells, privies, gutters, refuse heaps etc. To ensure houses with smallpox were sanitized, the Inspector of Nuisances also distributed disinfectants. Foston held the position for twenty-five years[464] and was also Chairman of the Lambert Charity, of which the Rev Hepworth was a trustee. Michael Smith, the committee clerk, had a background as a commercial clerk with previous experience as a grocer, draper and manager of the Cooperative department store. As an accountant, he was appointed clerk to Shepshed Urban District Council in 1903.[465] The Council met every month on a Tuesday night at The Town Hall.

The ramifications of the General Strike of 1926 were still evident, felt and absorbed by communities the length and breadth of the country. Shepshed experienced a high unemployment rate among men. The Council debated steps to attract new industries. The community expected tangible solutions, but there was no visible evidence that the Council was addressing the problem. The Chairman noted that there was sufficient work in the brickyards for twenty years, that the area had good clay, and that a brickyard could start employing three hundred men.[466] The Trades and Extension Committee had spent three months trying to lure new businesses to Shepshed. *The Loughborough Monitor and Herald* newspaper had begun to question what was taking so long in bringing new industries to Shepshed. Harley crafted how he would operate as a local councillor with transparency, constantly trying to provide

---

464 'One Hundred Years Ago 1913', St Winefride's Voice parish newsletter o. 5, Spring 2013.

465 David Stevenson, 'Written in Stone', www.mywesleyanmethodists.org.uk.

466 *Loughborough Monitor and Herald*, 28 July 1927.

answers to questions unwelcomed by his fellow councillors. He agreed with the newspaper, stating that:

> The Council had turned away factory after factory and I was told I had an axe to grind.[467] I complained about contractors claiming for 'extra' over their contract price and asked that such charges be brought before the entire Council. I endeavoured to speak again but was ruled out of order, and the matter dropped.[468]

Harley was appointed to the Trades and Extension Committee sub-committee with Councillors Blood and Martin.[469] His tenure on the Council henceforth became a constant battle with his fellow councillors, questioning their motives. Harley remarked:

> I noted that when a man had been on the Council for some years and then came along and offered Shepshed something, the people of Shepshed would ask why. It was most indecorous when a man standing for the Council should be approached in the street and told he was going on the Council for what he could get out of it.

Harley's verbal assault on the Council continued, and he popularized the phrase hush-hush policy[470] when a housing report submitted to the Council was going to be dealt with by the Council in Committee: 'I protested that were we ever going to be finished with this hush-hush policy?' Harley informed the other councillors that he was not only a councillor, but a journalist and proprietor of a newspaper that was going to be published in Shepshed that week. His verbal assault concluded:

---

467 Ibid.
468 *Monitor and Herald*, 29 September 1927.
469 *Shepshed Bulletin*, 28 September 1927.
470 Letter to Yale University from Jessie Cooke, Yale alumni records.

'You could stop the Loughborough Press, but from tonight, the hush-hush policy has got to end while I am a Councillor.'[471]

Harley now had a new tool with which to berate and belittle his fellow councillors. His first article in the *Shepshed Bulletin*, of which he was editor, reporter, printer and publisher, began:

> Are you a ratepayer? What do you think about the rotten rise in rates? Fair play requires knowing what improvements are about to follow - if none, why more money? Call a halt, get to know the inner working of the rate-machinery. How? The words on this page are a man you know will carry them out against the very gates of Babylon. In the hush-hush chamber where the predatory rates semi-annually overdose with sinister extract of yeast. Not for the misuse or abuse, but I come for your use. Use me, read the editorial articles. Hitherto the newspaper world has pulverised Shepshed by its compressed contempt. We in this disported little town have eaten humble pie for years, crawled in the dust, gone cap in hand, and stood shivering on the doorstep of Loughborough, Leicester, Nottingham, and even Coalville, if we remonstrated, surplus crumbs have been our lot. What I have printed I have printed.[472]

Harley's four-page newssheet, published in a ramshackle workshop at the back of his house, caused a sensation and fanned the flames of contempt, irritation and anger, exacerbating an already volatile relationship between him and his fellow councillors. He urged residents to shop locally, his newssheet carrying advertisements from local suppliers: H Danvers, for hand-sewn boots; Arthur Elliot's newsagents and stationery

---

471 *Monitor and Herald*, 12 January 1928.
472 'Shepshed Tells the World of Parson's Venture into Journalism', *Leicester Mercury*, 25 January 1928.

in Charnwood Road; John Gough newsagent in Field Street; petrol at Messrs Elliott, Haywood, Potter and Woolley; and J. Dainty, bakery, by penning this little ditty.

> Shop in a Shepshed shop; that's the style.
> Half-way to Loughhbro' stop, pause awhile
> Get out the red flip-flop
> Turn back - Shop in a Shepshed shop.
>
> Shop in a Shepshed shop, hold the fort
> Why help put Lough'bro on top?
> BE A SPORT.
> Cut out every red flip-flop.
>
> TURN BACK, Shop in a Shepshed shop
> Shop in a Shepshed shop; Summer's near.
> Give our Own shops a drop of Summer CHEER.
> How? Getting out of the beetroot flop.
> Summer shopping in a Shepshed shop.[473]

The newssheet was distributed for free at first, then later had a name change to the *Charnwood Bulletin* and a charge of one penny implemented.

Harley alleged corruption and moved that the Chairman's son resign his position on the Council. Mr Martin, the Chairman, stated there was no reason why his son should resign. With no seconder, the resolution fell through.[474] In the latter part of 1927, electric cables were laid in the streets by the Leicester and Warwickshire Electric Power Co for the supply of electricity to the public; Harley turned on the current on 15 November.[475]

---

473 *Charnwood Bulletin*, 27 April 1929, Harley's personal archive.
474 *Shepshed Bulletin*, 28 October 1927.
475 Freeman, *Shepshed Almanac for the Year 1927*.

The *Charnwood Bulletin*, written and published by Harley.
(Private collection)

Looking beyond the Urban District Council, Harley now stood as an Independent in the Leicestershire County Council elections on 3 March 1928, in opposition to the sitting Conservative member, C.G. Harriman.[476] Harley called a meeting in support of his candidature at the local school, but despite his efforts he could not get anyone to advertise his meeting. He went to the town crier in Shepshed, who told him he was ill. He drove to Loughborough, Kegworth and Hathern. At Hathern, there were two criers, but one was sick and the other blind. Nowhere could he get a town crier to advertise his meeting.

The result from the election was declared as follows:

Carlton Goodall Harriman polled 1,127
James Arthur Harley 1,104[477]

Harriman had spent a total of £18,19s 6d on his campaign compared to Harley's £3 16s 10d.[478] Harley requested a recount of the Shepshed Division, but without success. He had failed to become a County Councillor but was re-elected to the District Council.[479]

Harley continued to have several run-ins with his fellow Councillors over their handling of the Council finances and what he alleged was underhand dealing. He told them that the gravel used to grit the roads during heavy snowfall left a mixture of lemonpeel, rags and bones on the road and was not giving the ratepayers what they had paid for. He also requested that reports should no longer be pushed under Councillors' noses when they arrived for committee meetings, but that the various committees should compile the reports and send

---

476 *Leicester Mercury*, 23 February 1928.
477 *Leicester Mercury*, 5 March 1928.
478 *Leicester Mercury* 17 April 1928.
479 Henry Freeman, *The Shepshed Almanac for the Year 1928*, Freeman Press 1928.

them out in advance.[480] Harley even invited the public to come and hear what he termed the cuckoo chorus, councillors in session. The Council Chambers were crowded for the first time when nearly a hundred ratepayers experienced lively but brief entertainment. Frederick Clench denounced the tactics of 'the Rev Gentleman', expressing a desire to foster a better understanding between councillors and officials and stating complete confidence in the Council officials without exception. Clench said every Council member must know they had been insulted. Could they imagine anything more disparaging? He stated that Harley referred to him as 'Billy Clench'. 'For 46 years, his name had been Frederick.' Mr Harley had no right to call him 'Billy' and the town clerk 'Mike' or the Chairman of the Highways Committee 'Jack'. John Lacey, Chairman of the Highways Committee, said he had never seen a man he had not tried to understand and work with. He had tried to understand Harley, but when he 'talked nicely to them at the Council and published in his paper things directly opposite', he could not understand him.[481]

Harley related the events of the final meeting of the Urban District Council on 11 April 1928.

I seconded D.R Griffin's motion of thanks to the retiring members, Mr Martin and Mr Pallett. In seconding the motion, I said that there comes a time in the life of all when men have to hear criticism against themselves. No man can come here and do all that is right. I seconded this resolution as a man and a gentleman. Mr Pallett said that he was sorry that I had seconded this resolution. The speaker said that there always has to be a funny man in a show, whether he be a clown

480 *Leicester Mail*, 15 February 1928.
481 *Leicester Mercury*, 21 January 1928.

or a Black man, and pointing to me, there he sits. He continued I should like to thank all the members of the Council but the Reverend Mr Harley. Mr Martin said, 'Like Mr Pallett, no one regrets more than I do that the Reverend Mr Harley has seconded this resolution. His heart and tongue do not agree. No man has been abused or criticised more than I have, both in the Council Chambers and in the *Shepshed Bulletin*. At every opportunity, he has tried to plant his feet in the humble stomach of the working man. Everybody in Shepshed knows me, but not many know him. After I have taken myself from public life, I publicly give warning; if he continues to use my name and insult me in his dirty 'rag', he will have to put up with the consequences. I should like to thank all the members of the Council but the Reverend Mr Harley.[482]

Harley had certainly polarized opinion with his continual attacks in the Council Chambers and in the *Charnwood Bulletin*. The *Leicester Mail* newspaper proffered a few plain words to him:

Either through a quite excusable lack of knowledge or an easily understood lack of interest, the good people of Shepshed are not happy in possession of a particular species of bee that has found a tendency in the bonnet of Rev. J. Harley. Still, they have had frequent occasions to observe an extraordinarily eccentric and particularly truculent specimen. Wherever two or three are gathered to discuss public affairs, there the Rev Harley is sure to be observed giving all and sundry the benefit of his advice and applying to them the stimulant of his caustic

---

482 'A little plain-speaking', *Leicester Mercury*, 12 April 1928.

remarks. Not satisfied with these oral efforts, or perhaps a lack of attention on the part of his hearers, the Rev Harley has dropped into print much as Silas Wegg used to drop into pottery. For this purpose, he edits and publishes a paper called the *Shepshed Bulletin*, and in it, he tells readers just how sick Shepshed is, and into what a chronic condition of ill health the public life of the town has fallen. We do not enjoy the advantages of being regular subscribers to the paper but guardians of the public interest in Shepshed and district. We may yet be under the necessity of doing so. The publication is candid without being informative, amusing without being elevating. In it, the Rev Harley has a way of licking all and sundry with the rough side of his tongue and to this end has given nicknames to several gentlemen engaged in public affairs. As a minister, the Rev is frequently called upon to perform the duty of christening infants, but we have yet to learn that this carries the right or privilege to re-christen grown men. At all events, the people pilloried are not overloading his letterbox with letters of thanks for his rather too personal interest on their behalf. Under the influence of that class of communication that corrupts good manners, there are those in Shepshed who are disposed to give an Oliver for each of the Reverend gentleman's Rolands, and to this end, have re-christened the *Shepshed Bulletin*, the Rag. Long experience in journalism has made us familiar with the old gibe, but the Rev Harley appears to encounter it rather early in his journalism efforts. We offer the Rev Harley the sympathy of a professional practitioner to an aspiring amateur on this score. And out of our larger experience, we might venture a little advice too.

In the first place, then, in the cause of Shepshed, whose interest we quite frankly believe the Rev Harley is out to promote, it would be well if he banishes the bees that buzz so disconcertingly around his bonnet. People thus afflicted are as fire among stubble when they think it fit to drop into print. That some of the members of the Shepshed Council hold this view is evident in what occurs at the meeting. If things continue as they are, Shepshed is likely to become comicalities in public life. The Rev Harley may be quite right in his view that Shepshed requires rousing, but to be roused is one thing and to be unceremoniously ruffled is another. To go out to rouse is but to embark on the laudable take of awakening a dormant interest and quickening a latent enthusiasm. But to go out to ruffle unceremoniously is but to create and invite opposition, and that, we suggest, is what the Rev Harley is doing in Shepshed.[483]

The reporting of Council affairs was not limited to Shepshed and the greater Leicestershire area; local newspapers in the surrounding areas of Derbyshire and Nottingham also carried the Council reports. Harley's antics and constant questioning of his fellow councillors led to the awarding of the moniker the 'Stormy Petrel' to him by the *Leicester Mercury* newspaper.

There are two mythologies associated with the stormy petrel, with its sooty black plumage and a white rump:

1. A holy bird, named after the Apostle, St Peter the fisherman, for what appears to be its ability to walk on water (St Peter had 'walked' on the water to meet Jesus).

2. As a harbinger of doom, the reincarnation of sailors poorly treated by their captain. The sighting of a stormy petrel at sea indicated a storm would follow shortly.

---

483 'A few plain words to the Rev Harley', *Leicester Mail*, 26 June 1928.

This nickname was undoubtedly used as a device to draw readers to the otherwise dull and tedious reporting of Council meetings and their proceedings. The label had an additional significance - a metaphor to illustrate a person who has extreme views. Readers could follow the latest instalment of the Stormy Petrel's outbursts in the form of proposed resolutions, requests for information, demands for clarity on information and reports that might succumb to what he referred to as the hush-hush policy. Harley himself may not have interpreted the moniker as an insult but identified with the notion of a holy bird able to walk on water and with the words of the Russian Maxim Gorky's 1901 poem, 'Song of the Stormy Petrel'.

> The stormy petrel soars with a scream, a streak of black lightning, as an arrow pierces the clouds, on wing-tip slicing the wave froth.
>
> See him hover, like a demon - proud, the black demon of the storm - he laughs, and cries ... he laughs atop the clouds, he cries with joy!
>
> In the froth of anger - clever demon, - he has long heard weariness, he knows that the clouds will not cut the sun - no, the sun will triumph!
>
> The wind roars ... Thunder rumbles ...[484]

Harley may have seen himself as the streak of black lightning in his crusading mission to preach the Gospel and make Shepshed a better place.

Despite the attacks on him in the local press and the Stormy Petrel label, Harley recognized his privileged position and as such was determined to represent the people of Shepshed; he had earned his position, there was a reason he was elected, and he had a duty and responsibility to assist the electorate to the

---

484 M Gorky, Selected Short Stories, Progress Publishers, Maxim Gorky Internet Archive, www.marxists.org, 2002.

best of his ability and talents. His no-nonsense, if abrasive, approach may have found some favour with the townspeople. Still, his fellow Councillors by now resented him, his rhetoric and his newspaper, used at every opportunity to berate and belittle them. He had started to become intolerable, but, more importantly, his constant questioning of Council policy made inroads with the community. Harley continued his onslaught, despite ridicule in the press, mockery and even threats from his fellow Councillors of legal action.

His experiences and clerical training had equipped him with first-hand experience of the working-class poor and the soul-destroying nature of the cycle of poverty upon its victims. Still viewed by some as a ridiculous, bespectacled little man, Harley had now acquired the power to effect change; and he made sure that he did not abuse the trust and opportunity he had. The people of Shepshed may not have known it or fully appreciated his efforts, but his zealous campaigning on their behalf continued. He proposed many resolutions to elicit transparency. He gave notice to move resolutions in the following terms:

> Not to elect as councillors those who work for trade with the Council, in view of the unfair completion, undue influence, sly bribery, and insidious corruption, thereby tainting the atmosphere of so many local government bodies in nearly every nook and cranny in England. That this Council call upon any Councillor, who works for or trades with the Council at any time to ignore the disgraceful practice of the present: to remember the excellence custom of the past, and to resign his office of Councillor in common honesty rather than remain on the Council to grab all he can for himself while in office, by his office, and through his office surreptitiously.

It was, of course, outrageous and slanderous. Surrounded by a sea of white faces, by powerful local people with influence and long-held positions, Harley dared to confront and accuse them of back handers and corruption, and insist they resign forthwith. The Chairman, Mr Blood, invoked standing orders, which empowered him, if he considered any motion of business brought for the transaction to be of objectionable character, to ask the members, without any discussion, whether they should proceed with the matter. The Council expressed itself as unwilling to proceed further with the motion.[485]

Harley's gung-ho attitude overstepped the mark on more than one occasion. For a breach of standing orders in an alleged violation of confidence in reporting the committee's business in his *Charnwood Bulletin*, he was suspended from the Council and instructed that he would have to give a resolution in writing before being reinstated. Harley attended the next Council meeting and took his usual place. Asked by the Chairman if he had given his undertaking to keep the standing orders, Harley informed him he would abide by the rules while he was there. Several of his fellow Councillors told Harley that his resolution had to be in writing, and he had no right to be at the meeting and was asked to retire. Harley refused, claiming that the apology had not been requested in writing, and that the amendment was added to the minutes afterwards because they were all in a clique. He refused to retire; the Councillors then sent for a policeman to remove him from the meeting. Harley strode towards the door. The mover of the resolution Mr King said: 'I am A King and an Englishman'. Harley retorted, 'A what! A mudbug'.[486]

---

485 'Council Chairman forestalls Rev Harley', Monitor and Herald, 13 September 1928.
486 'Rev Harley walks out, someone goes for a policeman', *Monitor and Herald*, 12 December 1928.

Harley's one-line handwritten apology on the back of a visiting card delivered to the home of Mr Nelson, the Chairman, read simply, 'I undertake to carry out the standing orders of the Council'. An amendment was moved that Harley be reinstated, subject to the proviso that he should be suspended at any time he failed to keep within standing orders.[487]

Harley stood a third time as an Independent for the Leicestershire County Council elections in 1934. He managed his campaign, writing and producing copy for his election posters and had them printed by the Freeman Press in Market Place. The Freeman Press was run by Henry Freeman, born in Birmingham in 1857; at thirty-one, he established his printers and stationery business in Shepshed. Harley and Freeman's paths had crossed earlier; the latter held the office of Sunday School Superintendent and churchwarden at St Botolph's Church, site of Harley's first curacy.[488] Harley's central campaign theme was the wasting and frittering away of the electorate's taxes by the Council. His campaign material consisted of posters in garish colours to catch the voters' attention. His forthright rhetoric and commentary left no room for any misunderstanding. One of Harley's bright red A3 posters trumpeted five points to the electorate:

1. For 46 Years you have gone and voted for man after man

2. When they got into the Council, they joined the clique

3. They have ignored You: they have defied You

4. They have made your hard-earned money fly

5. They have for generations kept you in the dark

---

487 'The Rev. J.A. Harley Apologises', *Monitor and Herald*, 28 February 1929.
488 Freeman, *Shepshed Almanac*.

Now here is your chance. Think for yourself and cast your one and only vote for Councillor HARLEY
The Man, who lets you know.
The one and only Man you can rely on to let you know.

His posters communicated directly to voters, informing them of the state of his health, how the Council was undermining him and taking credit for his ideas and suggestions.

Councillor Harley says:

An attack of influenza has prevented me from visiting you this Election.

See how your money was squandered during only a few of those boasted 22 years: IN HUNDREDS: Bowley £20 Freeman £10, Randon £245-8'footpath £528-2-8 IN THOUSANDS: £350 for.... £450 for.... £1,000 for ... Councillor Harley stopped this.

Come to my Public Meeting in the Council Schools at 7 o'clock on Friday Night, February 23rd, and I will explain those shocking figures.
One Councillor said lately that Mr Harley asks questions publicly to get in the newspapers **the very things the other councillors don't want divulged RIGHT – VOTE FOR HARLEY!**

When I suggest, they refuse. then they do it later. Look: 1. White lines; 2. Public Seats; 3. Bull Ring Clock; 4. Carr Lane Baths last summer; 5. Recreation Ground; 6. The De-urbanisation Petition.
Vote for Harley—he never called his motor car a third-class railway.[489]

---

489 Election poster 1934, Harley's personal archive

Be sure to be one of the 1500 Voters who will roll up and give their ONE and only ONE VOTE to Councillor Harley.
The one and Only Man who lets you know!
The Made-to-Measure Man of the moment
For the whole town!

This is the independent candidate speaking
Imagine Saturday morning, March 3
Are you undecided or unwilling to vote?
Vote for Harley
Listen to the news
Charley calling, Shepshed calling All Leicester calling
If never again, if never before, come out to vote
Be a sport, ride or walk, Cars are public; Ballot is secret.
Vote for Harley[490]

To the 109 electors of the parish of Charley
Vote for Harley

Perhaps because of your small numbers, no county councillor has ever paid you the compliment of acknowledging your identity as a separate parish in the Shepshed Electoral Division.
It is not the number but the civic duty that matter.
If you elect me, I will conscientiously keep in touch with you, and equally with those of Shepshed, look after the best interest of Charley.
Vote for Harley.

In the end, Harley was defeated at the polls in the County Council elections but retained his seat on the District Council.

---

490 Election posters, Harley's personal archive.

Ten years after the Great War, Shepshed, like many towns and cities, was still experiencing social ills. The worldwide recession had a grip on the country, and nearly two million people were suffering from unemployment, poverty and destitution. Decent housing had become an issue throughout the nation: unaffordable rents, overcrowding and poor sanitation all contributed to people living in squalid conditions: Shepshed was no different. In one case drawn to the Council's attention, a bed stood on the landing where a fourteen-year-old girl slept alongside her two brothers aged nine and thirteen. The father, mother and two children, aged five and seven, and a baby slept in the other room.[491] Harley asked:

> What was going to be done in the matter, as the medical officer, Dr Bell, had been made aware of the facts years ago and that they could not allow such an abominable state of affairs to continue. Sanitation was dreadful. When I complained about the dumping of night soil in a hole in the town on behalf of one of my constituents and that the practice had to stop because the town had enough smallpox, Mr Nelson protested my abominable statements made in open Council and the matter should have been reported to the Chairman.

He continued:

> The Housing Committee ought to get together and see what could be done. Some time ago, I had moved the fixing of the rent at eleven shillings and sixpence because no one else in the Housing Committee would do so, and I was promised that rents would be reduced in a year's time. The Chairman pointed out that the Council had the recommendation to reduce the rents

---

491 *Nottingham Evening Post*, 29 June 1932.

by sixpence. They all agreed that the Council housing rents were too high for working men to pay. I termed it disgraceful to have houses for working men at such high rentals as were charged.[492]

The housing issue continued to plague tenants enduring slum conditions throughout the country; millions relied on poor law relief, paid for by local ratepayers. Ramsay MacDonald's National Government, dominated by eleven Conservatives out of twenty Cabinet members, implemented a process to support unemployment from national taxation. The Unemployment Act of 1934 introduced the intrusive scrutiny of the means tests subjecting poor people to further pressure when already struggling to survive.

Shepshed tenants were in dispute with the Council, rebelling against new housing legislation and the high rents introduced in 1934. At a large gathering of the tenants, Harley commented that the new housing law had put 'the tenants in the cart and the members of the Urban Council in the donkey cart'. As Chairman of the Housing Committee, he visited seventy-two residents with a joiner to ascertain what repairs they required. Harley's incisive action led to a heated debate at the Council meeting. Any repairs necessary on any housing estates required a tender. Mr Nelson observed that his action of going around asking what repairs were needed was a dangerous one. Mr Grain stated he had never known a chairman to take a tradesman around with him. All repairs had to wait until the expenditure amounted to £5. Harley had gone against the rule. He replied that as long as he was Chairman of the Housing Committee he would examine the houses, seeing what was required. The old rule respecting £5 had not been broken and he concluded he had done nothing that had not been done before. The

---

492 *Nottingham Evening Post*, 28 September 1932.

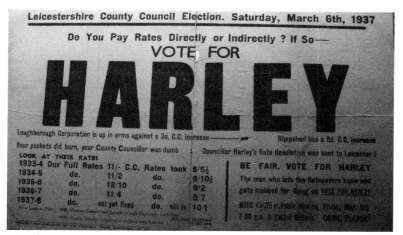

Harley's Leicestershire County Council election campaign poster, 1937.
(Private collection)

accusation 'was an abominable one'.[493] The outrage expressed by the other Councillors may have concealed a subtext. Harley had previous alluded to Councillors receiving undue favour in receiving contracts.

Harley's behaviour, perceived provocations and occasional disregard for Council rules did not alienate all his fellow Councillors; he had built political allies. Harley had brought his unorthodox style to his appointment as Chairman of the Housing Committee in 1934. He stood once again as an Independent candidate for Leicestershire County Council. Once more, his campaign was centred around the squandering of ratepayer monies, the focus reflected in his campaign literature.

> Do you pay rates Directly or Indirectly? If So, Vote for Harley. Loughborough Corporation is up in arms against a 3d C.C. increase. Shepshed has a 6d C.C. increase. Your pockets did burn, your County Councillor was dumb. Look at these rates

---

493 *Nottingham Evening Post*, October 1934.

1933-34 Our full rates 11/- C.C. Rates took 8/5½
1934-35   do.   11/2   do.   8/10
1935-36   do.   12/10   do.   9/2
1936-37   do.   13/4   do.   9/7
1937-38   do.   not yet fixed will be 10/1

Councillor Harley's rate resolution was sent to Leicester! Be fair vote for Harley. The man who lets the Ratepayers know and gets mobbed for doing so.

Said a friend to me, best of luck, Mr Harley. I thanked him then, and I thank you. Now to vote for HARLEY.

The man who dares fight the rate snatchers and the man who dares let you know.

Thanks to 693 voters last time.

Then came the result:

County of Leicester
Election of a County Councillor
For the Shepshed Electoral Division

I, the undersigned, DO HEREBY DECLARE that JAMES ARTHUR HARLEY.

Of 55 Sullington Road, Shepshed, Gentleman has been duly elected as a County Councillor for the said Electoral Division at the Election held on the 6th day of March, 1937.

State of the poll
Harley, James Arthur 886
Nelson, Charles Herbert 774

Given under my hand this 8th day of March 1937
County offices

Grey Friars
Leicester.
Lucas E. Rumsey
Returning Officer.

Thirteen months later, on 19 April 1938, William Wortley (Michael's father), a teacher and bookkeeper,[494] was elected to the Shepshed Urban District Council and voted in as Chairman of the Council for the ensuing year.[495] Harley was proposed and seconded to be appointed Vice-Chairman by Councillors Smith and Deacon. However, Mr Lacey moved an amendment to appoint Mr Martin as Vice-Chair. Seven votes to five carried the amendment.[496] Harley failed to be appointed Vice-Chair again the following year. Proposed by the same councillors, Harley was again scuppered by Mr Lacey, who proposed Mr Gough for the position. Five votes to three carried the motion.[497]

Harley had served eleven years on the Council, but his fellow Councillors ensured that his vice-chair appointment was blocked. Already seen as a controversial figure, his becoming Vice-Chairman of the Council was unacceptable to them. The position would further embolden what they saw as his inflated ego and grant him too much power and access to sensitive information. Harley was tolerated but not accepted, unlike William Wortley, who was appointed Chairman in his first year.

Harley, meanwhile, could see the unmistakable signs of war again. The unrest, invasions everywhere: first Austria, Czechoslovakia, then Hitler's forces marched right into Poland. On 3 September 1939, war with Germany began.

---

494 Freeman, *Shepshed Almanac for the Year 1922*.
495 Shepshed Urban District Council minutes, 19 April 1938, Leicestershire Record Office.
496 Ibid.
497 Shepshed Urban District Council minutes, 18 April 1939, Leicestershire Record Office.

Harley had suffered a seizure at the age sixty-four, but his poor health did not slow him down. Food, clothes, camp beds, homes for hundreds of bombed-out children all had to be found in his role as a member of the Billeting Committee. Shepshed was a reception area for the cities of London, Sheffield and Coventry. Parents followed children, and there were no houses to put them. He requisitioned empty halls and sourced beds, cooking utensils, blankets, sanitary arrangements. A member of the food control committee, he dealt with distribution, complaints, offences and prosecution when necessary.

Harley's time was taken up by his administrative work, attending committee meetings sixteen miles away several times a week. In addition to his wartime role, he was a member of the Education Committee, the Roads and Bridges Committee, the Public Assistance Committee and was a Governor of Loughborough College.[498]

The strenuous work of being a Councillor and his total commitment eventually took a toll upon his failing health. Harley suffered a second heart attack, curtailing his Council activities for 1942. The Chairman welcomed him back to the meeting of 26 January 1943.[499] Harley suffered a third heart attack on 12 May 1943; he died at home, three days shy of his seventieth birthday. The Stormy Petrel's song would no longer be heard in the Council chambers of Leicestershire.

*

Harley was buried on 15 May 1943 at the Oaks-in-Charnwood cemetery on his seventieth birthday. His granite headstone

---

498 Jessie Cooke to Yale University, 1943, Yale University Archives.
499 Shepshed Urban District Council minutes, 1943, Leicestershire Record Office.

The grave and headstone of James Arthur Harley, Oaks-in-Charnwood Cemetery. (Private collection)

indicates his many qualifications - Diploma Anthropology (Oxon), BA Harvard (Dist), MA Oxon - in raised black letters. As in life and replicated in death, his grave is towards the front of the cemetery.

The *Leicester Mercury* obituary tribute to Harley read:

Death of the Rev J.A. Harley

One of the most prominent figures in Shepshed public life for the past 15 years, the Rev. James Arthur Harley, died at home, Sullington Road, Shepshed, on Tuesday, at the age of 69. His death created a vacancy on Shepshed Urban Council and Leicestershire County Council. The Rev. J.A. Harley was first associated with Shepshed in 1909 when he was appointed curate at Shepshed Parish Church. He left in the following year to take up an appointment at Deal.

He returned to Shepshed about 1924, and after living a life of comparative seclusion for two or three years suddenly took an active interest in the political life of the town. He was elected as a Labour member of Shepshed Urban Council in 1927 and soon became well known for his outspokenness and strong criticisms.

Defeated at the polls in 1930, the Rev. Harley regained his seat as an independent member two years later and held it until his death. In the early stages of his Council career, he caused a mild sensation by publishing his newspaper, which he called 'Shepshed and Charnwood' Bulletin. The paper, which was printed at his home, consisted of a single news sheet, and the reading matter was largely composed of criticism of the Council and his views on local current affairs.

Organised petition

During the greater part of this Council career, the Rev. Harley adopted a strong individualistic attitude, as a result, found himself, at some time or other, at variance with most of his fellow councillors.

He was twice suspended for failling to submit to the ruling of the Chairman. He had, however, always the interest of the town and the welfare of it citizens at heart, and when Shepshed was threatened with de-urbanisation, he organised and carried out, at his expense, a petition of the whole town against this taking place.

A great scholar, the Rev. Harley's knowledge was at the disposal of anyone who cared to consult him, and many young Shepshed young people, with scholastic ambitions, had greatly benefited from his tuition. In 1937 the Rev. Harley created another surprise in local political circles by defeating Mr C.H. Nelson, the retiring member at Leicestershire County Council elections, and he represented the town on that body until his death. He served on several committees of the County Council, including the Education Committee and the Board of Governors of Loughborough College.

The Funeral

The funeral took place quietly at Oaks-in-Charnwood on Saturday, the service being conducted by the vicar, the Rev. A.C. Holden. Shepshed Urban Council was represented by Councillors T.K. Walker (Chairman). L.E. Batten, F.A. Smith, Mr H.W. Barrisford (clerk), and Mr H. Bintcliffe (sanitary inspector). Others present included Miss Cooke, Dr L.C. Griffin, Dr L.M. Smith, Mr E. Marktin and Mr A. Peberdy.

The service was choral. Mr W.G. Thurman being at the organ. The floral tributes included wreaths from the chairman and governors of Loughborough College, Transport and General Workers' Union and Shepshed Urban Council. The grave was decorated with flowers and foliage by the Rev. A.C. Holden.

The two-line sentence of his will uses only five letters to describe him: CLERK, leaving the sum of £279 12s 1d. These five insignificant letters do an injustice to the full life that he led - scholar, anthropologist, Reverend and politician.

*

Harley's story does not end with the final closing of his eyes on 12 May 1943. He left an indelible mark on Shepshed, his adopted home and final place of rest. The rich tapestry of his life lived on through conversations in the homes of Shepshed residents for years to come as local history and folklore. Whether remembered by the townspeople as the eccentric councillor, recalled with affection by the Cooke sisters, friends and colleagues, or reviled by his fellow Councillors as a constant thorn in their side in the Council Chambers, Harley remained a presence.

After his death, Jessie Cook, his close friend and confidante, took Harley's leather suitcase with his papers, mementoes, letters and clippings and entrusted it to William Wortley. Why did she not keep the suitcase herself? Other than her sister, a spinster, she had no close family and must have concluded that the suitcase would be discarded as junk after her or her sister's death. William Wortley had sat on the Council in the latter stages of Harley's life. He had become a Justice of the Peace affording him authority in the town. He was also something of a local historian and had a family to which he could pass down information. William Wortley became the unofficial custodian of Harley's archive.

It is poignant to note that Harley's legacy lived on fifty-four years after his death. In 1997, property developers Westley Development applied for planning permission for a single development of fifteen homes on land off Ring Fence Road, which merged into Sullington Road, where Harley had lived. Harley's name was put forward to the street naming committee at Shepshed Town Council for consideration for the new development. His name had to be proposed by either a parish or local councillor and unfortunately there are no details of who submitted his name for this visible honour. The former editor of the *Loughborough Echo*, John Rippin, wrote:

In memory of an amazing speaker.

A road is to be named after one of the most remarkable people ever to live within our circulation area. Shepshed Town Council has recommended that the new development be called 'Harley Close'. Here, Here! I say. For a memorial to the Rev. James Arthur Harley is long overdue.

In the days when I was *Echo's* Shepshed reporter, there was still plenty of folk around who could remember the multi-talented West Indian. So colourful were the stories that I was promoted to write a long feature article, headed '*Was fiery MA Shepshed's man of the century?*'[500]

The small cul-de-sac off Ring Fence Road has neat rows of compact new build houses with well tendered gardens, home to a new generation of families in Harley Close.

---

500 *Loughborough Echo*, 21 November 1997.

21. Ivanhoe

'All men who have turned out worth anything have had a chief hand in their own education.'

Sir Walter Scott

A multi-layered, complicated, intriguing man, there is one more layer in Harley's story to be revealed. After his death in May 1943, Jessie Cooke, the headmistress who lived in the cottage next to his in Shepshed, embarked upon a letter-writing campaign, extolling his virtues and qualities. She wrote to Yale and Harvard Universities and Leicestershire County Council. In her letter to Yale, she wrote:

> I feel proud too that it has fallen to my lot to fill in the questionnaire for the late Reverend Harley as far as I am able. In writing an appreciation of the Rev Gentleman's work here in this town, I could never do him justice, for his good and generous deeds outstrip description by any plea. However, they will live on as a lasting memorial to him and the great universities though he has passed, among them Yale.[501]

In her letter to Harvard, she wrote:

> Dear Sir,
>
> It seems right and proper that Harvard should know something of the life work of Rev. James Arthur Harley, one of her sons, since this cannot but make her glow with pride as she adds one more to her long list of world personalities that she has helped to shape.

---

501 Jessie Cooke to Yale University, September 1943, Yale University Alumni records.

Jessie Anne Cooke. M.R.S.T.

Miss Cooke attached a detailed letter headed 'An appreciation of the Rev. James Arthur Harley by one who has known him personally for thirty years'.

Her two-page A4 typed letter, accompanied by a five-page handwritten communication, outlined Harley's academic career, his time in Shepshed as a reverend and independent councillor, the contribution made to both World Wars and the miners' strike of 1926. She concluded her appreciation testimonial with:

> The people of his adoption sincerely miss and mourn him, one, the like of which will never come their way again, for he was a man of the century, nay of a thousand years. They recognise that one of the Great Ones of the Earth has passed from their midst. Harvard may well be proud of her part in fashioning this Man among men as James Arthur Harley.[502]

In her letter to Leicestershire Council, one month after Harley's death, she made an interesting statement alluding to and revealing another fascinating aspect of his life.

> The sender of the enclosed clipping begs the Chairman of the Leicestershire County Council to pardon her seeming presumption in writing to him. Still, in fairness to her late County Councillors, she feels that the 'appreciation' should not escape the eyes of that august body on which the late Rev. J.A. Harley served so faithfully. May she, in all modesty, suggest, therefore, that Sir Robert (Leader of Shepshed Council) will of

---

502 Letter of appreciation from Ms Cooke to Harvard University, 1943, Harvard University Archive, Box 433, Harley.

his goodness bring it to their notice as a small mark of respect to one descended from *noble* (her emphasis) British stock who so humbly sat in their midst to serve others.

She followed her letter to the County Council with a note to the editor of the *Coalville Times*.

Dear Sir,

Knowing you to have been very friendly towards the late Rev. J.A. Harley, I am venturing to send you a copy of a clipping taken from a London daily recently.

Few people in Leicestershire know the Harley mentioned in the clipping that the late Rev. Gentleman was descended, so I hope you will reserve a space in your valuable paper to print the account.

The clipping:

An observant friend walking along with Vere Street W1 today saw that the notice board was missing from St. Peter's. This use to recall that the church was built in 1722 as a private chapel to the Earl of Oxford. The board is being painted, and I am told that when it reappears this bit of history will be omitted. When St. Peter's was built, the Earldom of Oxford was held by the statesman Robert Harley. This title has been held by three different families; the Veres held it from 1141 until 1703 when Aubrey de Vere the 20th Earl died, and the title became extinct. In 1711, Harley became Baron Harley of Wigmore and Earl of Oxford and Mortimer. The title became extinct in this family in 1853 on the death of the 6th Earl. It does provide yet once again for Mr Asquith who became Earl of Oxford and Asquith. The present holder is Mr Asquith's grandson Julian. It seems a pity that St. Peter's will no longer inform the passer-by of this interesting fact of its history.

Descended from noble British stock - what did Jessie Cooke know? What had Harley intimated to her, what had their long conversations into the night yielded? In the questionnaire from Yale University, a section asked for Harley's lineage; she wrote, 'he told me his father was Robert Harley, the Earl of Oxford.' Now, Henry James Harley, as we know, was documented as his 'father', but who was Henry James Harley, and was he a direct descendant of that Robert Harley, Earl of Oxford? Why did Harley tell Jessie his father was the Earl of Oxford? He must have been told this version of events by family in Antigua, and the information would have been passed down through generations by oral history. Was this question of lineage and heritage anything more than a fanciful Nancy story?[503] And did this account for traits in the character of a man who was loquacious, opinionated, self-righteous, bombastic and grandiose?

The Harley family took its name from the Shropshire village of Harley, the ancient seat of the family,[504] and were significant in national and political life. Malcolm de Harley became chaplain to Edward I and Sir Richard was the first Harley elected to Parliament as Knight of the Shire for Shropshire in 1300. The latter's eldest son, Sir Robert, married Margaret, eldest daughter and heir of Brian de Brampton, in 1309, thus acquiring the seat of Brampton Bryan in Herefordshire. He died in 1349. The estate descended via Sir Robert's second son and from then on from father to eldest surviving son through eleven generations directly to Sir Robert Harley, first Earl of Oxford and Mortimer.[505]

---

503 A Nancy story is, in Caribbean oral tradition, a far-fetched tale.
504 Clyve Jones, 'The Harley Family and the Harley Papers', *British Library Journal*, 1989, p. 125.
505 Ibid.

Robert Harley, the eldest son of Sir Edward Harley, was born in 1661 in London's Bow Street. In 1682, at the age of twenty-one, he entered the Inner Temple but was not called to the Bar. Instead, he continued his family's political tradition. The family had established political associations with the counties of Radnorshire and Hertfordshire from the fourteenth century as Members of Parliament. Five generations of the Harley family sat as MPs from 1604 to 1802. They all represented local seats of New Radnor Boroughs, Radnorshire, Herefordshire, or Leominster.

Robert Harley's life was just as colourful, with twists and turns, as James Arthur Harley's. Robert Harley entered politics as a Member of Parliament for Tregony, Cornwall, in 1689 before finally acquiring a seat representing the borough of New Radnor in 1690.[506] He had a very distinguished political career; he became Speaker of the House for four years between 1701 and 1705 and in 1710 was appointed Chancellor of the Exchequer and Chief Minister. On 23 May 1711, he became Baron Harley of Wigmore in the county of Hereford and Earl of Oxford and Earl of Mortimer. A year later, on 25 October, he became Knight of the Garter.

He survived an assassination attempt when stabbed with a penknife by the Marquis of Guiscard. For an alleged crime of high treason, Harley was impeached and imprisoned for two years in 1715 in the Tower of London. He died in May 1724 at his home in Albemarle Street, Mayfair, London.

His political adventures never took him to the Caribbean or Antigua, but his son, Edward, the second Earl of Oxford, whose great uncle was Sir Robert Harley (1626-73), had interests in plantations in Barbados, Suriname and Antigua and connections with other slave trading companies.[507]

---

506 Edward Stanley Roscoe, *Robert Harley Earl of Oxford, prime minister 1710-1714: A Study of Politics and Letters in the Age of Anne*, London: Methuen, 1902.

507 Sheryllynne Haggerty and Susanne Seymour, 'Slavery Connections of Bolsover Castle (1600-c.1830)', Historic England, 2010.

Sir Robert Harley was involved in property development and ownership with William Byam, founder of a planter family in Antigua, and Francis, Lord Willoughby, and all held colonial positions. Sir Robert was in Barbados in the 1660s for his colonial duties.[508] Despite his trading activity, he was facing financial problems in the early 1670s. A 1663 agreement refers to creating a forty-acre plantation to grow plantains, yams, cassava, potatoes, sugar cane and corn in the vicinity of Torarica, former capital of Suriname. Byam and Captain George Strange, then in Suriname, were to 'fall, clear and plant' the land 'all clean and well planted'. At the same time, Sir Robert was responsible for delivering the enslaved African workforce. The agreement made was for him to 'pay ye said persons [Byam and Strange] in able Negros, to the Value [value] of Thirty thre[e] Thousand pounds of merchantable Muscovado Suger' by the following February, with the earlier delivery of 'Four able young Negros, two men and two women at Taurarica by the end of July 1663'.[509]

Robert Harley's plantation in Suriname was lost after the colony was ceded to the Dutch in 1667, and Byam moved on to Antigua, his correspondence with Sir Robert containing references to estates at St John's and Parham. Sir Robert Harley died in 1673, aged forty-seven, just three years after his marriage and without children. Sir Robert's brother, Sir Edward Harley (1624-1700), paid debts for him in the 1670s, and he sold most of his property to pay off the remainder.

Two centuries after Sir Robert Harley's death in 1673, Henry James Harley fathered a child with Josephine Eleanor Lake. Was Henry James Harley a direct descendant of the famous Harley family or was this just coincidence in a name? There are two possibilities concerning the lineage of Harley's father, and

508 Ibid.
509 Ibid.

therefore, James Arthur Harley's ancestry. Edward Harley, the Fifth Earl of Oxford and Earl of Mortimer, or his son, Alfred, Sixth Earl of Oxford, may have sired a child. Edward Harley (1773-1849) married the daughter of Rev James Scott in 1794 and had seven children. His firstborn, Edward, Lord Harley, died aged twenty-eight. The second son, Alfred, the Sixth Earl of Oxford, married the first Marquess of Westmeath, George Nugent's illegitimate daughter, Eliza Nugent, but the union did not produce any legitimate children. The period would fit, but firstly there is no evidence of either Edward Harley or his son Alfred being in Antigua. Secondly, Alfred did not have any children.

Oral history had undoubtedly passed this complicated story from generation to generation over two hundred years, eventually perhaps for James Arthur Harley to believe that his family was descended from the Harleys of Shropshire. But there existed the real possibility of this oral history becoming distorted, embellished or romanticized.

Harley always described his father's occupation as landlord on any official documentation from his university applications to his Deacon's Orders. For a man who wrote and spoke eloquently, providing copious information to elevate his status, he never offered any additional information or provided specific details of any sugar estates in Antigua. There are no records in the Antiguan archives of a Harley family owning any plantations.[510] However, the name of Harley is on the documentation of land ownership at Clare Hall Estate.[511] Originally belonging to the Nugent family, Clare Hall became one of the plantations owned by Codrington. The distinguished lineage of the Nugent family can be traced back to tenth-century Normandy. Warin

---

510 J. Johnson, *An Historical and Descriptive Account of Antigua*, London: Henry Baylis, 1830.
511 Certification of title,1946, Antigua National Archives.

de Belesme first adopted the Nugent name, Lord of Domfront, Montaigne and Nogent, around 1020. The 'de' was dropped, and Nogent was Anglicized, creating Nugent.

The family disappeared from France and settled in Ireland in 1172. Centuries later, Captain Walter Nugent, who had inherited his family estates at Westmeath, found himself on the losing side at the Battle of the Boyne in 1690, where Protestants defeated Catholics led by the deposed monarch James II, causing his estates to be forfeited. He set sail from Liverpool around 1718 to Antigua, establishing the family there. Walter's son, Oliver Nugent, inherited 500 acres in Antigua known as 'Nugent's' and built Clare Hall, commemorating and honouring the family links with County Clare in Ireland.[512] The Certificate of Title states:

> Know all men to whom these presents shall come, that Henry Walter Munroe Harley, Administrator of the Estates of Sygualine Britannia Harley, deceased, is registered proprietor of that parcel of land
>
> Forming part of the Clare Hall Estate in the Parish of Saint John's on the island of Antigua, now commonly known as Lot W at St. Johnston's Village, containing 5000 square feet.[513]

A further subtle clue as to how Harley communicated or acknowledged his assumed lineage is the use of his pen name - Ivanhoe. Harley used his pen name on several essays at Harvard, notably on his award-winning essays about Japanese Shintoism for the Pierre Jay Prize at the Cambridge Theology School. Ivanhoe was a fictionalized character created by the author Sir Walter Scott in 1820 for his novel of the same name.

---

512 V.L Oliver, *The History of the Island of Antigua from 1635 to the Present Time*, London: Mitchell and Hughes, 1894.
513 Antigua National Archives.

Set in twelfth-century England, the book tells the story of the hero Sir Wilfred of Ivanhoe, a Saxon knight. His support for the Norman King Richard the Lionheart brings such animosity between him and his father that his father disinherits him. Did Harley draw parallels from this historical novel and Ivanhoe's disinheritance by his father? Harley may have felt cheated out of an entitlement that could have eased his path throughout life. It is hard to determine what Harley thought or knew, but he researched the Harley family.

One Kitty Day wrote to Harley in 1937:

31 Arthur Street
Peckham SE15

Dear Sir,

I have which I wish to Sell:(sic) and feel sure will appeal to and interest you a Pedigree History of this family of Harley. This is sound and unique also in excellent presentation. As I feel sure were you only to see this that you would like to possess the same. I may forward it on approval with a view to your purchasing.

Thank you in anticipation
I am Yours obediently
K. Day

Kitty Day was a spinster who lived with her father Ernest Day, a wastepaper dealer, and perhaps his trade involved second-hand books.[514] Kitty may have responded to an advertisement placed by Harley requesting further information about the Harley family. It is unknown if the book she mentioned was ever sent or purchased by Harley; there is no evidence of any material relating to the Harley family in his archive.

---

514 Wells Archives.

There are many tantalizing teasers as to Harley's assumed lineage:

- Signing himself as J. Arthur, instead of James Arthur
- Using his pen name Ivanhoe
- Telling Jessie Cooke his father was Robert Harley, the Earl of Oxford
- His search for additional information about the Harley family

During my research in Antigua, a family named Harley, located in the Potteries area, made themselves known to me. Arthritis and old age did not impede the razor-sharp mind and memory of Amelia Harley, the ninety-year-old matriarch of the family. She recalled her mother's grandfather as Robert Harley. Another passing down of a name, or just a coincidence?

These are all tenuous links and based on oral narratives with little documentary evidence to confirm or substantiate Harley's ancestry. But one element that should be weighed in Haley's favour and given serious consideration as regards his claim, lies in a dirty old brown suitcase. In this battered suitcase, Harley stored fragments from his life: theology degree from Jesus College, Oxford, copies of his Matthew Scholarship certificates from Harvard, Deacon's Orders, Ordination certificates and campaign posters. Without these papers illustrating the full life he led, would the little black man who ventured from the small Caribbean Island present a believable narrative of his academic and political achievements or would he be dismissed as a victim of delusions of grandeur? What would he have hoped to gain with this fanciful story? The removal of the stain of being perceived as a bastard? A form of ammunition to repel the insults and taunting as a young mulatto boy growing up in a country that valued colour and respectability? The prestige of claiming the Earl of Oxford as his father. Whatever Harley knew or tried to find out, he took it with him to his grave.

22. Loose Ends

This chapter addresses the loose ends and answers the questions: what became of the people and places Harley intersected and interacted with throughout his life? These include Bishop Satterlee, the Lawsons, Alain LeRoy Locke, Horace Kallen, the Archbishop of Canterbury, Rev Hepworth, Rev Kent, Jessie Cooke, and finally his wife, Josephine.

Antigua

Betty's Hope
The Codrington family retained ownership of Betty's Hope until 1944 when they sold the property to the Antigua Sugar Estate Ltd. Today, Betty's Hope is a historical and tourist site with trails and a visitor centre managed by the Antigua Museum. The site is undergoing a restoration process under the guidance of Dr Reginald Murray, Chair of the Betty's Hope Project.

All Saints Church
The original church Harley attended was destroyed by a hurricane. The current church was rebuilt in 1974, retaining its position on the corner of the crossroads.

The Teachers' Training College
The College remained open until 1959 when it merged with the Golden Grove Technical College to form the Antigua State College.[515]

---

515 Hewlester A. Samuel. *The Birth of the Village of Liberta, Antigua*, Fort Lauderdale FL: Llumina Press, 2007.

America

St John's Mission Church, Boston

Harley taught at the mission church of St John the Evangelist in 1903 while studying at Harvard University. It became a parish church in the Episcopal Diocese of Massachusetts in 1985. In 2014, a residential property developer purchased the church and mission house for $4.5 million and it underwent transformation into houses, the money raised used to pay for the restoration of the Cathedral Church of St Paul.

Henry Yates Satterlee, First Episcopal Bishop of Washington

Satterlee provided several references for Harley during his academic career. The President at King Hall, Satterlee was instrumental in establishing one of the most prominent and visible signs of the Anglican presence in the United States - the National Cathedral in Washington DC. Satterlee died on 22 February 1908 in Washington and is buried in the Bethlehem Chapel.

Josephine Lawson Harley

In 1912, at the age of twenty-seven, Josephine returned home to America, escaping her marriage with Harley. She resumed her teaching career at several Historically Black Colleges and Universities (HBCUs), primarily in Virginia. She applied her skills to creating a new generation of teachers at the Bluefield Normal School in Mercer County, West Virginia, renamed Bluefield State Teachers' College School in 1931 and Bluefield State College in 1943. The school was founded in 1895 as the Bluefield Colored Institute created to educate the young minds of the coal miners' children. Josephine had a short tenure there before embarking on a five-hundred-mile journey to the capital of Delaware, Dover, where she worked at the State College for Colored Students (SCCS) teaching Latin and as assistant matron.[516] The College was created because of the second Morrill Act. The Morrill Acts, spearheaded by Justin Smith Morrill, a Republican Senator, enacted a land-grant bill to fund a system of industrial colleges in each state.[517]

A year before Josephine's arrival at the College, the curriculum students could study changed to Academic, Agricultural, Mechanic Arts and Domestic Science, leading to a Bachelor of Pedagogy.[518] The Faculty President mentioned Josephine in his report to the Members of the Board of Trustees for the year ending 31 May 1914:

> Mrs Josephine L Harley was elected after Mr Alonzo H. Long decided to retain his position. Her services were entirely satisfactory, not only in the classes she was employed in but also as a teacher in other branches to which she was assigned during the year.

Josephine's mental health improved and her resilience started to grow. She slowly began recovering from her traumatic experiences in Marshside with her return to the safety and comfort of her family, the familiarity of a country she knew, and the knowledge that she could now resume her career.

The only known image of Josephine Maritcha Lawson, perhaps at her Oberlin College graduation, 1907. (Private collection)

516 State College for Colored Students catalogue 1914.
517 State College for Colored Students 1891-1947, Delaware State University and special Collections.
518 Ibid.

In the summer of 1914, Josephine engaged the services of attorney L. Melendez King to file for divorce from Harley. Divorce was a serious undertaking at this time, the granting of a divorce requiring proof that the accused spouse had committed adultery, abuse or abandonment. Josephine accused Harley of adultery, citing the co-respondent as Ada Young, and demanding a divorce on those grounds.[519]

Who was Ada Young? When and where did the alleged affair take place? Ada Young was the wife of Frederick Young, the papermaker at Wookey Hole, Somerset. The Harleys had stayed with the Youngs as boarders in the April of 1911. Josephine's allegation thus raised a major question. Did Harley know the Young family, and Ada in particular, from his time at Wookey Hole, or from his unitarian ministry work for Manchester College?

There is no evidence of Harley contesting the divorce. On 9 July 1914, Josephine was granted a divorce in a Washington DC court.[520]

Josephine remained at the State College for Colored Students until 1915. That year, her nomadic lifestyle brought her to St Paul Normal and Industrial School in Lawrenceville, County of New Brunswick, Virginia. The one-room school in the vestry room of St Paul's Chapel was established in 1883 by the newly ordained Protestant Episcopal Deacon Rev James Solomon Russell when he arrived in Lawrenceville in 1882. The school serviced the educational and spiritual needs of the region's black community. Josephine found some solace and peace at St Paul's; this was her longest tenure, remaining at the school for six years until 1921.

She returned home to Washington, living at the family home in LeDroit Park and taught for a year at the institution founded by her parents, the Frelinghuysen University. She eventually settled as an English teacher at the school she and her mother had attended, the M Street School, now named

---

519 *Daily Washington Law Reporter*, vol. 42, 1914, p. 459.
520 Ibid.

after the African American poet Paul Dunbar and known as the Dunbar High School. In completing information for inclusion in her Oberlin yearbook, a question asked for her husband's details and Josephine wrote, 'I do not know if he is living or not.' Josephine did not remarry and remained a divorcee. On 30 December 1934, the Secretary of Oberlin College, George Jones, opened a handwritten note. It read:

> Dear Mr Jones,
>
> It is my sad duty to record the death for college alumni on Tuesday, December 4, 1934, of Josephine Lawson Harley, class 1907. Teacher of English in Dunbar High School, Washington.
>
> Very truly yours,
> Anna. J. Cooper.

Her cause of death was attributed to nerve depression.[521] Josephine's experiences in England undoubtedly had a traumatic effect on her mental health and general well-being; the loss of a precious child, the claustrophobic conditions of Marshside and dealing with Harley all left their scars.

Her obituary stated she was married to an English man. Whoever placed the notice reported him as such, not a black man of Caribbean descent; the interpretation - he was white, a conspiracy of pretentiousness the family was happy to indulge.

Forty-one years after Josephine returned to America, Harley received a short notice about her death at his home in Sullington Road, Shepshed. The correspondence indicated that he had to communicate with a member of the family. Josephine is buried next to her father in the historic Woodland Lawn Cemetery in Benning Ridge, Washington DC, one of the most prestigious burial grounds for black Washingtonians.

---

521 Josephine Lawson file, Oberlin College Archives.

Josephine's brothers: James and Edward Lawson

Josephine's eldest brother, James, was an alumnus of Howard Medical School and became a doctor. He married Ms Lula Love; the couple had a daughter, Anna Rosetta Lawson, who married Earl Wylie Renfroe and, before they divorced, had a son, who lived in Maryland, Earl Wylie Renfroe.[522] Edward, her younger brother, had three sons, Edward, Victor and Charles. The birth of Edward's daughter, Hilda, caused an upset in the family. After returning from England, Josephine became known as a bitter and angry woman. Edward decided not to name his daughter Hilda Josephine, just plain Hilda. as the family did not want the child identified with Josephine's bitterness.[523] Hilda received a PhD from the University of Illinois and married Lincoln University professor Dr Sidney J. Reedy in Washington DC at St Augustine's Catholic Church on 11 September 1941 and lived in Jefferson City, Missouri.

Josephine's father: Jesse Lawson

Jesse Lawson carried on with his work at the Pension Bureau and campaigned for equality and civil rights for African Americans. Jesse and his wife Rosetta founded Frelinghuysen University in 1906. Jesse passed away on 8 November 1927. He is buried at Woodland Lawn Cemetery, next to his daughter. His headstone sits immediately behind that of Blanche K. Bruce, the first black US Senator and beside his friend, John Langston Mercer, the first head of Howard University Law School.

The Frelinghuysen University

The University started life in the home of the Lawsons at 2011 Vermont Avenue, Washington, as a school for Bible study in 1906. The school grew, and soon classes were being held in various centres around the city, offering a full academic

---

522 Mikki Taylor personal archive.
523 Ibid.

curriculum. It established itself as the Inter-denominational University of Washington DC and on 22 February 1917, at a Board of Directors meeting, the University was renamed Frelinghuysen University, recognizing the life and work of New Jersey Senator Frederick Theodore Frelinghuysen, Secretary of State in President Chester A. Arthur's administration.[524] Jesse Lawson had written that Frelinghuysen had been 'of great service to the cause of the Colored people, while a member of the United State Senate and in the reconstruction days following the close of the Civil War. He had seen to it that Colored Americans were written into the statutes of the United States.'[525]

The mission of the University was to empower the people. The founders recognized that parents worked hard, holding down two or three jobs to enable their children to have a good education that would not condemn them to menial work at the expense of their educational development. As social activists, the founders brought programmes to local communities as Frelinghuysen became a centre for adult education. The underlying principle of the University was 'a practical education for efficient service'.[526] 'Such is the way to the stars - or to immortality' was adopted by the founders as the University's motto. The University advertised its classes, ceremonies and graduations in Washington's various black newspapers, including the *Washington Herald* and *Evening Star*.

The University also advertised for potential students. The following advertisement appeared in the *Evening Star* on 31 March 1921.

---

524 Frelinghuysen University catalogue 1920-1921, Hathi Trust, Library of Congress, Washington DC.
525 The House History Man: Anna Julia Cooper & Frelinghuysen University, http://househistoryman.blogspot.com/
526 Frelinghuysen's University catalogue 1920 – 1921 Hathi Trust, Library of Congress.

The Frelinghuysen University
1800 Vermont Avenue
Washington D.C.

An institute adapted to the needs of the people.
Incorporated under the Laws of District of Columbia

Day and evening classes
Terms very reasonable
Office: 2011 Vermont Avenue
Phone North 5864

School of Liberal Arts
School of Applied Science
School of Fine Arts
School of Stenography and typewriting

Jessie Lawson A.M. LLB. PhD.
President: Wallace McCarry R.D.

The University sought sizeable endowments for its various colleges and schools:[527]

The College of Applied Science $200,000
The College of Liberal Arts $200,000
The College of Agriculture $200,000
School of Sociology $25,000
School of Fine Arts $50,000
The Catherine Fergusson School of Applied Christianity $200,000
Interdenominational Bible College $25,000
The College of Mission $100,000

---

527 Ibid, Library of Congress.

Frelinghuysen's curriculum had developed, and by 1926 the school's offering ranged from courses in business, including aspects of business English and simple banking procedures, office skills: short-hand and the touch system of typing, bookkeeping, and filing from junior to college level. After Jesse Lawson passed away, Anna Julia Cooper took up the University's mantle as an advocate for education, a supporter of the Lawsons and the University's work since its inception. The daughter of a enslaved mother and white landowner father, Cooper was a scholar, activist, orator and author, publishing her first book, *A Voice from the South: By A Woman from the South*, in 1892. A graduate of Oberlin College in 1884, she earned a master's in mathematics a year later. She taught at M Street School, becoming its principal in 1901.

Under her leadership, students secured sponsorships to Ivy-League colleges. Her progressive methods and successes brought her to the attention of the Washington School Board. They required the school 'teach' students to a mediocre level only; it was not her role to impart wisdom and knowledge that would equip them to compete at the same schools and colleges as whites.

Anna Julia Cooper, second President of Frelinghuysen University: image from *A Voice from the South*. (Library of Congress, Washington DC)

Outraged at her refusal to capitulate to what they expected for black children, the School Board dismissed her as principal in 1906, although she remained with the school. In 1925, at the age of sixty-four, Cooper completed her dissertation, earning DPhil. She became the fourth African American woman to do so. In 1931, when the University ran into trouble and lost its downtown premises, Cooper stepped in and rented her home at 201 T Street to the University. On 15 June 1930, Cooper became Frelinghuysen's second president.

Cooper's former adversary, the Washington Board of Education, held the fate of the University in its hands. It was the only agency that could independently recognize a university. Almost to avenge an old grudge against Cooper, the board refused accreditation for Frelinghuysen - it lost its charter in 1937.

Cooper continued to fight to keep the University open. In 1935, at the age of seventy-five, she applied for a position in the Education Division of the Works Progress Administration. Her valiant efforts could not compete against the racist infrastructure increasingly limiting the institution's future, and in 1940 it became the Frelinghuysen Group of Schools for Colored Working People. Cooper became its registrar and remained as President until 1941. The University was finally dissolved in the late 1950s.

Rosetta Coakley Lawson

Rosetta continued her work with the Frelinghuysen University as a dynamic social activist and a strong campaigner for education for poor blacks. Inspired by the Chicago Young Women's Christian Association (YWCA). She had the vision to start a YWCA for black women and girls in Washington. Rosetta's literary group, the Booklovers Club, was instrumental in helping to organize the YWCA. In two rented rooms, the nascent YWCA, named after Phyllis Wheatley, the first black woman to produce a published book of poetry *Poems on Various Subjects, Religious, and Moral*, in 1873, welcomed hundreds of black women arriving in Washington to look for employment. It provided them with care, housing and guidance. In 1923, the organization received incorporation as the Phyllis Wheatley Young Women's Christian Association.

As National Organizer for the Woman's Christian Temperance Union for Coloured People Movement, Rosetta toured the Southern states in March 1910,[528] undertaking a six-week trip to South Carolina and Georgia.[529] As Vice-President of the Alley Improvement Association, Rosetta worked with the Association to carry out work in thirty-five alleys in Washington, provided a summer vacation Bible and Industrial school, and conducted mothers' and children's temperance prayer and open-air gospel meetings in twenty-five alleys. The Association also offered summer outings for children and their parents. An active member of her church and Sunday School, Rosetta worked in Bands of Mercy for Children and as financial agent for Stoddard Baptist Church Old Folk's Home. Rosetta died on 19 April 1936, aged eighty-two. Her funeral took place at Nineteen Avenue Baptist Church on 22 April and she was laid to rest next to her husband and daughter at the Woodland Lawn Cemetery. When political, social and economic forces were almost entirely obstructive to the efforts of black women, Rosetta Coakley Lawson's role in the advancement and empowerment of black people, especially women, cannot be overestimated for the great strides she made.

---

528 *The Washington Bee*, 23 April 1910.
529 *The Washington Bee*, 26 March 1910.

The Lawsons' home: 2011 Vermont Avenue, Washington DC

The Lawsons family home is still standing on Vermont Avenue. The house is currently divided into two apartments.

1800 Vermont Avenue: Frelinghuysen University

The ex-University is now the private home of Mr and Mrs Ronald and Gloria Carlson. They purchased and remodelled the house in 2007 to its former architectural elegance and glory. The couple placed the house on the National Registry. The former University features as a stop on the African American Heritage Trail operated by Cultural Tourism DC.

The LeDroit Park district

The neighbourhood where the Lawsons resided and where Josephine and her brothers grew up saw dramatic and transformational changes. The white families moved out of the neighbourhood during World War I. The proximity of Howard University and the U Street Corridor continued to be a magnet for the black intelligentsia in the 1940s, 1950s and 1960s. However, drugs and crime adversely affected the neighbourhood, making it a no-go area. LeDroit Park acquired official recognition on the National Register of Historic Places in 1974 as the LeDroit Historic District.[530] A ninety-minute LeDroit Park Heritage Trail opened on 17 October 2015. The trail features sixteen signs illustrating the neighbourhood's history and highlighting places of interest.

---

530 Washington D.C. National Register of Historic Places Travel Itinerary, National Park Service Department of the Interior.

Oxford

Alain LeRoy Locke

After the devastating and humiliating experiences of his hasty removal from the University of Oxford for failure to settle his bill for £600 and the rejection of his dissertation, Locke wrote 'Oxford Contrasts' about his views and his time at Oxford in July 1909. The article was published in *The Independent* and republished in September of the same year in *The Colored American* titled 'Oxford: By a Negro Student'.[531] In 1910-1911 Locke travelled to Germany to study the philosophy of Immanuel Kant at the University of Berlin and toured Eastern Europe. He earned a Bachelor of Letters degree. In 1911, he travelled with Booker T. Washington throughout the racist Deep South. After his travels, he wrote:

> Returning home in 1911, I spent six months travelling in the South - my first close range of the race problem and there acquired my lifelong avocational interest in encouraging and interrelating the artistic and cultural experience of Negro life, for I have become deeply convicted of its efficacy as an internal instrument of group integration and morale and as an external weapon or recognition and prestige.[532]

Locke joined the faculty at Howard University with the help of Booker T. Washington on 12 September 1912,[533] teaching English literature, ethics and logic. In 1916-1917 he took a sabbatical from Howard as an Austin Teaching Fellow at Harvard. During this period, he produced his 236-page dissertation, *The Problem of Classification in the Theory of Value*, and was awarded a PhD from Harvard in 1918.

---

531 Zoeller, *op. cit.*
532 Christopher Buck, *Alain Locke*, American Writers, Supplement 14, Academia, 2004, p. 199.
533 Buck, p. 200.

As a direct result of his experiences with racism in the South, Locke resolved to promote the interests of African Americans, using culture as a strategy. Having studied African culture and traced its influences on western civilization, he urged black painters, sculptors and musicians to look to African sources for identity and to discover materials and techniques for their work. He encouraged black authors to seek subjects in black life and to set high artistic standards for themselves. He also set about establishing Howard as the country's pre-eminent African American university, a training ground for African American intellectuals and a centre for African American culture and research on racial problems.

The burgeoning movement, known as the Harlem Renaissance, started to flourish during the 1920s and 1930s, producing artists such as Langston Hughes, Zora Neale Hurston, Florence Mills and Aaron Douglas. Locke became known as the movement's father, promoting the underlying concept that African American literature, art and music could challenge racism and promote social integration. Locke familiarized American readers with the Harlem Renaissance by editing a special Harlem issue of *Survey Graphic* (March 1925), which he expanded into *The New Negro* (1925), an anthology of fiction, poetry, drama and essays. The Harlem Renaissance impacted cities across the US, contributing to the Civil Rights Movement. Locke remained at Howard until retiring in 1953. He moved to New York to continue work on his primary project, *The Negro in American Culture* (published posthumously).

Locke died on 9 June 1954 at Mount Sinai Hospital in New York from heart complications and was cremated at the Fresh Pond Cemetery, Little Village, Long Island. On 11 June, his memorial service at Benta's Chapel, Brooklyn, was presided over by Dr Channing Tobais. The discovery of his ashes in 2007 in a filing cabinet at the Moorland-Spingarn Research Center archives was a shock. Finally, interred at the Congressional Cemetery on Capitol Hill, his headstone reads:

> The beloved son of Pinny Ishmael Lock and Mary Hawkins Locke. Philosopher, Educator, Cosmopolitan. Herald of the Harlem Renaissance, Export of cultural pluralism, philosophy chair, Howard University. First African American Rhodes Scholar.

Alain Locke Hall at Howard University is dedicated and named in his honour.

Pixley Seme

In 1910, back in South Africa, Seme set up a legal practice in Johannesburg, where his clients included the Swazi royal family. He produced an seminal text entitled 'Native Union' in 1911, appearing in various newspapers. It called for making a modern African political organization and became the founding document for the South African Native National Congress. On 8 January 1912, Seme and several of his colleagues convened a convention that led to the South African Native National Congress (SANNC), later renamed the African National Congress (ANC) in 1923. Seme suggested that the new organization should be modelled on the US Congress. He became its treasurer general. The Queen Regent of Swaziland provided Seme with the funds to launch the ANC newspaper *Abantu-Batho*. Printed in Zulu, Xhosa, Sotho and English, the paper achieved nationwide circulation and continued publication for over twenty years. Seme's record with the newspaper was mixed, and he ran it through a turbulent period. In 1930, he became the ANC's president general. In 1928, Columbia University awarded him an Honorary Doctor of Law (LLD). Seme married the daughter of Dinizulu, paramount chief of the Zulus. They had four sons and one daughter. He died in Johannesburg in 1951. Seme's 'Native Union' speech of 1911 proclaimed:

> The South African Native Congress is the voice in the wilderness bidding all the dark races of this sub-continent to come together once or twice a year to review the past and reject therein all those things which have retarded our progress, the things which poison the springs of our national life and virtue; to label and distinguish the sins of civilization, and as members of one household to talk and think loudly on our home problems and the solution of them.

Horace Kallen

Kallen studied philosophy at the Paris-Sorbonne University after leaving Oxford. He returned to Harvard and received his PhD in 1908. He taught philosophy at Harvard and logic at Clark College (1910) until he received an instructorship at the University of Wisconsin in 1911. Credited with developing the concept of cultural pluralism, Locke initially used the term in discussions between them while at Oxford. He affirmed that each ethnic and cultural group in the US had a unique contribution to make to the variety and richness of American culture and thus provided a rationale for those Jews who wish to preserve their Jewish cultural identity in the American melting pot.

He continued at Wisconsin until 1918, when he was forced to resign because of his support of the rights of pacifists during World War I. This incident increased his belief in the necessity of intellectual freedom and the right to speak out on controversial issues.[534] In 1919, together with James Harvey

---

534 Papers of Horace Meyer Kallen (1882-1974). Centre for Jewish History, New York.

Robison, Charles A. Beard, Thorstein Veblen, Alvin Johnson and Robert Bruerre, Kallen founded the New School for Social Research in New York City. The institution was founded as a kind of refugee camp for America's intellectuals and academics amid fears concerning academic and intellectual freedom. Kallen was the author of more than thirty books and numerous pamphlets and articles. He was active in liberal, educational and Zionist movements. He wrote on consumerism and environmental control long before they became significant topics. He was an outstanding leader in the adult education movement in America. Kallen died on 16 February 1974 aged ninety-one.[535]

Manchester College
The Unitarian College has grown from its original size, with new additions to accommodate twentieth- and twentieth-first-century demands. The College became a Hall of the University of Oxford in 1990. With the granting of a Royal Charter in 1996, the College became the thirty-ninth College of Oxford. Following a merger with two other Oxford Colleges, Templeton College and Green College. Lord Harris of Peckham, a businessman who successfully developed his family's carpet business, made a generous endowment to the College, which became known as Harris Manchester College. Harris Manchester College is now the thirty-seventh College of the University of Oxford. The College changed its admittance of students and currently only accepts mature students over twenty-one.

Pitt Rivers Museum
On the upper gallery floor, two glass cabinets display the flints Harley collected from Wookey Hole, Somerset.

---

535 Ibid.

Shepshed

Michael Wortley

Michael sadly passed away in 2017. A memorial to him was unveiled in December 2021 in the corner of the Shepshed Library. The memorial featuring a brass plaque commemorates his life as a very well-known Shepshed historian.

The suitcase

Harley's archive housed in the battered suitcase is still uncatalogued and undeposited. It remains in the possession of the Wortley family. In 2014, I was the catalyst for an exhibition at the Pitt Rivers Museum entitled *A Well-Documented Life: James Arthur Harley* https://www.prm.ox.ac.uk/harley.html. Some of Harley's archival material can be viewed here.

Reverend Hepworth

Upon his retirement Rev Hepworth went to live in Cheltenham. He died on 1 September 1918 and his funeral took place on 4 September. His body was brought from Cheltenham to Shepshed. The chief mourners were his son, brother and granddaughter.[536]

The Cooke sisters: Jessie Anne and Lucy

Jessie Cooke retired in 1949 after thirty years of service to the Hall Croft Primary School in Shepshed. An avid admirer of Shakespeare, the culmination of her career was a visit with eight students and staff to see *A Midsummer Night's Dream* at Stratford-on-Avon on 29 June 1949. Lucy Cooke remained as the Head of the Infants' Department for twenty-two years. Both sisters retained their interest in the school during retirement and were active in woodworking, making a set of rostrum steps in their classes which they used when invited to jointly open the Evening School Exhibition held in Garendon Road Centre. Jessie died in

---

536 Griffiths, p. 141.

1957.

Lucy continued to do her woodwork until the year before her death. She died in 1974. The sisters lie together in the corner of Bethesda Chapel Graveyard, close to the Ingles footpath, where local folklore poignantly notes, they can hear the children pass on their way to and from school.[537]

Shepshed Lace Manufacturing Company/Munitions Factory
The factory in Sullington Road now operates as Charnwood Oaks, a care home specializing in care for older people with dementia.

Marshside, East Kent

The Mill House, Chislet
The little cottage lived in by the Harleys during their time in Marshside was occupied twenty-eight years later by the English scientist, engineer and inventor, Sir Barnes Neville Wallis,

The Mill House, occupied by the Harleys, 1909 -1910. (Pamela Roberts)

537 Mallory, *op. cit.*

inventor of the bouncing bomb. Wallis' device was developed to destroy the dams in the Ruhr area of Germany during World War II. Wallis and the RAF 617 Squadron, 'the Dam Busters', tested the bombs at Reculver using the shoreline to practise dropping them at the right height and speed above the water. Operation Chastise, the bombing campaign to attack the dams of Möhne, Edersee and Sorpe, took place in May 1943.

Chislet windmill

The windmill remained a working mill until 1916, when the cap and sails blew off in a gale. Fire destroyed the windmill on 15 October, 2005. A replica mill was constructed on the old mill site in 2011 as part of a new house.

Reverend Reginald Arthur Kent, Vicar, Chislet

Rev Kent remained as the vicar of the parish of Chislet for a further nine years until 1920 before becoming Vicar of Doddington and Wychling until 1927. He is buried in Harton Chapel, Chartham, Canterbury.

St John's Church, Marshside

The little clapperboard church Harley served as a curate under Rev Kent is now a private residence. The crucifix at the top of the roof remains as a feature. The pews from the church were relocated to the Gate Inn in Boyden Gate and used as restaurant seating.

The Gate Inn Public House, Boyden Gate

The public house is still in the village; the metal signs for the bakery are now a pub feature.

Randall Davidson, Archbishop of Canterbury

The Archbishop preached at Geneva before opening the Third Assembly of the League of Nations.[538] In October 1928, he

---

538 Bell, *op. cit.*

received the Freedom of the City of London. The Archbishop retired at eighty and passed away on 25 May 1930, aged eighty-two. He is buried in the Cloister Gardens, Canterbury Cathedral.

Bibliography

Archives Referenced

James Arthur Harley personal archive

The James Arthur Harley personal archive I have referred to in the book is a miscellaneous collection of his papers, certificates and associated press cuttings in a battered suitcase. The archive is not catalogued in any order or by any subject heading, for example, educational, clerical career or political. The archive is undeposited and remains in the care of the Wortley family in Shepshed, Leicestershire.

The Talley archive

Makiel Talley is the great-grandniece of Josephine Lawson, Harley's wife. Makiel kindly shared oral histories, photographs and information about her family. I have referred to this collection in the book as the Talley archive.

Antiguan National Archives, Antigua
Bodleian Libraries, University of Oxford, Oxford
British Library newspaper archive
Canterbury Cathedral Archives, England
Harris Manchester College Archives, Oxford
Jesus College Archives, Oxford
Lambeth Palace Archives. London
Leicestershire Records Office, Wigston Magenta, Leicester, England
Liddell Hart Centre for Military Archives, King's College, University of London
Moorland-Springarn Archives, Howard University, Washington DC
The National Archives, Kew, England
The University of Oxford Archives, Bodleian Library, Oxford
Pitt Rivers Museum Archives, University of Oxford
Wells Archives, Somerset, England
Yale University Archives

Books and Articles

Cain, Rudolph Alexander Kofi, *Alain LeRoy Locke: Race, Culture and the Education of African American Adults*, Leiden: Brill, 2004

Alexander, Shawn Leigh, *An Army of Lions: The Civil Rights Struggle before the NAACP*, Philadelphia PA: University of Pennsylvania Press, 2012.

Bell, G.K.A., *Randall Davidson, Archbishop of Canterbury*, Oxford: Oxford University Press, 1935.

Carter, Jacoby Adeshei and Leonard Harris, *Philosophic Values and World Citizenship: Locke to Obama and Beyond*, Lanham MD: Lexington Books, 2010.

Carlson, Tucker, 'Washington's Lost Black Aristocracy', *City Journal*, New York, Autumn, 1996.

Charnwood Borough Council, *Shepshed Conservation Area Character Appraisal*, 2007.

Danesh, John and Seena Fazel, *Search for Values: Ethics in Baha'i Thought*, Los Angeles CA: Kalimat Press, 2004.

DeFerrari, John, *Historic restaurants of Washington D.C.*, Mount Pleasant SC: Arcadia Publishing, 2013.

Ethnic Heritage Center, 'An Ethnic History of New Haven: Pre-1638 to 2000 and Beyond', New Haven CT, n.d.

Fergus, Howard A, *A History of Education in the British Leeward Island 1838-1945*. Kingston: University of the West Indies Press, 2003.

Fifty Years of Lace: The Shepshed Lace Manufacturing Company Ltd, Loughborough: Reprint, n.d.

File, Nigel and Chris Powell, *Black Settlers in Britain 1555-1958*, London: Heinemann, 1981.

Fisher, Russell, *Soldiers of Shepshed Remembered 1914-1919*, Market Harborough: Matador, 2008.

Freeman, Henry, *The Shepshed Almanac for the Year 1928*, Freeman Press 1928.

Gatewood, Willard B, *Aristocrats of Colour: The Black Elite 1880-1920*, Fayetteville AR: University of Arkansas Press, 2000.

Haggerty, Sheryllynne and Susanne Seymour, 'Slavery Connections of Bolsover Castle (1600-c.1830)', Historic England, 2010.

Harris, Leonard and Charles Molesworth, *Alain L. Locke: The Biography of a Philosopher*, Chicago IL: University of Chicago Press, 2010.

Heeney, Brian, 'On Being a Mid-Victorian Clergyman', *Journal of Religious History*, 7, 1973.

Henle, Ellen and Marlene Merrill, 'Antebellum Black Coeds at Oberlin College', New York: CUNY, 1979.

James, Winston, *Holding Aloft the Banner of Ethiopia: Caribbean Radicalism in Early Twentieth Century America*, London: Verso, 1998.

Jones, Clyve, 'The Harley Family and the Harley Papers', *British Library Journal*, 1989.

Kerr, Audrey Elisa, *The Paper Bag Principle: Class, Colourism, and Rumour and the Case of Washington D.C.*, Knoxville TN: University of Tennessee Press, 2006.

Lightfoot, Natasha, *Troubling Freedom: Antigua and the Aftermath of British Emancipation*, Durham NC: Duke University Press, 2016.

Lowes, Susan, '"They Couldn't Mash Ants": the Decline of the White and Non-White Elites in Antigua 1834-1900", in *Small Islands, Large Questions: Society, Culture and Resistance in the Post-Emancipation Caribbean*, ed. Karen Fog-Olwig, London: Frank Cass, 1995.

Mallory, G.H., *The First 100 Years: The Founding of the Old Shepshed British School and its Subsequent History. 1875-1975*, www.crbcshepshed.org.uk/britishschool

McHenry, Elizabeth, *Forgotten Readers: Recovering the Lost History of African American Literary Societies*, Durham NC: Duke University Press, 2002.

Mellone, Sydney Herbert, *Liberty and Religion: The First Century of the British and Foreign Unitarian Association*, London: Lyndsey Press, 1925.

Mitchell, Kenneth, 'The Story of Dunbar High School: How Students from the First Public High School for Black Students Influenced America', Washington DC: Georgetown University thesis, 2012.

Mitchell, Sir Lewis, *The Life of Rt. Honourable Cecil John Rhodes*, Ithaca NY: Cornell University Library, 1912.

Moore, Jacqueline M., *Leading the Race: The Transformation of the Black Elite in the Nation's Capital*, Charlottesville VA: University of Virginia Press, 1999.

Perkins, Linda M., 'The Role of Education in the Development of Black Feminist Thought, 1860-1929', *History of Education*, vol. 22, 1993.

Quinn, Frederick, *A House of Prayer for All People: A History of Washington National Cathedral*, New York: Morehouse Publishing, 2014.

Riviere, Peter (ed), *A History of Oxford Anthropology*, Oxford: Berghahn, 2009.

Roscoe, Edward Stanley, *Robert Harley Earl of Oxford, prime minister 1710-1714: A Study of Politics and Letters in the Age of Anne*, London: Methuen, 1902.

Sacks, Marcy S., *Before Harlem: The Black Experience in New York City Before World War I*, Philadelphia PA: University of Pennsylvania Press, 2006.

Samuel, Hewlester A., *The Birth of the Village of Liberta, Antigua*, Fort Lauderdale FL: Llumina Press, 2007.

Smith, Jessie Carney, *Notable Black Women: Book II*, Detroit MI: Gale, 1996.

Sollors, Werner, Caldwell Titcomb and Thomas Underwood, *Blacks at Harvard: A Documentary History of African American Experience at Harvard and Radcliffe*, New York: New York University Press, 1993.

Sterling, Kelsey, 'The Education of the Anglican Clergy 1830-1914', PhD. thesis, University of Leicester, 1982.

Stewart, Jeffery, *The New Negro: The Life of Alain Locke*, Oxford: Oxford University Press, 2017.

Sturge, Joseph and Thomas Harvey, *The West Indies in 1837. Being the journal of a visit to Antigua, Montserrat, Dominica, St. Lucia, Barbadoes, and Jamaica; undertaken for the purpose of ascertaining the actual condition of the negro population of those islands*, London: Hamilton, Adams and Co, 1838.

Tweedy, Margaret T., 'A History of Barbuda under the Codringtons 1738-1833'. M.Litt thesis, University of Birmingham, 1981.

Weinfeld, David, 'What Difference Does Difference Make? Horace Kallen, Alain Locke, and the Development of Cultural Pluralism in America,' PhD thesis, New York University, May 2014.

Williams, Paul K., *Greater U Street (Images of America),* Mount Pleasant SC: Arcadia Publishing 2002.

Walrond, Eric, *Winds Can Wake up the Dead: an Eric Walrond Reader*, Detroit MI: Wayne State University Press, 1998.

Wrathall Susan, An Historical Tour of the Close. A History of the Building of the General Theological Seminary of the Protestant Episcopal Church', *Church History*, April 2006.

Zoeller, Jack C., 'Alain Locke at Oxford: Race and the Rhodes Scholarships', *The American Oxonian*, Spring 2007,

Websites

Methodist and Moravian Relationships in the North-East., http://www.methodistheritage.org.uk/missionary-history-neal-methodist-moravian-

Lewis Harold, West Indian Anglicans: Missionaries to Black Episcopalians – yet with a steady beat, the African American struggle for recognition into the Episcopal Church.

Collection: Papers of Horace Meyer Kallen (1882-1974 .... http://digital.cjh.org/webclient/DeliveryManager?pid=1278441

Phi Beta Sigma Fraternity, Inc., Western Region. https://www.pbswest.org/sigmatrailblazers/locke.html

The Anglican Communion, Episcopal Church Archives

Afro-Anglican History Episcopal Archives

St Thomas Church, Washington Website

Newspapers and Journals

The Afro American

The Antigua Standard

Boston Guardian

The Cambridge Tribune

The Colored American

Daily Express,
Daily Washington Law Reporter
The Deal Mercury
Leicester Chronicle
Leicester Mail
Leicester Mercury
Liverpool Echo
Loughborough Monitor and Herald
Nottingham Evening Post
South Wales Echo
The Sun, New York
Taunton Courier and Western Advertiser
The Times
The Washington Bee
The Washington Post
Whitstable Times & Herne Bay Herald

Pamphlets and leaflets

Rhodes Scholarship information, Rhodes House Trust, University of Oxford

General Theological Seminary information leaflet.

Index